# THE MEDIEVAL IMAGINATION

JACQUES LE GOFF

# THE MEDIEVAL IMAGINATION

TRANSLATED BY

ARTHUR GOLDHAMMER

THE UNIVERSITY OF CHICAGO PRESS

CHICAGO AND LONDON

JACQUES LE GOFF, director of the Ecole des Hautes Etudes en Science Sociale, Paris, is the author of *Time, Work, and Culture in the Middle Ages* and *The Birth of Purgatory*, both published in translation by the University of Chicago Press.

Originally published in French as *L'imaginaire médiéval*, © Editions Gallimard, 1985.

The University of Chicago Press, Chicago 60637
The University of Chicago Press, Ltd., London

© 1988 by The University of Chicago
All rights reserved. Published 1988
Printed in the United States of America

97 96 95 94 93 92 91 90 89 88    54321

Library of Congress Cataloging-in-Publication Data

Le Goff, Jacques, 1924–
    The medieval imagination.

    Translation of: L'imaginaire médiéval.
    Bibliography: p.
    Includes index.
    1. French literature—To 1500—History and criticism.  2. Marvelous, The, in literature.
3. Fantastic literature, French—History and criticism.  4. Imagination.  5. Philosophy, Medieval.
I. Title.
PQ155.M27L413   1988      840'.9'15      88-4787
ISBN 0-226-47084-9

# CONTENTS

# TRANSLATOR'S NOTE

This book is a translation of *L'Imaginaire médiéval*, published by Gallimard in 1985. Three essays contained in the French edition have been omitted. Two of these have appeared elsewhere in English:

"The Learned and Popular Dimensions of Journeys in the Otherworld in the Middle Ages" was published in Steven L. Kaplan, ed., *Understanding Popular Culture* (New York: Mouton, 1984).

"Is Politics Still the Backbone of History?" appeared in *Daedalus* (Winter 1971): 1–19, and has since been reprinted in F. Gilbert and S. Graubard, *Historical Studies Today* (New York: Norton, 1972), pp. 337–55.

The third omitted essay, "Une collecte ethnographique en Dauphiné au début du XIIIe siècle," has not appeared in English. (See pages 40–56 of the French edition.)

# INTRODUCTION

The essays collected here form the sequel to my earlier collection, *Time, Work, and Culture in the Middle Ages*, published by the University of Chicago Press in 1978. They extend, elaborate, and deepen the results of my efforts to elucidate a new view of medieval history. Three themes link the two collections: that of time, the historian's primary object of inquiry; that of historical political anthropology, a new discipline whose content is still being defined and whose aim is to provide theoretical guidance for work in political history, interest in which has revived of late; and, finally, that of the relations between high and popular culture. Despite recent criticism from such excellent scholars as Pierre Bourdieu, Peter Brown, and Roger Chartier, I persist in my belief that high and popular culture are meaningful and useful terms with an objective foundation.[1]

Over the past several years I have become increasingly interested in *imagination* as a dimension of history. The term being rather vague, a definition is called for, and I shall attempt to give one by distinguishing between imagination and three related but nevertheless distinct terms: representation, symbolism, and ideology.

By *representation* I mean any mental image of a perceived external reality. Representation is related to the process of abstraction. The representation of a cathedral is our idea of it. Semantically, imagination and representation are related, but imagined images are created rather than reproduced from external objects; they are poetic images in the etymological sense. To evoke an imaginary cathedral one must have recourse to literature or art: to Victor Hugo's *Notre Dame de Paris* or to Claude Monet's forty paintings of the Cathedral of Rouen or to the "cathédrale engloutie" of Claude Debussy's *Preludes*. Imagination is therefore more comprehensive than representation. Fantasy is not limited by the intellect.

Another related concept is *symbolism*. An object is symbolic if it makes reference to an underlying system of values; whether historical or ideal. The kings of France who stand above the royal portals of French cathedrals symbolize the ancient kings of Judea (or vice versa). In Gothic sculpture the woman with bandages over her eyes symbolizes the Synagogue. Such symbolic sculpture expresses the correspondence between the Old and the New Testament, between the royal world of the Middle Ages and the world of the Bible, between the fig-

ures of art and the ideas of religion. Victor Hugo describes Notre
Dame as seen by Quasimodo: "For him the cathedral was not just society but the whole world, indeed all of nature." He thus creates not
only a symbolic cathedral that mirrors Quasimodo's three worlds but
also an imaginary cathedral: "About the whole church there was something fantastic, supernatural, horrible. In it, here and there, eyes and
mouths stood open." Thus, even though the symbolic and the imaginary may to some extent overlap, it remains legitimate and necessary
to distinguish between them in order to think clearly about the objects
in question.

It is equally necessary to distinguish between imagination and ideology. Ideology distorts representation by imposing upon it a conception of the world that alters the meaning of both material "reality" and
that other reality that I am calling the imagination. When medieval
clerics used the image of two swords, temporal and spiritual, to distinguish between royal and pontifical power, they were not describing
society but imposing upon it an image intended to set the clergy apart
from the laity, indeed to set the former above the latter, for the spiritual sword was supposed to be superior to the temporal sword. When
the same clerics identified seven deadly sins, they were not describing
the forms of wickedness but forging a weapon with which to combat
vice in the name of Christian ideology. Although ideological systems
involve conceptual innovation, concepts of social classification elaborated by reigning orthodoxies (or their adversaries) are not imaginary
systems in the proper sense of the word. Once again, however, it is
difficult to trace an exact boundary. When Jean de Meung evoked the
golden age and the origins of political authority in the *Roman de la
Rose,* was he availing himself of imagination or ideology? Obviously
both. But the task of literary critic and historian alike is to circumscribe the limits of each and to say how they are related.

Many of the documents with which the historian works contain
some element of imagination. In form as well as content even the most
prosaic of charters may yield traces of the imagination. Parchment,
ink, writing, seals, and the like embody not just a representation but
an imagination of a society's culture, administration, and government.
The imaginary is different when it comes to us in written form rather
than in records of words spoken or monuments or images. Ritual initial phrases, final clauses, dates, and lists of witnesses, to say nothing
of the text itself, reflect not just concrete circumstances but ways of
imagining power, society, time, and justice.

Yet the history of the imagination has its own primary sources, and these quite naturally are the products of the imagination: literary and artistic works. Such sources are difficult for the historian to exploit, in part because he lacks the technical competence and training. The academic disciplines are scandalously specialized, not only in France but in most other countries as well. This poses obstacles to interdisciplinary research, making all but inevitable failures to which those who have done everything in their power to make success impossible then point with unseemly amusement. More than that, specialization has created insuperable barriers even within the historical profession, making it impossible to carry out meaningful synchronic studies. The Middle Ages as reconstructed by our scholars is a Middle Ages without literature, art, law, philosophy, or theology. Fortunately, "pure" historians have been able to collaborate fairly successfully with archaeologists studying medieval life. Fortunately, too, some courageous medievalists have dared to look beyond the disciplinary boundaries, and a few openminded specialists from other disciplines have been willing to educate them or supply them with information. But a historian must have the stature of a Georges Duby before he can dare to write a book like *The Age of Cathedrals,* which, by the way, is a brilliant success. In order to bring about an interdisciplinary conference on a particular period such as the Spoleto Weeks founded thirty years ago by a group of Italian medievalists for the study of the early Middle Ages, historians must be not only enlightened but also powerful. Although matters have improved somewhat in recent years, we must still ask when France will have its own Institute for the Middle Ages or a Center for Medieval Studies.

Pure medievalists, doing the best they can without professional training or specialist advice, use works of the imagination as evidence but generally not in a very satisfactory manner. They scour the sources for "historical" information, that is, information relevant to the subject matter of traditional history: events, institutions, major personages, and, more recently, marking progress of a sort, *mentalités* [mental outlook as expressed in discourse and artifacts].

A genuine history of the imagination must first, however, take account of the unique nature of works of the imagination, which were not produced to serve as historical documents but are a historical reality unto themselves. Such works, whether mediocrities or masterpieces, cannot be interpreted according to the same rules as the archival sources with which historians are accustomed to working, for their motivations and purposes are different. It is important whether the work is typical or atypical and whether it was produced for a high or a low audience. The masterpiece is no more valuable as evidence than the mass-produced mediocrity, provided that each is properly interpreted. Aesthetic values and ideas of beauty are in themselves historical constructs.

Another valuable historical source is hagiography. Progress has been made in hagiographic interpretation, which has been rescued from the pure positivism of the Bollandists (to whom, it should be added, we owe so much). Hagiography is now treated as a specific genre, a product of popular beliefs and practices as well as of the attitude of the Church toward that fundamental but changeable Christian hero, the saint, to the understanding of whom Peter Brown has recently made an outstanding contribution.[2] Much remains to be done, however, before historians learn to make proper use of literature and art. Here I offer no more than a few tentative suggestions for the study of historical works.

Third, in order to understand the imagination we must make the simple observation that among other things it is a matter of *images,* this being one of the things that distinguishes the imagination from representation and ideology, which are often purely intellectual. True images are concrete and have long formed the subject matter of a specialized discipline, iconography. In the time of Emile Mâle[3] iconographers classified themes and studied their evolution (and, secondarily, the evolution of style); they compared works of art with texts. More recently, depth has been added to the subject by the substitution of iconology for iconography, as exemplified in the works of two great scholars, Erwin Panofsky[4] and Meyer Schapiro.[5] They succeeded in defining the relation between iconology and art history; they also introduced semiology into the study of images and used images to shed light on the intellectual and cultural enviornment. Today, individual and collaborative research efforts are transforming iconography into a fully historical scientific and intellectual enterprise.[6] The establishment of icon libraries and computerized data banks will ultimately yield great benefits, but for the present the historian can only wait. Analysis will eventually concern the totality of an image: not merely themes and structures but also such aspects as color, location in the manuscript, situation on the page, and relation to the text, with the aim of understanding how images function in culture and society. One weakness of the present collection of essays is the absence of images and iconographic studies, although the reader will find implicit references to images throughout.

I am well aware that the imagination is today the object of a great deal of research. Certain collaborative research projects are important and in many respects pathbreaking and enlightening. I have my doubts, however, about the use of psychoanalytic methods, particularly those influenced by the suspect ideology of archetypes.[7] I prefer to study the imagination by means of science, not mystification.[8]

Why, then, do I propose a new kind of history, the history of the imagination?[9] In the first place because growing numbers of historians recognize that everything in the life of men and societies is a suitable subject for history. Nature itself has been annexed to the "territory of the historian," as exemplified by Emmanuel Le Roy Ladurie's *History of Climate*[10] and Robert Delort's *Animals Have a History,*[11] which sees itself as a zoological history, a history as told from the point of view of nature and her beasts rather than of man. The history of the imagination is rather less audacious, for it remains wedded to man's world. But psychoanalysis, sociology, anthropology, and the study of the media have taught us that the life of men and societies depends just as much on images as it does on more palpable realities. All mental images are important, not just the iconographic and artistic. The images of interest to the historian are collective images as they are shaped, changed, and transformed by the vicissitudes of history. They are expressed in words and themes. They are bequeathed in traditions, borrowed from one civilization by another, and circulated among the various classes and societies of man. They are a part of social history but not subsumed by it. Paul Alphandéry and Alphonse Dupront have shown that what the western Christians who made the Crusades possessed was above all an image of Jerusalem.[12] The history of the imagination is an elaboration of the history of conscience, whose awakening in the Middle Ages was so brilliantly analyzed by Father Chenu.[13] The imagination nourishes man and causes him to act. It is a collective, social, and historical phenomenon. A history without the imagination is a mutilated, disembodied history.

It has always been a concern of mine that my historian's tools, for the most part forged after the Middle Ages, have an intimate relation to the mental structures of the men of the past whom I was studying. This is not the place to go into the medieval concepts of *imago* and *imaginatio*. The word *imagination* first appeared in Old French in the twelfth century. But the clerics of the Middle Ages always saw a connection between external sensibility and *internal* sensibility. Medieval Christianity was one long effort of internalization, which ranged, beyond Augustine and Boethius, from Gregory the Great's *Moralia in Job* (late sixth century) to the mystical visions and ecstasies of the twelfth to sixteenth centuries. Beyond the outer eye and ear are the inner eye and ear—far more important because what they perceive is the divine vision and the divine word, the whisper of a world more real than this one, a world of eternal truths. It is in that inner world that images are perceived and work their effects, whether as introjections of external forms or direct intuitions of spiritual forms.

Augustine, in the tenth book of his *Treatise on the Trinity,* has left a theory of the genesis and power of mental and spiritual images, in which he alludes to certain extreme situations that seem to have come up frequently in the Middle Ages in the lives of men and women who, as it seems to us, had greater difficulty than we do in drawing a boundary between material reality and imaginary reality. By our way of reckoning it was easy in the Middle Ages to veer off into dream, madness, or mysticism. In Augustine's words: "The force of love is such that those objects in which the soul long delighted in thought and to which it has bound itself through its concern, are carried with it even when it turns inward in some fashion in order to think. Having loved those bodies outside itself through the intermediary of the senses, it has mingled in them through a kind of long familiarity, but since it cannot transport them within itself, into what is as it were the domain of spiritual nature, it enrolls their images and draws those images made of itself into itself. . . . It assimilates those images not through its being but through thought. In it subsists the power to judge, which causes it to distinguish the body, which remains exterior, from the image that it carries within itself, unless those images externalize themselves to the point where they are taken to be sensations of foreign bodies and not internal representations, which frequently occurs in sleep, madness, or ecstasy." [14]

To study the imagination of a society is to go to the heart of its consciousness and historical evolution. It is to go to the origin and the profound nature of man, created "in the image of God." Man's growing awareness of his human nature in the twelfth century animated the rise of medieval humanism, which influenced all aspects of medieval society from economic performance to the highest cultural and spiritual creations. [15] All the great "images" of the Middle Ages—man as microcosm, the "mirror," [16] the Church as mystical body, society as organism, danse macabre, symbols of social rank from clothing and furs to coats of arms, symbols of power such as flags and oriflammes, royal investitures and entries—this entire corpus of images simply reproduces in outwardly visible signs the profound mental images of medieval men and women, more or less sophisticated according to their social status and level of culture.

Chronologically, this book is concerned with the traditional Middle Ages, that is, with the Middle Ages created by humanists at the end of the fifteenth century and institutionalized by humanist and classical scholars, mostly German, in the sixteenth and seventeenth centuries, including the philologist and historian Christophe Keller (Cellarius), the historian Georg Horn in his *Arca Noe* (1666), and the celebrated French scholar Du Cange in his *Glossarium mediae et infimae latinitatis* (1678). These men saw history as divided into three periods: antiquity, the Middle Ages, and the modern age. For Keller the Middle Ages stretched from the founding of Constantinople in 330 to its fall in 1453; for Horn the period began in 300 and ended in 1500. In the nineteenth and twentieth centuries university curricula have consecreated this chronology. In France the modern age is subdivided into two periods, one covering the time from the Renaissance to the French Revolution, the other from the Revolution to the present. For a time it was fashionable to mark boundaries within the curriculum by specific dates, usually those of major political events or battles. Thus the beginning of the Middle Ages was generally set in 476, the year in which Romulus Augustulus transferred the imperial insignia from Rome to Constantinople, and the end was usually fixed at some point in the second half of the fifteenth century, either 1453, when Constantinople was taken by the Turks, or 1492, when Columbus discovered America, or 1494, when the French invaded Italy. Since the sixteenth century it has been traditional to see the Middle Ages as having been followed by a period called the Renaissance, characterized by "humanism" and "Renaissance art." During the Enlightenment the Middle Ages were commonly referred to as the Dark Ages to emphasize their inferiority to the Renaissance.

In the nineteenth century the Italian Carlo Cattaneo praised the civilization of Renaissance Florence: "The cities of Tuscany, and especially Florence, were characterized by the fact that respect for the law and civil dignity had spread to the lowest orders of the population. . . . The Florentine artist was the first in Europe to share in the culture of science. A close relation developed between the mechanical arts and the fine arts. . . . The eye and the hand laid the groundwork for the science of the intellect, and all thought gradually became oriented toward a speculation that was no longer proud or sterile but rather what Bacon would later call *scientia activa*. . . . This was the true inner force that raised modern Europe above antiquity and the Middle Ages and carried it beyond the rigid and static knowledge of the past. When applied to social life as a whole, this developed into the idea of progress, which is the faith that unites the civilized world." But what Cattaneo says about Renaissance Florence can also be said about much of Christendom in the thirteenth century, and the notion of progress did not take hold in scientific circles before 1620 and was not assimilated by history, philosophy, and political economy until after 1740.[17]

This chronological—and pejorative—definition of the Middle Ages has been under attack for decades, and in recent years with particular intensity. The even more pejorative term *Bas-Empire,* Low Empire, that Montesquieu and Gibbon applied to the final centuries of the Roman Empire has been replaced by the more objective late antiquity, which is now seen as a time of change, ferment, and creativity.[18] After all, this was the period during which Christianity became established in the West, and the transition from Roman to barbarian rule cannot be described simply as a regression. That being the case with late antiquity, how can the Middle Ages be any different? The rehabilitation of late antiquity implies that of the Middle Ages.

But the judgment of history—and of historiography—can also swing too far in the other direction. It is undeniable that technologically, demographically, economically, and culturally the period from the third to the seventh century was one of depression—the longest the West has ever known. Yet during this time the groundwork was being laid for the dramatic advances of the tenth and especially the eleventh century.

Given these changes in our view of the Middle Ages, what becomes of the year 476? It is downgraded from a turning point to a mere episode, a sidelight on the main thrust of history. At the other end of our period the situation is more complex. The Middle Ages–Renaissance dichotomy has been challenged from many angles. For some, such as Armando Sapori whose attention was focused mainly on Italy, the Renaissance begins in the twelfth-century and continues to the end of the sixteenth century, and the medieval period should therefore be limited to 300–1100. This view has certain points in its favor. For one thing, it brings out the tremendous advances that were made in the Middle Ages, particularly from the twelfth century on. For another, it clarifies the reasons for rejecting the view of the Swiss historian Jacob Burckhardt (expressed in two books, *The Civilization of the Renaissance in Italy* [1860] and *Considerations of Universal History* [1905]) that the Italian Renaissance was the height of civilization, a view still widely accepted, if not by historians then at least by a large part of the educated public. Sapori's brilliant paper shows that Burckhardt's view of the Renaissance was shaped by a vision of history according to which the only "essential features of society are the state, culture, and religion." In particular the economy does not exist for Burckhardt, whose view, even of those areas upon which he focuses in ultraidealist fashion, is that of a bourgeois professor indifferent to material, social, and even intellectual realities. The political, cultural, and religious life of the "Renaissance" was shaped not by neo-Platonism, Albertism, Machiavellianism, Erasmism, and other esoteric doctrines but by movements far more profound and diverse.[19]

One can certainly agree with Krzysztof Pomian that any periodization is a straitjacket for the historian. Periods overlap. History moves at a different pace in different domains: for example, the history of culture and the history of the economy do not generally coincide. There are marked differences between civilizations and regions. Mesopotamian civilization flourished while much of Europe still lived in prehistoric conditions. When Columbus's Spaniards and the Indians of America discovered one another, firearms determined which would be the victor. Thus disparities in historical time have real consequences. I have no quarrel with any of these observations. Still, when one takes a broad view of human evolution, it is clear that certain slowly developing systems or phases persist for relatively long periods. These enduring realities are useful to historians in their efforts to articulate a rational scientific account of the past. No doubt the past will resist any attempt to impose a periodization upon it. But certain ways of dividing it up are more illuminating than others.

I, for one, feel that it is of no use in understanding historical change to single out a period called the Renaissance. Most of the characteristic signs by which it is supposedly distinguished appeared well before the fifteenth century. The "return to antiquity" was under way as early as the thirteenth century, by which time Aristotle had invaded the universities and ancient sculpture had made its influence felt in Pisa, Pistoia, and Florence. The "Machiavellian" state existed in France under Philip the Fair. Perspective was known in optics as well as painting by the late thirteenth century. Reading was widely practiced before Gutenberg, and literacy—the really important cultural phenomenon—did not await the arrival of printing. At the turn of the thirteenth century individualism was already as powerful a force in Italy as it would be in the Quattrocento, and, as I hope I have shown,[20] the triumph of

Purgatory was also that of the individual, whose fate was sealed at the moment of posthumous individual judgment, although I do not agree with Aaron Gourevitch that the individual triumphed alone.[21] Nor do I agree with Max Weber and R. H. Tawney when they see a connection between Protestantism and the "religion" of work. For the latter existed as early as the thirteenth century, as can be seen, for example, in the accusations leveled at the mendicant orders by Guillaume de Saint-Amour and other secular masters at the University of Paris as well as in the reactions against praise of idleness stirred up by such works as the fabliau of Cockaigne (ca. 1250). As for religion, the mendicant orders introduced greater changes to Christianity than the Council of Trent. Conversely, as Lucien Febvre has shown in his study of Rabelais's religion, the Middle Ages not only survived but thrived "in the religious heart of the sixteenth century" in the work of this genius who, more than any other man of his time, claimed modernity for the sixteenth century.[22]

It is high time, therefore, that we let the air out of the inflated concept of the Renaissance. I shall make an even bolder proposal than Armando Sapori's: that the Middle Ages, defined in terms of a set of slowly evolving structures, endured from the third century until the middle of the nineteenth century. Only then, under the combined effects of the Industrial Revolution, European domination, and mass democracy (of which the ancient city-state had provided only a glimmer), did there come into being a truly new world, and even then a certain legacy of the old, a certain continuity of tradition, remained.

Seventeen centuries cannot pass without some kind of change, and it is therefore useful to distinguish subperiods in these very long "Middle Ages." So let us call the period from the third to the tenth century "late antiquity." Or, if that prospect is too alarming, let us say that late antiquity ended in the seventh century and that the High Middle Ages extended from the eighth to the tenth century. Then, around 1000, a period of tremendous advance inaugurated the central Middle Ages, which lasted until the middle of the fourteenth century. The late Middle Ages began with the Great Plague (1348) and continued into the sixteenth century, when the Reformation (and nothing so vague as the Renaissance) ended the Church's monopoly on the Christian religion. The last phase of this extended medieval period would then consist of what is now called early modern history, from the Reformation to the Industrial Revolution, a time of political and economic stagnation coupled with cultural innovation (the birth of modern science, the Enlightenment, the idea of progress, and of course the French Revolution, whose effects would not be felt until the nineteenth century).

Contemporary history begins in the middle of the nineteenth century. A period of expansion (Industrial Revolution, mass democracy, European domination) is followed by a period of crisis (two world wars, the rise of fascism, Soviet totalitarianism and expansionism, American imperialism, the Great Depression, and modernism in culture and the arts). For the past quarter-century we have been witnessing the painful beginnings of a new era in human history, marked by the advent of a global economy, the population explosion, a revolution in communications, decolonization, revolutionary advances in science and technology, worldwide economic crisis, major changes in culture, attitudes, sensibilities, and behavior, and the division of the world into hostile camps—East and West, North and South. How long will this new period last? As history accelerates, periods become shorter and shorter.

The essays in this book are actually concerned with the period from the fifth to the sixteenth century—already an extension of what is traditionally called the Middle Ages. A few ("The Wilderness in the Medieval West," "The Repudiation of Pleasure," and "Christianity and Dreams") are concerned primarily with late antiquity, a time when new spaces, values, and practices, profoundly marked by if not actually the result of Christianity, were being established. I have always been fascinated by questions of birth and genesis and little interested in questions of origins, decline, and decadence. For origins are often no more than illusions dependent on some form of determinism, whereas the notion of decadence derives from a pessimistic, moralistic ideology that I do not share, for I am convinced that in history few things ever die. History is a matter of transformation and memory, memory of a past that continues to live and to change as one society succeeds another. What moves me is the birth of a society or a civilization, which is partly or even wholly a matter of chance.

This collection begins with an essay on the concept of "the marvelous," which stands at the crossroads where religion, literature and art, philosophy, and sensibility meet.[23] Many aspects of the medieval imagination involve the marvelous, both in this world and the next, in nature, man, animals, and objects, in geography and history. I have proposed several classifications of marvelous occurrences, at times making use of categories that Jack Goody has shown were fundamental to knowledge.[24] Nevertheless, I have not bound myself to a single

model, for to do so would be to transform a mere analytical convenience into an ontological reality. The historian should be free to choose
his method as necessary to grasp the nature of the object of inquiry.
Hence in one case I have used a classification based on the "vehicles" of
the marvelous, whether animate or inanimate objects, while in another case I classify marvelous occurrences in terms of the sources
from which they derived: biblical, ancient, barbarian tradition, oriental tradition, and folklore. In still another case I rely on the nature and
function of the marvelous, distinguishing between the routine marvel,
the symbolic marvel, the scientific marvel (defined by Gervase of Tilbury as "that which surpasses our understanding even though it be
natural"), and the political marvel (in which a product of the imagination becomes an instrument of earthly power). Reputations not only
of individuals but even more of families, lineages, and dynasties were
based on marvels. One reason for my interest in the marvelous is the
system by which supernatural events were interpreted from the late
twelfth until the sixteenth century. The "marvelous" was in a sense a
natural form of the supernatural, a middle term between the divine
supernatural (that is, the *miraculous,* which depends solely on God's
saving grace) and the diabolical supernatural (or *magic,* governed by
Satan's destructive activity). After the thirteenth century the marvelous seems to me to gain ground on the miraculous and the magical.
Miracles become rarer, and magic is more hotly contested. Does it
make sense to speak of a "secularization" of the supernatural?

The phenomena of the imagination are embodied in words, hence
analysis of vocabulary can reap major dividends. Every idea is embodied in words, and every word reflects some reality. The history of
words is history itself. When terms appear or disappear or change
their meaning, the movement of history stands revealed. The marvelous interests me because it reveals changes in underlying attitudes
and sensibilities. Christianity brought about changes in the concep-
tualization and utilization of the marvelous, as did the social changes
of the twelfth and thirteenth centuries. Marvels in dreams were particularly affected by these historical sea-changes.

The first essay in this collection was originally presented as a paper
at a conference on "The Strange and Marvelous in Medieval Islam"
held at the Collège de France in 1974. That the concept of the marvelous permits comparisons between civilizations is not the least of its
virtues.

After considering the marvelous, I turn to the question of space and
time, the essential dimensions of history. This approach is rewarding

because space and time provide a conceptual framework for viewing both the "real" and the imaginary. Proceeding in this way points up the inadequacy of the Marxist theory of base and superstructure, a reductionist hypothesis incapable of explaining the complexity of historical phenomena. In my *Civilisation de l'Occident médiéval* (1964) I described the medieval world view in terms of interlocking but causally distinct spatiotemporal structures, that is, material and mental realities elaborated upon the facts of space and time. For medieval men and women space was composed of forests, fields, gardens, seigneuries and cities—geographical as well as imaginary realities. In each of these places work was done and social practices enacted, yet they were also powerful symbols, objects of fear and desire and subjects of dream and legend. The Middle Ages also knew many kinds of time: liturgical time, bell time, the time of rural labors, the time of the urban worksite, the academic year, the calendar of holy days. Each of these was associated with various images and myths. History, too, had its own time scale or, rather, scales: the epochs of the terrestrial city, which followed the generations; the series of kings and bishops; the succession of pagan empires and Christian monarchs, some historical, others legendary ("in the time of Charlemagne," people said, but they also said "in the time of King Arthur"). Sometimes these sequences were not continuous; there are gaps, silences that cannot easily be overcome. Mechanical clocks seemed to provide a relatively tractable measure of time, apparently objective, but even this became grist for the imagination and inevitably became mixed up with eschatological time, with the end of the world and the Last Judgment and even the end of time itself: eternity.

Thus, the structures of space and time were fragile and vulnerable. The men of the Middle Ages not only cleared new land in this world, they created a new space and time in the next. Every Christian looked forward to this "appendix" to his biography and in doing so focused his attention on the time of his death. Meanwhile, changing religious practices and new developments in art, literature, and music opened up a new space-time within each man: that of conscience. The Church took control of this as it had done with Purgatory, ensnaring the conscience in the confessional and pursuing it by every available means, including torture.

For my first object of study in this section, I chose a space around which swirled symbols and passions: the forest, the western equivalent of the eastern desert. I then turned to the example of a royal bureaucracy establishing control over space and time: the organization of the

Second Council of Lyons in 1274. It assumed the existence of an imaginary Christendom, newly recentered in Europe after the loss of the Holy Land and the waning of the crusader spirit. Perhaps the richest images of space and time are associated with travel. Rather than examine the travel of pilgrims, crusaders, colonists, warriors, vagabonds, or merchants, however, I chose to examine journeys that were imaginary in their very essence: voyages to the other world. Finally, I turned my attention to the question of literary time, examining the temporal structures of a modest but highly effective pastoral genre, the *exemplum*, which was designed to establish a link between narrative time and eschatological time.

Historians in recent years have begun to take an interest in the body.[25] Shaped by the imagination (as well as by symbolism and ideology), the body occupies a central place in the medieval system of thought. The Church defined itself as the mystical body of Christ, and the nascent state saw itself as a living body with the monarch as its head, an ancient image revived by John of Salisbury in his *Policraticus* (1159) and thereafter borrowed by many other writers. Bodily imagery played an important role in defining the three orders of the tripartite society. Priests formed a *corps* (body) consecrated by ordination, which excluded anyone who was handicapped or crippled. The corps of warriors was ennobled by its prowess in battle and tourney. And the corps of laborers, stooped beneath their heavy burden, was nevertheless exalted in the sculpture of cathedral portals, which depicted peasants engaged in the labors of the months and artisans engaged in the various occupations of the active life.

To be sure, it was Christian doctrine, oft-repeated, that the body is contemptible, an "abominable vestment of the soul," as Gregory the Great put it. Monastic rules proposed that the body be humbled and tamed through asceticism, continence, and abstinence. In the late Middle Ages the Church increasingly exalted the image of the suffering body, in imitation of Christ. By his willingness to endure suffering, to accept sickness and embrace asceticism, Saint Louis acquired the image of a Christlike king, a suffering king, and therefore a saint. I have tried to show how the rejection of pleasure originated with Stoicism in late antiquity and was subsequently enforced by Christianity.

According to Church prescription, however, body and soul were inseparable, or, rather, they would separate only for that instant of time that stood between the moment of death and the final resurrection. Even in Purgatory the soul was supposed to be wrapped in a body capable of feeling the devilish tortures. Ultimately the body would live again. The truth is that salvation was possible only with and through the body. Bodily imagery alternated between misery and glory, humiliation and ecstasy. In medieval Christian philosophy the external senses were supplemented by internal senses, by an inner eye and ear. The external senses functioned properly only if agumented or, rather, inspired by these internal senses. I have tried to shed some light on the ambiguity of medieval attitudes toward the body and its relation to the soul.

I also examine one extreme case of bodily symbolism. In the twelfth and thirteenth centuries a code of gestures was elaborated under the supervision of the Church. This was a highly symbolic language, whose symbolic significance was heightened in Purgatory, an emergent space in which the gesticulations of the souls on trial were passive responses to the perverse gestures of the devils administering their torture.

At this point I must confess that there is a gap in my discussion of the medieval imagination, for I have become more and more convinced that its center, its pivot, was Satan, medieval Christianity's most important creation.[26] Satan was the orchestrator of feudal society. Admittedly his power depended on the will of God, and medieval man had to choose between God and the Devil, Heaven and Hell—an imaginary choice but nonetheless very real for the men and women of the time. In this world, however, Satan called the tune, as I hope to show in a subsequent work.

Anyone interested in the imagination of a period must look at the products that typify that imagination: literature and art. For lack of competence, however, I avoided tackling works of art, although I looked at and meditated upon a great many. I did nevertheless venture into the domain of literature, examining the period from about 1150 to 1250, a century of decisive change. I looked at a number of literary genres: the courtly romances of Chrétien de Troyes, a theological summa, an exemplum. My research focused on certain key themes, in which material and social realities were closely intertwined with fancies of the imagination: the forest, the city, clothing, food, tournaments. I looked at these themes with an anthropologist's eye for myths of the forest and city[27] and codes of dress, diet, and ideology. The time has come to abolish the academic barriers between "pure" (meaning truncated) history, literary and linguistic history, and art history. The history of law, science, and technology must also be integrated into general history, with due respect for their particularities.[28] In all these fields imagination had a role to play.

For the past twenty years I have been exploring an area in which the imagination frequently manifests itself, namely, dreams. The influence of dreams on the life of the individual and of society has been a subject of literature from the Bible to Freud. Some time ago I published a paper on the relevance of dreams for the study of history.[29] Here are two more recent contributions on the subject. One is an extensive analysis of the changes in attitudes toward dreams and traditions of dream interpretation that were brought about by the advent of Christianity. Having condemned the ancient techniques of oneiromancy, the Church in both theory and practice revealed not only a weakness for dreams but also a fear of their consequences. In the Middle Ages the dream was one of the primary battlegrounds on which God contended with the Devil for the possession of man's soul. Satan, God, body, and soul were the actors in a struggle whose stakes were eternal salvation and knowledge of the future in both this world and the next. The Church at first attempted to restrict dreams to an elite but ultimately, I think, moved toward greater freedom for dreams and dreamers; interest in dreams was "democratized" as their sources were "naturalized."[30] Increasingly it was the body that was singled out as the source of human dreams, although many were still thought to be of diabolical origin, hence deceptive and sometimes fatal, while others were inspired by God, hence prophetic, premonitory, or even salvational.

I also give one example of a literary dream that is closely bound up with a specific social and cultural group: the peasants and clergy of Bavaria and Austria in the thirteenth century. A young peasant courts damnation by becoming a brigand. His father, who shares the same name (an identity that suggests a mirror structure to the story), seeks to save his profligate son by dreaming "true" dreams, but the oneiric assistance is rejected.

A jaundiced observer might feel that the essays collected here have been unduly influenced by recent intellectual fashions in France. Like Roland Barthes, I am prepared to come to fashion's defense. An interest in novelty, that driving force of modernity, can be an instrument of renewal, an historical agent. It can of course be perverted into mere snobbery, although even such perversity is moving testimony to man's desire to overcome the passage of time and the menace of death through an ultimately foolish and hopeless effort to be always up to the minute. A series of rapid changes can hide the fact that time marches on. But fashion is an expression of the spirit of the time, the visible manifestation of underlying historical change. Carefully analyzed, fashion is a key to understanding the secrets of history. That said, I should add that a glance at the dates of these essays will, I think, show that they generally anticipated rather than followed fashion.

I have organized the essays in this collection in what I think is a coherent fashion, and I hope that this introduction will serve as a guide to the reader. Yet I am bound to acknowledge that many of these papers were influenced by the occasion for which they were written: a tribute to a scholar or a commission from a conference or journal. These are recent papers, and I have made a minimum of corrections. One of the more pleasant risks of historical work is that one is vulnerable to progress in historiography as well as to the history of one's own time. What is history, after all, if not a more or less successful way of establishing order in a world of accident and happenstance? It would be dishonest to remove the patina of time that has accumulated on these essays, except in cases where more recent research has demonstrated flagrant errors of fact or method. These essays are all aspects of my continued efforts to ponder the medieval imagination. I firmly believe that the imagination will become an increasingly important subject not only of historical science but of science in general.

# FOR AN EXTENDED
# MIDDLE AGES

When the Italian humanist Giovanni Andrea, the pope's librarian, invented the term *Middle Ages* in 1469, he did so in order to draw a contrast between the "ancients" of that era and "the moderns of our time," that is, the men of the Renaissance. He outlined a purely secular and terrestrial periodization of history but let stand the old Christian chronology of six ages since the creation of the world. The ancient-versus-modern distinction had been made in the early Middle Ages but as a neutral description; increasingly, however, it came to connote a difference of values. Originally *modern* simply referred to the present time. But from the end of the thirteenth century it also connoted an idea of progress, of struggle against the past. The term *ars nova* suggested that the new music of the fourteenth century was superior to that of previous periods. *Logici moderni* and *theologi moderni* marked the rejection of Aristotelianism that caused such turmoil in thirteenth-century universities. And Marsilio of Padua, in outlining the foundations of a politics separate from religion, of a state separate from the Church, in his *Defensor Pacis* (1324) used the word *modern* in the sense of innovative. Giotto considered himself and was considered by others to be *modern* as opposed to Cimabue and the Byzantine-influenced painters of his time. The *devotio moderna,* which helped shape religious practice in the twelfth and thirteenth centuries, marked a break with superstitious religion on the one hand and scholastic rationalism on the other. By affirming modernity yet presenting it as a return to true antiquity, to the antiquity of Greece, Rome, and, as is too often forgotten, the Bible, the humanists created something they called the Middle Ages, which they saw as a sort of dark tunnel linking two brilliant epochs whose lights shone in science, the arts, and letters. By contrasting "modern times" with the Middle Ages they were advertising nothing less than a cultural revolution.

In the seventeenth century German scholars divided the history of mankind into three periods: Antiquity, the Middle Ages, and Modern Times. Georg Horn in *Arca Noe* (1666) situated the *medium aevum* between 300 and 1500. (The idea of a *century* had been invented in the interim.) The great French scholar Du Cange placed his stamp of

First published in *Europe* 654 (1983): 19–24.

approval on the idea when in 1678 he published his monumental *Glos-sary* "of middle and lower Latinity." The Latin language was thus di-vided in two: ancient Latin was opposed to the decadent Latin of the Middle Ages.

In the eighteenth century the term High Latin (*latin savant*) came into wide use, and a tripartite periodization became current. To the men of the Enlightenment the Middle Ages were Dark Ages. The Ro-mantics "rehabilitated" the Middle Ages and positivist historians viewed the period as no different from any other, indeed as a time of progress, but to no avail: *medieval* acquired a pejorative connotation. Today, in our highly developed societies, we take a complex and ambivalent in-terest in the Middle Ages, but centuries of scorn lie just below the sur-face. We view the Middle Ages as primitive, attractive, perhaps, like African art but definitely barbarous, a source of perverse pleasure and a way of revisiting our origins. Even nations and civilizations that never experienced the Middle Ages raise the specter only to ward it off. President Chadli of Algeria stated recently that his country must never return to the Middle Ages, by which he meant rule by religious fundamentalists.

Fundamental to the very conception of the Middle Ages is the his-torical watershed of the Renaissance. I have no intention of reviving the interminable quarrel over the Renaissance versus the Middle Ages. I ask only that the Renaissance be seen in proper proportion, as a bril-liant but superficial interlude. In history there is no such thing as re-birth. There is only change, in this case camouflaged as a return to antiquity. Between antiquity and the time when modernity was fully embraced (the middle of the nineteenth century) renaissance was a re-current phenomenon: the Carolingian renaissance in the eighth and ninth centuries, the renaissance of the twelfth century, the "great" Re-naissance that began in Italy in the twelfth to fourteenth centuries and triumphed in the rest of Europe in the fifteenth and sixteenth cen-turies, and the renaissances of the eighteenth and nineteenth centuries in art, literature, and theology (neoclassicism, Gothic revival in which the Middle Ages played the role of antiquity, neo-Thomism, and so on). Thus renaissance was not a phenomenon marking the end of the Middle Ages but a recurrent feature of a very long period of time during which men were constantly seeking authority in the past, in a previous golden age. No precise date can be ascribed to the great Re-naissance, which spans some three or four centuries across Europe. What is more, a number of significant historical phenomena transcend it. Historians are increasingly inclined to view the onset of the Black

Plague (1347–1348) as the great watershed in European history, dividing a time of growth from a time of crisis, a period of certainty from a period of doubt. But bubonic plague was a longlived phenomenon. It endured for three and a half centuries, oblivious to the Renaissance, until its final lethal outbreak in Marseilles in 1720. During that time it had a major impact on the demography, biology, and psychology of the Western world.

When Marc Bloch was casting about for a longlived phenomenon that he could study from its inception to its decline, he chose the royal miracle, that is, the belief that the kings of France and England could by their touch cure scrofula (tuberculous adenitis and other ailments marked by swollen ganglia in the neck). The belief in miracle-working kings endured from the eleventh (or perhaps the twelfth) century until the eighteenth century. In France it is attested for King Louis VI (1108–1137) and was practiced for the last time by Charles X after his anointment in 1825. Bloch showed that the belief in "sacred kingship" was shared by both common folk and elites.

An essential part of the coronation of a French king was his anointment with an oil said to have come from heaven. It was this rite that distinguished the king of France from the other monarchs of Christendom and that earned him the epithet "most Christian king." The oil used in the coronation ceremony at Reims was not simply oil consecrated by a high Church dignitary but a miraculous fluid. The king of France was truly anointed by God. Now, the legend on which the Christian notion of sacred kingship was based from the ninth to the seventeenth century derived from the same model. Hincmar, archbishop of Reims in the ninth century, was the first to record the legend that became the cornerstone of the coronation ritual: a dove (the Holy Spirit) in the late sixth century had delivered an ampulla of divine oil with which Saint Remigius baptized Clovis. The Holy Ampulla had been preserved in the church at Reims, where it was used to consecrate all subsequent kings of France. Early in the fourteenth century, the kings of England, seeking to rival the French monarchy, gave currency to the legend that in the second half of the twelfth century, Thomas à Becket, exiled in France, received from the Virgin a vial containing a supernatural oil intended for use in anointing the fifth king of England after the one reigning at the time (Henry II), in other words, King Edward II. Finally, in 1594, when Henry IV was forced to hold his coronation at Chartres because Reims was in the hands of the League, royal agents transported from the Abbey of Marmoutier near Tours an oil that an angel was supposed to have delivered to Saint

Martin late in the fourth century to help soothe him following injuries incurred in a fall occasioned by the devil. Earlier the Holy Ampulla of Marmoutier had been sent to the bedside of the dying Louis XI.

Bernard Chevalier, in *Les Bonnes villes* (Aubier, 1982), has studied French cities that were sufficiently powerful and wealthy to represent, alongside the clergy and nobility, a third "estate" in the kingdom. They were privileged partners of the king, to which the monarch turned for military and financial support. Royal policy toward these cities alternated between respect for their privileges and efforts to increase royal control. The phrase *bonnes villes* (good cities) to refer to this privileged group of towns first appeared in the thirteenth century and had all but disappeared by the seventeenth century.

Were any of these phenomena altered by the Renaissance? More generally, one can argue that certain fundamental structures persisted in European society from the fourth to the nineteenth century, bestowing a coherent character on a period of some fifteen centuries.

Marx proposed an interpretation of this period in terms of the concept of a feudal mode of production. Without examining this in detail, one must acknowledge the power of a concept that links technology to the economic regime and social structures (where technology is defined in terms of an unequal contract between the lord and those who maintain him, primarily peasants, the bulk of the surplus value being absorbed in feudal rents). The entire system is designed not for growth but for simple reproduction. On this view of the matter, the Middle Ages, identified with feudalism, extends from antiquity, characterized by the slave mode of production, to the modern era, characterized by the capitalist mode of production. In other words, the Middle Ages extends from the end of the Roman Empire to the Industrial Revolution.

Looked at in this way, the Middle Ages were shaped by a dominant ideology that was neither a reflection of the material base nor an idealist motor of history but an element essential to the operation of the feudal system. This was an age dominated by Christianity, by a Christianity that was at once a religion and an ideology and that therefore enjoyed a very complex relation to the feudal world, which it both contested and justified. By this I do not mean to suggest that Christianity today is dead or moribund, only that since 1850 it has not played the same key role that it played between the fourth and nineteenth centuries. It has lost the near monopoly that it once held in the realm of ideology. Hence no useful study of the Middle Ages can fail to ascribe a role of the utmost importance to the Church and religion. Over a very long period of time life was dominated by the struggle, in man or

around him, between two powers, God and Satan, that were in practice almost equal in strength even if in theory one was subordinate to
the other. The Middle Ages, in the extended sense intended here, were
a time of struggle between God and the Devil. Satan was born at the
beginning of the Middle Ages and died at the end.

The extended Middle Ages can also be approached in less sweeping
terms. It is, for instance, the period during which Georges Dumézil's
trifunctional schema appeared (or reappeared) in the West. Evident in
England as early as the ninth century, the trifunctional model triumphed in the eleventh century with the formula "*oratores, bellatores,
laboratores*" (those who pray, those who fight, those who work): priests,
warriors, and peasants. It endured down to the time of the French
Revolution with its three estates. The Industrial Revolution established a trifunctionality of quite another order: the primary, secondary, and tertiary sectors invented by sociologists and economists.

From the standpoint of transportation and domination of space, the
Middle Ages are the period of the horse and wagon, preceded by the
human and bovine traction of antiquity and followed by the railway of
the nineteenth century.

In regard to sickness and health, the Middle Ages fall between the
destruction of the ancient baths and the inception of the modern hos-
pital. The era was one of sorcerer-physicians, of bodies martyred or
scorned, without stadiums or sports, a period during which the hospi-
tal was at first more like an asylum and later more like a prison than a
place of cure.

From the standpoint of culture, the Middle Ages fall between the
end of the schools of the ancient world and the mass education of the
nineteenth century. The period saw slow progress in literacy, belief in
miracles, and enduring struggle between high and popular culture,
which borrowed from one another. It was a time of storytelling, written as well as oral, and of tales such as the exemplum, the edifying
anecdote that was a gift from the monks of the East in the fourth century to the Western world where it flourished from the twelfth to the
eighteenth century. And such themes as the angel and the hermit were
passed on from the fabliaux of the twelfth century to Voltaire's *Zadig.*[1]

To be sure, the extended Middle Ages can be divided into subperiods. One might, for example, choose to call the period from the
fourth to the ninth century the early Middle Ages, a time when the
ancient world was still on the wane and the feudal system was just coming into being. The tenth to the fourteenth centuries, or central Middle
Ages, were a time of great progress. And the late Middle Ages, the

fourteenth to the sixteenth century, were a time of crisis. What one might call the Ancien Régime—the waning of the feudal regime—stretches from the English Revolution to the French Revolution, from what Pierre Chaunu calls the time of a "finite world" (which Europeans attempted to conquer with their ships, entrepreneurs, soldiers, and missionaries) to the Industrial Revolution.

One may agree with Krzysztof Pomian that no periodization is adequate because, as Witold Kula nicely puts it, every age exhibits a "coexistence of asynchronisms."[2] Because different kinds of historical phenomena are always "out of sync," it is best to base historical explanation on models, and feudalism, or the feudal system, is perhaps the most instructive model of all.

Why should we be interested today in the concept of an extended Middle Ages? For one thing, it dispels a misleading contrast between two equally false images of the Middle Ages: that of the Dark Ages and that of a golden age of religious faith, corporatist social harmony, and a flourishing art of the people. No one would argue that a Middle Ages that begins with the barbarians was an ideal era, and no one can deny that a Middle Ages that ends with the Enlightenment was a period of progress. By taking a long view we can better comprehend the ambition of an era that knew not only famine, epidemic, pauperism, and religious persecution, but also cathedrals and castles; that invented or discovered the city, the university, work, the fork, furs, the solar system, the circulation of the blood, tolerance, and other things too numerous to name.

Second, we must bear in mind that the process of civilization described by Norbert Elias is still in its first phases, despite the threat of a new apocalypse in the form of nuclear self-destruction. By taking a very long view of the period, we focus on a history that moves more slowly than the history that is perhaps more familiar from tradtional texts. But a history of the evolution of deep structures, both material and psychological, can perhaps tell us more than a rapid-moving but superficial history of events.

Finally, there is widespread interest today in the Middle Ages as the source of what we are today: our roots, our childhood, our dreams of a primitive harmony that was only recently within our grasp, what Peter Laslett has dubbed "the world we have lost." Lost, yes, but we cling to nostalgic memories of what our grandparents still knew. The sound of living voices still binds us to the Middle Ages.

# PART ONE

# THE MARVELOUS

# THE MARVELOUS IN THE
# MEDIEVAL WEST

## I. Remarks and Problems[1]

The question of marvels must be approached by way of vocabulary. No serious study is possible until the semantic field of the word *marvel* has been circumscribed. As always in the historical sciences, we must compare our own vocabulary with that of the historical societies under study. The study of marvels offers fruitful comparative possibilities. We must ask ourselves first how we understand the term and second how the men of the Middle Ages understood and expressed what we now call marvels. My impression is that in the Muslim world the lexicon of the marvelous was quite rich. This is an advantage but perhaps also a disadvantage. It is an advantage because we possess fairly detailed knowledge of what Muslims, especially intellectuals and scholars, classified as marvelous. But I wonder if the Muslim world possessed a word to express what, *mutatis mutandis*, we call marvelous. The medieval West did have such a term. Among scholars, at any rate, the word *mirabilis* was used in almost the same way as our marvelous. But medieval clerics did not possess a psychological, literary, or intellectual category that corresponds exactly to what, in French, we call *le merveilleux, the* marvelous. Where we see an intellectual construct or literary genre, medieval clerics and their students saw a world of objects, a collection rather than a category.

There is also a problem of etymology. The root of *mirabilia* is *mir* (as in *miror, mirari*), which implies something visual. It is a question of looking. Not all *mirabilia* were things that men admired with their eyes, things upon which they gazed with eyes wide open, but originally there was, I think, an important reference to the eyes—important because a whole world of the imagination, a whole series of visual images and metaphors is implied. As Pierre Mabille makes clear in *Le Miroir du merveilleux* (1962), the men of the Middle Ages drew a parallel between *mirari, mirabilia* (marvel) and *mirror* (in Latin, *speculum,* but the affinity with *mirabilia* was clear in the vulgar tongue), thus linking

First published in slightly different form in *L'Etrange et le merveilleux dans l'Islam médiéval,* ed. M. Arkoun, J. Le Goff, T. Fahd and M. Rodinson (Paris: Editions J.A., 1978), pp. 61–79.

the marvel to the complex of images and ideology associated with the mirror.

In order to understand how the medieval mind understood marvels, we must look not only at the learned Latin of the clerics but also at the vulgar languages. A word akin to *marvel* can be found in the literature of all the Romance languages as well as in Anglo-Saxon but not in the Germanic tongues, where the word *Wunder* took its place. Philologists, so far as I know, have yet to explore this area.

Concerning medieval marvels there are, I think, three important questions. First and foremost, what was the attitude of medieval men and women toward the marvelous tradition? Tradition is of course a general problem in the history of culture and civilization. It makes sense to study traditions rather than sources or origins because the concept of a source implies a necessary and almost automatic development, a notion incompatible, in my view, with the reality of concrete historical situations. A tradition exists; it is not created. Yet tradition presupposes a collective as well as individual effort of appropriation, modification, or rejection. This is particularly true in Christian societies, for Christianity embraced a diversity of ancient cultures, and more than other aspects of culture and folklore the marvelous drew upon these ancient strata. To some degree every society produces a concept of the marvelous, but this concept is dependent upon its predecessors, on older notions of what a marvel is. I do not presume to define the Christian sense of the marvelous. My ambition is simply to circumscribe an idea that, admittedly, played no essential role in Christian thought. Medieval Christians developed a concept of marvels, I think, because an influential tradition of the marvelous already existed. Hence Christians had to have an opinion on the subject, to take sides. By contrast, the supernatural and the miraculous are central concepts of Christianity, and these seem to me different from the marvelous in both nature and function. They did, however, influence Christian thinking about marvels.

Within Christianity, then, the marvelous is essentially embodied in tradition, elements of which we encounter in beliefs, literature, and hagiography. The roots of the marvelous are almost always pre-Christian. The traditions in question being continuous, medieval Christianity was obliged to confront them throughout its history. We can trace Christian attitudes toward the marvelous by examining the evolving views of spiritual and intellectual leaders.

For the early Middle Ages, roughly speaking from the fifth to the eleventh century, it is difficult to give any precise cultural chronology.

On the whole I would argue that the marvelous was if not actually rejected then at least repressed during this period. From a cursory study of early medieval, particularly Merovingian, hagiography, I reached conclusions quite similar to those of Frantisek Graus in his much more ambitious study of the same materials.[2] For the student of folklore, early medieval hagiography proves to be rather disappointing, revealing little ethnographically relevant material. Clearly the Church was out either to transform the significance of traditional materials so profoundly as to alter the nature of the phenomenon entirely or to conceal or destroy what it considered the most dangerous elements in traditional—what the Church called pagan—culture. Certainly the marvelous exerted a fascination on some minds; this was one of its social and cultural functions.

By contrast, in the twelfth and thirteenth centuries the marvelous suddenly makes an appearance in high culture. I shall not venture a lengthy explanation of this phenomenon here. Suffice to say, first of all, that I agree with Erich Köhler's view that courtly literature was bound up with the class interests of a rising but already threatened social stratum, namely, the lower and middle ranks of the nobility, the knightly strata. It was the desire of this group to oppose the culture of the Church and its ally, the aristocracy, by erecting not a counter-culture but an alternative culture that was more its own, hence more amenable to its wishes. It therefore drew upon an extant reservoir of culture, namely, the oral culture of which the marvelous was an important component. That the marvelous plays such a large part in courtly romance is no accident. It is intimately associated with the idealized knight's quest for individual and collective identity. The knight is tested by a series of marvels. Marvels such as magical charms aid in his quest, while others such as monsters must be combatted. Accordingly, Erich Köhler draws the conclusion that the knightly adventure itself, the demonstration of prowess in search of identity, was itself nothing other than a marvel.[3]

Another reason for the emergence of the marvelous in this period, I think, is that the Church no longer had the same reasons to oppose it as it had had in the early Middle Ages. The marvelous had become less threatening, and the Church felt that it could tame it or turn it to advantage. Thus, pressure from certain secular social groups combined with increased tolerance on the part of the Church accounts for the emergence of the marvelous in the Gothic Age.

The third phase is somewhat different from the first two. A sociological explanation is still in order, I think, but something needs to be said first about what I have elsewhere called the aestheticization of the marvelous, that is, its increased use as ornament. This was a literary and artistic development, a question of style.

So much for medieval attitudes toward the marvelous. Let me turn now to a second major problem, that of the role of the marvelous within monotheist religion. Here my research is far from complete, my reading is insufficient, and I cannot even venture to state a tentative conclusion. What is needed, I think, is a comprehensive survey relying to some extent on statistical analysis. Nevertheless, I do want to note what I think is a diversification, noticeable first at the level of vocabulary, in the world of the supernatural in the twelfth and thirteenth centuries. This phenomenon helps to provide a better grasp of the relation between the marvelous and the Christian religion.

In recent years the concept of the marvelous has been influenced by Todorov's very interesting work on the literature of the fantastic. In particular, Todorov draws a distinction between the marvelous and the strange. The latter can be dispelled by reflection, whereas the former always leaves a supernatural residue, as it were, and can never be explained in other than supernatural terms. But there is something more than this in the medieval concept of the marvelous.[4] My own view is that in the twelfth and thirteenth centuries supernatural phenomena were divided, in the West, into three categories, fairly clearly delineated by three adjectives: *mirabilis, magicus, miraculosus.*

*Mirabilis* corresponds to our notion of the marvelous, with its pre-Christian origins. Below I attempt to catalogue the phenomena that may be classed as marvelous in this sense.[5] *Magicus* was in theory a neutral term, for there was both black magic, influenced by the devil, and white magic, which was considered legitimate. In fact, however, magicus very quickly came to be associated exclusively with evil, with Satan. It referred to the maleficent supernatural, to the Satanic forces. There was also a specifically Christian supernatural, to which one might refer as the Christian marvelous: *miraculosus.* But the miracle (*miraculum*) was I think only one element—and, I would add, one relatively circumscribed element—in the vast domain of the marvelous. Yet miracles tended to overshadow marvels.[6] The Church, which slowly worked to dismiss marvels as "superstition," needed to distinguish clearly between the two.

One characteristic of the marvelous is of course that of being produced by supernatural forces or beings (note the plural), and one finds something of the sort in the plural *mirabilia* of the Middle Ages. The marvelous embraces a world of diverse objects and actions behind which lies a multiplicity of forces. Now, in Christian marvels and miracles there is an author, to be sure, but that author is God, in the singular. In other words, the status of the marvelous is problematic in any religion, but particularly in a monotheistic religion. As rules develop to define what may legitimately be considered miraculous, the marvel is "rationalized" and stripped of its essential unpredictability.

Etymologically the word *marvel* (from the Latin *mirare,* to look at) suggests a visual *apparition.* The miracle depends only on the will of God, in which respect it may be distinguished from natural events, which are of course also willed by God but are determined once and for all by the regularity that God has built into his creation. Nevertheless, the miracle is also subject to God's plan and to regularity of a certain kind. Many miracles are obtained through the intercession of saints, for example. Despite changes in the nature and sources of hagiography, I think it is possible to detect a growing lassitude in medieval man's attitudes toward the saints: the moment a saint appears, one knows what he is going to do. Given the situation, there is no doubt that he will multiply loaves or raise the dead or exorcise a demon. There is no surprise about what will come to pass. In other words, at some point hagiography ceased to partake of the tradition of the marvelous. Probably some of the difficulty that Christians had in accepting marvels had to do with the fact that there are very few biblical examples.

Of course we must distinguish, as medieval Christians did, between the Old and the New Testament. The latter contains more miracles than marvels. But even in the Old Testament, at least as it was read and understood by the men of the Middle Ages, the marvelous played a relatively limited role. Admittedly, the classic studies of Frazer, Saintyves, and others on the folklore of the Old Testament turned up a variety of marvelous legends and tales.[7] In the Old Testament there are episodes, even entire books, that contributed substantially to the Christian West's fund of marvels, but as it was read, felt, and lived by the men of the Middle Ages there are few marvels as such. The New Testament contains one of the major sources of medieval marvels, the Book of Revelation. But the Bible, while not the universal source, was indeed the universal reference. When the marvelous did finally reemerge, it enjoyed a certain independence, precisely because it was impossible to find for it what medieval Christians were always seeking: a biblical reference.

The third problem that I wish to consider is the function of the marvelous. There is little point in describing and analyzing the marvelous unless we know why it was produced and consumed, what it was used for, and what demand it satisfied. One function of the marvelous was obviously to serve as compensation for the banality and predictability of everyday life. But the way in which this worked varied from society to society and epoch to epoch. In the medieval West the *mirabilia* tended to create a world that was a sort of inverted mirror image of the real world, a world in which food was plentiful and people went naked, enjoyed sexual freedom, and did not work. It is no accident that one of the few medieval inventions was that of never-never land, which first appeared in the thirteenth century. One can trace earlier roots or roughly equivalent notions, but the thing itself was a creation of the Middle Ages. Marvels also turned time around, reviving the idea of an earthly paradise or a golden age but at the end rather than the beginning of time. In this the Book of Genesis was influential, but it was a Genesis in which the pre-Christian elements were emphasized. One looked forward to millenarian utopias not as to future glory but as a return to the origins.

It is not farfetched to say that the marvelous was one form of resistance to the official ideology of Christianity. This was not its only function, but it was one of the most important. Consider briefly the catalogue of the marvelous. In Muslim tales involving marvelous animals, plants, and objects, there is nearly always some reference to man. In the medieval West the opposite is true. The world is largely dehumanized. Marvels feature a world of animals, minerals, and plants. There is a rejection of humanism, a central notion of medieval Christianity based on the idea that man is created in the image of God. In opposition, therefore, to what has been called Christian humanism (or Carolingian or Romanesque or Gothic humanism), which increasingly exploited an anthropomorphic image of God, the marvelous became the focal point of a form of cultural resistance.

The marvelous rarely existed in pure form. At times it grew to extravagant proportions. Marvels often occurred in routine situations but without any real connection to them (like modern surrealism or fantastic Romantic art). People continued to stare at them wide-eyed, but their pupils no longer dilated to quite the same degree. The marvelous remained unpredictable but ceased to be extraordinary.

In Caesarius of Heisterbach's early thirteenth-century *Dialogus Miraculorum*, a young noble who has become a lay brother of the Cistercians is tending sheep in one of his abbey's barns when there appears before him a cousin of his who has recently died. He asks quite simply: "What are you doing?" And the cousin replies: "I am dead. I have come because I am in Purgatory. You must pray for me." The shepherd replies: "What is necessary will be done." The apparition then flees across the meadow and disappears into the landscape as though a part of nature. The world remains undisturbed. The *Otia Imperialia,* a somewhat earlier thirteenth-century text, mentions any number of *mirabilia.* Its author, Gervase of Tilbury, who is living at that time in Arles, reports that in the cities of the Rhone Valley there are evil creatures called *dracs,* which, though generally not ogres, attack children. They steal into locked houses by night, snatch babies from their cribs, and deposit them in streets and marketplaces, but in the morning the doors of the houses are found still to be locked. Anthropologists are quite familiar with this changeling theme. The coming of the dracs is all but imperceptible. The marvel barely ripples the tranquil surface of daily life. What is perhaps most troubling about medieval marvels is precisely the fact that they merge so easily with everyday life that no one bothers to question their reality.

Marvels also played a role in political life. Medieval rulers used them for political ends. Royal dynasties attempted to trace their origins to some mythical past. Noble families and even cities followed their lead. What is surprising, however, is that the myths often involved troubling if not downright suspect marvels. Melusina, who was probably a survival of some fertility goddess, was claimed as an ancestor or a sort of totem by various noble families, of which the Lusignans were the most successful; in fact, she had no name until she took up with them, as it were, whereupon she adopted the clan's name as her own. Thus marvels became an instrument of political power.

The best example of a political marvel is from the early thirteenth-century writings of Giraud le Cambrien.[8] It concerns the "Melusinian" forebears of the Plantagenets. According to Giraud, the Plantagenets were descended from a female demon. From other sources we learn that this legend was widely known and that Richard the Lion-Hearted referred to it to explain his seemingly ignoble concealment of some of the more extravagant aspects of his policy as well as to account for the scandalous hostilities within the dynasty, which pitted father against son. "We sons of the demon," he used to say. What is less well known is that Philip Augustus attempted to use this myth of marvelous origins against the Plantagenets, especially John Lackland. In particular, when he was laying plans for his son Louis to lead an army against England, he mounted a campaign of psychological warfare in which the emissaries and defenders of France spread the notion that it was high time to do away with the children of the demon once and for all.[9]

Finally, there were at least three ways in which the marvelous was reclaimed for other ends: Christian, scientific, and historical. Christians on the one hand recast marvels as miracles and on the other used them as moral symbols. The evolution of the Latin texts of the *Physiologus* provides a good example. The earlier versions tell of animal marvels without ascribing any symbolic significance to them. But later versions incorporate so much moral symbolism that the marvelous intent is all but lost.

Certain clerics, possessed of what we would nowadays call the scientific spirit, scrutinized marvels with a scientific eye. They looked upon *mirabilia* as extreme or exceptional but not unnatural occurrences and considered them to be true even if not sanctioned by the Bible. To my mind, the best example of this attitude is again Gervase of Tilbury, who in his prefaces to the *Otia Imperialia* (texts of great interest to the historian of science) dwells at length on a naturalistic hence scientific view of mirabilia: "Mirabilia vero dicimus quae nostrae cognitioni non subjacent etiam cum sint naturalia" (We call marvels those phenomena that surpass our understanding even though they be natural).[10]

Marvels were reinterpreted not only scientifically but also historically. They were associated, in other words, with specific dates and events. But there can be no marvel if there is no temporary suspension of time and history. Hence the historicizing tendency worked against the tradition of the marvelous. This may well have occurred in other cultures in other parts of the world. Or it may be peculiar to Christianity, which combined symbolism and moral interpretation with scientific and historical rationalism.

## II. A Preliminary Catalogue of the Marvelous in the Medieval West

### Introduction

DEFINITIONS

*a. Current:* According to Tzvetan Todorov, *Introduction à la littérature fantastique* (1970), the marvelous differs from the strange in that it "remains unexplained" and presupposes the "existence of the supernatural." But this definition is not applicable to the concept of the marvelous as it was understood in the Middle Ages. Compare P. Zumthor, *Essai de poétique médiévale* (1972), pp. 137ff. Todorov's definition requires an "implicit reader," who opts for either a natural or supernatural explanation. But the medieval marvelous rules out an implicit reader; it is presented as something objective, conveyed by "impersonal" texts. Note: all the texts that Todorov considers are from the nineteenth or twentieth century with the exception of Perrault's *Tales* and *The Thousand and One Nights*.

*b. Medieval:*  The word *marvelous* belongs to the medieval vocabulary. The Latin *mirabilia* (low Latin: *miribilia*) has derivatives in English and the Romance languages but not in German (where it is replaced by *Wunder, wunderlich*). In particular, in eleventh-century French we find the adjective *merveillos* (in the *Chanson d'Alexis*) and the verb *merveiller* (to admire, in the *Chanson de Roland*). See also Wace, line 1155. But note that the adjective *merveillos* is never used as a noun (as in contemporary French: *le merveilleux*, rendered here as "the marvelous"). The term that best corresponds to the current noun is the plural *mirabilia* (marvels).

*c. Medieval works that allude to the marvelous in the title:*  1. In ancient and urban contexts: *Mirabilia Romae* (mid-twelfth century). See A. Graf, *Roma nella memoria del Medio Evo*, 1915. There is also a description of the "marvels of Naples" in Gervase of Tilbury.

2. Geographical marvels and monsters: Gervase of Tilbury, *Otia Imperialia* (ca. 1210). *Mirabilia uniuscuisque provinciae* (The Marvels of All Countries). Marco Polo, *The Book of Marvels* (1305).[11]

3. The marvelous and Christian ideology: Raymond Lull, *Libre des meravelles* (1288), in Catalan.

*d. The marvelous in popular literature.*  See M. L. Tenèze, "Du conte merveilleux comme genre," in *Approches de nos traditions orales* (Paris, 1970).

## I. Marvels, Magic, Miracles
### THE MARVELOUS AND CHRISTIANITY

In Christian ontology the marvelous is classed as supernatural, but Christian marvels are embodied in miracles in which the marvelous element is limited:

a. because a miracle has a single author, God;

b. because the Church controls the occurrence of miracles;

c. because Christianity rationalizes the marvel, substituting an orthodox view of the supernatural for the essential unpredictability of the marvelous.

Unlike miracles, magic, despite the distinction between white magic and black, is generally considered illicit or deceptive, and its

origins are traced to the devil. The place of the marvelous is between
the miraculous and the magical. It is neither good nor evil and Christianity can therefore tolerate it, but its roots are in a traditional, pre-
Christian system. It draws upon folklore, even where folkloric sources
have been altered by contact with high culture. For medieval man
what was astonishing about marvels was that they were tolerated by
the Church.

The Christianization of the marvelous: see *Huon de Bordeaux* (ca. 1220).
Oberon, the "fairy," is a midget with marvelous powers that he attributes to Jesus (line 3673). Saints, angels, and demons are the agents of
the marvelous. Distortions and changes of function: the Grail (from
magical cup to chalice).

Medieval Christianity incorporated some aspects of the marvelous:
see Keith Thomas, *Religion and the Decline of Magic* (1971). But the
marvelous also resisted.

II. Catalogue of Medieval Marvels

*a. Sites:* Natural sites included mountains (especially hollow mountains) and rocks (Gargantua), springs and fountains, trees (Joan of
Arc's "tree of fairies"), and islands (Islands of the Blessed, islands in
medieval cartography). Sites of human action included cities, castles,
towers, and tombs. See A. Graf, "Les merveilles du Paradis terrestre,"
in *Miti, leggende e superstizioni del medio evo,* 2 vols. (Turin, 1892–1893).

*b. Humans and anthropomorphs:* Giants and midgets (Oberon). Fairies:
see A. Maury, *Les Fées du Moyen Age* (1847). L. Harf-Lancner, *Les Fées
au Moyen Age, Morgane et Mélusine, La Naissance des fées* (Paris: Honoré
Champion, 1984). Also, men and women with physical peculiarities,
such as Bertha with the large feet, Henno with large teeth, and the
children of Melusina. See Jean d'Arras, *Mélusine* (Paris: Stock, 1979).
On human monsters, see C. Bologna, ed., *Liber monstrorum de diversis
generibus* (Milan: Bompiani, 1977), and the book by C. Lecouteux
listed in the bibliography at the end of this section.

*c. Animals:* There are "natural" animals such as Yvain's lion, the horse
Bayard that belonged to Aymon's four sons, and the pelican as a symbol of Christ. And there are also imaginary animals such as the unicorn, griffin, and dragon or the animals that figure in Charlemagne's
dream in the *Chanson de Roland.*

*d. Mischwesen:*  Half-human, half-animal creatures, such as Melusina or the sirens or Yonec in Marie de France's *L'Oiseau bleu* or werewolves (see Metamorphoses in section IV below). The griffin also falls under this class, as do automata. Ultimately we find creatures that are half-living, half-inanimate, as in the paintings of Hieronymus Bosch.

*e. Objects:*  There are protective objects, such as rings that make a person invisible, and productive objectives, such as the cup in *Oberon* or *The Holy Grail* or the horn of plenty in *Oberon* and the *Chanson de Roland*. There are also objects that give strength, such as swords and belts. The bed is sometimes considered a "sacred space" (compare the walled garden).

*f. Historical personages.*  Those who become figures of legend or "scientific" marvels, such as Alexander in the medieval romances that depict him in the heavens or beneath the sea. See C. Settis-Frugoni, *Historia Alexandri Elevati per Griphos ad Aerem: Origine, iconografia et fortuna di una tema* (1973).

## III. Sources and Repositories of Medieval Marvels

See E. Faral, "Le merveilleux et ses sources dans les descriptions des romans français du XIIe siècle," in *Recherches sur les sources latines dans les contes courtois du Moyen Age* (Paris, 1913), pp. 305–388.

### A. SOURCES

*a. Biblical marvels*  See the folklore of the Old Testament, especially Genesis: Eden, Noah's Ark, the Tower of Babel, the crossing of the Red Sea.

The Book of Revelation.

*b. Ancient marvels*  Mythology: Vulcan, Minerva, the Fates, Venus, Alexander, Virgil.

The Seven Wonders of the World.

Pliny's *Natural History* (1st century).

Solinus's *Collectanea rerum memorabilium* (3d century).

*c. Barbarian marvels*  German mythology.

See A.-H. Krappe, *Etudes de mythologie et de folklore germaniques* (1928).

On Breton material, see J. Marx, *La Légende arthurienne et le Graal*

(Paris: Presses Universitaires de France, 1952), and *Nouvelles recherches sur la littérature arthurienne* (Paris, 1965). On Myrddin-Merlin, see P. Zumthor, *Merlin le Prophète* (Lausanne, 1943).

*d. Oriental marvels*   The *Thousand and One Nights*.
*Panchatantra,* a collection of Indian folktales and fables (6th century).
Peter Alphonsi's *Disciplina Clericalis* (ca. 1100), a collection of Arab moral tales by a Spanish Jew converted to Christianity.
*Kalila and Dimna,* an Arabic version of the Persian translation of the Panchatantra (9th century).

*e. Foklore*   See P. Delarue, *Le Conte populaire français,* vol. 1 (1957).
On folklore in exempla, see Jean-Claude Schmitt's essay in *L'Exemplum,* ed. Jacques Le Goff and Jean-Claude Schmitt (Turnhout: Brepols, 1982).

B. REPOSITORIES

*a. The Celtic repository*   Breton material and courtly romance. On adventure as marvel see E. Köhler, *Der altfranzösischer hofische Roman* (Darmstadt: Wissenschaftliche Buchgesellschaft, 1978).

*b. The oriental repository*   On the Orient and especially India as a source of marvels, see Jacques Le Goff, "L'Occident médiéval et l'océan Indien: un horizon onirique," in *Pour un autre Moyen Age* (Paris: Gallimard, 1977), pp. 280–298 [English translation, pp. 189–200]. On Ireland and Sicily as sites of Purgatory, see Jacques Le Goff, *La Naissance du Purgatoire* (Paris: Gallimard, 1982) [translated by Arthur Goldhammer as *The Birth of Purgatory* (Chicago: The University of Chicago Press, 1984)].

IV. Techniques: Ways and Means of Medieval Marvels

*a. Dreams, apparitions, visions*   On the end of the ancient system of dream interpretation (Macrobius) and the uncertain interpretation of dreams, see Jacques Le Goff, "Les rêves dans la culture et la psychologie collective de l'Occident médiéval," in *Pour un autre Moyen Age* (Paris: Gallimard, 1977), pp. 299–306 [English translation, pp. 201–204], as well as the present volume.

*b. Metamorphoses*   See Jacques Le Goff, "Mélusine maternelle et défricheuse," in *Pour un autre Moyen Age* (Paris: Gallimard, 1977), pp. 307–334 [English translation, pp. 205–223]. Werewolves are also of interest.

*c. Magic* On sorcery see A. Danet, trans., *Le Marteau des Sorcières* (Paris, 1973). On sorcery and heresy, in particular an episode in Reims (1176–1180), see Ralph of Coggeshall, *Chronicon anglicarum,* ed. J. Stevenson (1875), pp. 121–125. See also Michelet on sorcery.

*d. On the marvelous in literature* Hagiography.

Journeys in the other world (the Irish *imran* and *Navigatio Sancti Brendani*).

Bestiaries: the *Physiologus.* See M. Ayerra Redin and N. Guglielmi, *El Fisiologo, Bestiario Medievila* (Buenos Aires, 1971), and G. Bianciotto, *Bestiaries du Moyen Age* (Paris: Stock, 1980).

The *Imago mundi.*

*e. On the marvelous in art* See J. Baltrusaitis, *Le Moyen Age fantastique: Antiquités et exotismes dans l'art gothique* (Paris, 1955), and *Réveils et Prodiges: Le Moyen Age fantastique* (Paris, 1960).

## V. Growth and Limits of the Marvelous in the Middle Ages

As marvels appeared in new and unexpected aspects of the culture, their nature was transformed.

*a. Everyday marvels* Marvels were easily and seamlessly integrated into daily life. See, for example, the episode of the *dracs* in Provence in Gervase of Tilbury, *Otia Imperialia,* Decisio 3, chap. 86, and that of the ghost in the meadow in Caesarius of Heisterbach, *Dialogus Miraculorum,* Decisio 12, chap. 33.

*b. Symbolic and moralistic marvels.* See the *Physiologus.*

*c. Political marvels* The myth of origin was used as a political tool. The Lusignan clan, for instance, traced its origin to Melusina. Richard the Lion-Hearted and the Plantagenets claimed to be sons of a demon (see Giraud de Barri, *De Instructione Principis*).

*d. Scientific marvels* See Gervase of Tilbury. There was a tendency to characterize marvels as rarities rather than supernatural phenomenon, as unexplained rather than inexplicable events. Marvels took place on the fringes of this world, not in another world.

*e. Marvels and history: the exemplum* See A. Jolles, *Formes simples* (1972), p. 193: "The moment the folk tale took on historical traits . . .

it lost a part of its force. Historical localization and dating brought the tale closer to immoral reality and sapped the power of the natural and necessary marvel."

VI. Functions of the Medieval Marvel

a. *Compensation*   The world turned upside down; Never-Never Land. Abundance of food, nudity, sexual freedom.
Paradise regained: Eden and the golden age.

b. *Challenges to Christian ideology*   Antihumanism:
—The savage
—Monsters
—*Mischwesen,* half-men, half-animals
—Opposition to the idea of man *ad imaginem Dei*
The rejection of Manichaeanism:
—Domesticated or not, the marvelous remained ambiguous, neither wholly good nor wholly evil. See, for example, the dragon of St. Marcel of Paris in Jacques Le Goff, *Pour un autre Moyen Age,* pp. 236–279.
Optimism: the marvel and the happy ending.

c. *The Accomplishment*   Mirari, Mirror, Marvel.
On the mirror as a theme of literature, see D. Poirion, *Etude sur le Roman de la Rose* (1974), chap. 2.
The marvelous tale.
On the marvelous not as escape but as accomplishment: see Pierre Mabille, *Le Miroir du merveilleux:* "Marvelous journeys offered more than just pleasure, satisfaction of curiosity, amusement, escape, terror, and enjoyment; they offered a more thorough explanation of the whole of reality than was available anywhere else."

CONCLUSION
Periodization of medieval attitudes toward the marvelous:
  1. The early Middle Ages and the repression of the marvelous
  2. The emergence of the marvelous: 12th–13th centuries
  3. The aestheticization of the marvelous: 14th–15th centuries

## III. Revelations and Speculations

Marvels consisted in large part of enlargements or distortions of the normal, natural world. Giants, midgets, and creatures with extra appendages were not common but were basically natural. So were fabulous and mythical beasts and, stretching a point, *Mischwesen* and some of the more extreme monstrosities found in the paintings of Bosch, half-human, half-inanimate. Insofar as these were creatures that did not exist but whose existence was possible, they were marvels only to the first degree. But the marvelous was not content merely to surpass nature; there was something in it that was very much antinature. The exaggeration and extravagance of marvelous creatures extended beyond the quantitative into the realm of the qualitative. *Metamorphosis,* one of the profound features of the marvelous, eludes characterization in terms of the devices used to produce simple "static" marvels: accentuation, multiplication, association, or distortion. In the Christian system marvels were scandalous because they transformed human beings, created "in God's image," into animals.

Curiously, the transformation of humans into plants was far less common in the Middle Ages than in antiquity. Medieval marvels of plant transformation were generally based on a bookish tradition. Yet most of the medieval literature of the marvelous drew on oral and "popular" tradition. The werewolf, treated in a long series of medieval texts, is an interesting case in point. At bottom Gervase of Tilbury and many others anticipated Shakespeare in saying that there is more in heaven and earth than is dreamt of in philosophy, notwithstanding the problems that such a view poses for Christianity. At times Gervase is shockingly bold, as in one extraordinary passage where he says that Genesis omits some aspects of Creation. But the marvelous as such is not really compatible with rational explanation. One characteristic of the marvel is its dreamlike instability. In other words, one awakens from a marvel as from a dream; with the return of cognition the marvelous either vanishes like smoke or is transformed by rationalization into knowledge of another kind.

Western Christendom was also familiar with the purgative function of the marvelous, in which strangeness is associated with foreignness and all disturbing fantasies are shifted into another world, namely, the East (leaving aside the Celtic case, which is special). For the men of the West the East was the great repository of the marvelous, the focal point of Western dreams and magic. The East represented the *truly foreign,* and had done so for the Greeks and Romans, at any rate, since antiquity. From the East came both good and bad, marvels and heresies. The men of the West were well aware of this, at times with surprising consequences. Paradoxically, when Marco Polo traveled to the East and reported what he had seen, mixing truth with falsehood but in any event telling something of the truth, the men of the West refused to believe him. In the late Middle Ages his account of his travels was viewed as a book of fables, a fantasy, and it was referred to as the "Book of Marvels," where in this case *marvel* has the sense of mirage. It was as if occidentals were unable to believe in the reality of the marvels of the Orient.[11]

Exaggerating somewhat, one could almost say that Christianity, or at any rate medieval Christianity, was allergic to the marvelous. Of course I am well aware that the house of the Lord has many mansions and that even the relatively unified Christianity of the Middle Ages was capable of accommodating considerable diversity. Still, Saint Bernard expressed what I think was the fundamental Christian view when he criticized Romanesque art for its figuration of the marvelous. The clergy believed in miracles but not in marvels. Images were another thing entirely; Tzvetan Todorov has written a fine book on the subject, but it is useless for my purposes because the medieval mind knew nothing of the *fantastic*. When Baltrusaitis speaks of the "fantastic in the Middle Ages," he is making anachronistic use of a concept borrowed from the Romantics and Surrealists.

Another important question is whether Christianity's especially intense fantasies and taboos can account for some aspects of medieval marvels. I am thinking not only of sexual marvels but also of alimentary ones. Prodigious appetites, dietary taboos, and the ingestion of hallucinogens and aphrodisiacs are only a few aspects of this complex phenomenon. Concupiscence and gluttony were linked in the Christian mind. There was also an obsession with idleness, with what one might call the marvel of unemployment. An ideology of hostility to work may lurk in medieval marvels.

"Popular" and "learned" marvels were dialectically related in ways that are difficult to unravel because the boundaries between high and popular culture were constantly shifting. The rather crude periodization that I proposed earlier is applicable mainly to high culture. The cultivated clergy was initially rather successful in obscuring much of the tradition of the marvelous that existed in popular culture, glimpses of which can be seen in other sources. Later, in the twelfth and thirteenth centuries, high culture proved more receptive to popular traditions, which it assimilated and reworked. Still later there was a tendency to take an aesthetic view of the marvel, and the dialogue or struggle between high and popular culture ceases to be so prominent. But how can we study the popular traditions of the early Middle Ages, since these were transmitted primarily by oral means? Van Gennep does not look back any further than the late Middle Ages partly because few documents have survived from earlier periods and partly because a new popular culture imbued with Christian influence had by then been born. Earlier sources—perhaps above all iconographic sources—must be collected and scrutinized with care.

Folktales involving marvels are especially rich mines of information. As history progresses these tales are subject to revealing changes, especially as regards the relation between the ordinary and the extraordinary or the natural and the supernatural, as I have attempted to show in my study of Melusina.

Some readers may find fault with my contention that the Bible contains few marvels. Think of the words of Isaiah that Christians interpreted as applying to the Messiah: "*Vocabitur nomen ejus admirabilis*" ("he will be called the Admirable," sometimes translated as: Marvelous) or of Saint Paul's words in the Second Epistle to the Thessalonians" *Cum venerit admirabilis fieri in omnibus qui crediderunt* ("When he shall come . . . to be admired in all them that believe," 1 : 10).

Between *admirabilis* and *mirabilis,* however, it seems to me that there is an important distinction. For medieval Christians the life and person of Christ were not marvelous but miraculous and admirable. The "religion of the marvelous" was not the religion of the Middle Ages. There is, however, at least one marvel in the New Testament, connected with the Nativity of Jesus, in which the presence of the East is significant. This is also the only passage in the New Testament in which dreams and visions play an important role.

A marvelous interpretation of the New Testament would have been branded as Gnostic, and medieval clerics ostensibly preferred a narrower reading. But the reality is certainly more complicated than this view suggests. Significantly, even the most orthodox medieval Christians read not only the New Testament recognized by the Church but also the Apocrypha, through which they absorbed the Gnostic influence and, with it, elements of the marvelous. Once again, however, it is images to which students of the subject must direct their attention.

## Bibliographic Note

The following important works appeared after this essay was completed:

Kappler, Claude, *Monstres, démons et merveilles à la fin du Moyen Age.* Paris: Payot, 1982.

Lecouteux, Claude. *Les Monstres dans la littérature allemande du Moyen Age (1150–1350).* 3 vols. Göttingen, 1982.

Meslin, Michel, ed. *Le Merveilleux: L'imaginaire et les croyances en Occident.* Paris: Bordas, 1984.

Poirion, Daniel. *Le Merveilleux dans la littérature française au Moyen Age.* Paris: Presses Universitaires de France, 1982.

# PART TWO

# SPACE AND TIME

# THE WILDERNESS IN THE
# MEDIEVAL WEST

Scholars have attempted to demonstrate a connection between religious phenomena and the desert, or wilderness. They have asked themselves whether there is perhaps a religion of the desert and whether the desert favors one kind of religious experience over another. Some have argued that wilderness encourages mysticism. A century ago, Ernest Renan in his *History of the People of Israel* (1887) boldly asserted that "the desert is monotheistic." Such simplistic geographic determinism is untenable today.[1]

But the desert-wilderness, whether real or imagined, has played an important role in the major religions of Europe and Asia: Judaism, Islam, and Christianity. Because it usually represented values opposed to those of the city, it is a subject of great interest for social and cultural history.

The medieval West took its cultural models first of all from the Bible, that is, from the East, and in the Bible the desert is both a symbol and a historical and geographical reality—an ambivalent reality. Abel's murder leaves Adam and Eve with two sons, Seth and Cain. From Seth stems religion, for Seth's son Enos is the first "to call upon the name of the Lord" (Genesis 4:26). And from Cain stems civilization, especially material civilization in its four principal forms[2]: urban life (Cain himself builds the first city); the pastoral civilization of the desert through Jabal, descendant of Enoch, Cain's son, "the father of such as dwell in tents, and of such as have cattle" (Genesis 4:20); art, through Jabal's brother Jubal, "the father of all such as handle the harp and organ" (Genesis 4:21); and craft, through Tubal-Cain, "instructor of every artificer in brass and iron" (Genesis 4:22).

In ancient Israel the desert long rivaled the city of Cain in prestige. Despite the difficulties of crossing the desert as described in Exodus, the Hebrew people clung to their memories of desert life, as Yahweh observed when he established the holy day of tabernacles (Succoth): "Ye shall dwell in booths seven days . . . that your generations may know that I made the children of Israel to dwell in booths, when I brought them out of the land of Egypt" (Leviticus 23:42–43).

Originally published as *Traverses/19: Le désert* (Paris: Centre Georges-Pompidou, Centre de création industrielle, 1980), pp. 22–33, with illustrations.

In the same vein, Yahweh maintains a balance between the city in which Sarah and Isaac remain and the desert into which Hagar and Ishmael are sent in exile: "Let it not be grievous in thy sight because of the lad, and because of thy bondwoman; in all that Sarah hath said unto thee, hearken unto her voice; for in Isaac shall thy seed be called. And also of the son of the bondwoman will I make a nation, because he is thy seed" (Genesis 21:12–13). Even after the Hebrews had settled in towns and the urban symbolism of Jerusalem and Zion had replaced the older symbolism of the desert, ambivalence toward desert values persisted. In the psalms Yahweh is praised as a builder (Psalm 147:2: "The Lord doth build up Jerusalem"), but bittersweet memories of the desert remain (Psalm 136:16: "To him which led his people through the wilderness: for his mercy endureth forever"). But the desert to which positive value is ascribed in the Old Testament is a place not of solitude but of trial and above all of rootless wandering.

The changing image of the desert in the Old Testament is a complex subject and beyond the scope of this essay. Much could be said, for example, about the contrast between the desert in Genesis, initially the desert of the primordial chaos and later the antithesis of Eden, into which Adam is sent as a punishment, and the desert in Exodus, the Sinai of Moses and the Jewish people, a wilderness experienced collectively and scene of Yahweh's most important revelation.[3]

Other scholars have called attention to the close ties that exist among the desert, the ocean, death, and *sheol*, the hellish abode of the dead.[4] These associations are specific to ancient Judaism and were not adopted by Christianity, although it is possible that the medieval Celtic hermits who went to sea in search of the desert were encouraged by their reading of the Old Testament.

In the New Testament the biblical image of the desert changes. It is now not just a place but "an epoch in religious history during which God educated his people."[5] For Jesus of Galilee, the desert of Judaea in which John the Baptist lived, an almost empty wilderness of arid mountains rather than sand, was a dangerous place, a place not so much of trials as of temptations.[6] It was an abode of unclean spirits (Matthew 12:43) and the scene of Satan's first try at tempting Jesus: "Then was Jesus led up of the spirit into the wilderness to be tempted of the devil" (Matthew 4:1). But it was also the place where Jesus sought refuge and solitude (Mark 1:35, 45). In Revelation 12:6–14, the wilderness is the refuge of "the woman," that is, of Zion, of the holy people in the Messianic age, the Church of believers.

The fourth century saw the beginning of what has been called

Christianity's "desert epic" in the East.[7] The major works of desert hagiography and spirituality formed part of the tradition of the Roman Catholic Church as well as of Orthodoxy. The earliest of these was the *Life of Anthony* by the Greek Athanasius, bishop of Alexandria (ca. 360), which enjoyed almost instantaneous success in the West in a variety of Latin translations.

Anthony's primacy among eremites was soon challenged by Saint Jerome, who between 374 and 379 wrote the *Life of Paul of Thebes, the First Hermit,* in the Calchis desert east of Antioch in Syria. Which of the two saints came first is of little importance. Christians in the West looked upon both as exemplars of the desert ideal. Jerome hit upon the ingenious idea of having Anthony, at age ninety, pay a call on Paul, by then over a hundred, in his retirement. In an atmosphere more delirious than anything in Victor Hugo's most unbridled romantic imagination, the nonagenarian pays homage to his elder, tries to outdo him in reverence, and returns to wrap him in a winding sheet fetched from his own hermitage.

Paul's wilderness consisted of "a mountain, a cave, a palm, and a spring." Clad in palm leaves, he lived on half a loaf of bread brought him each day by a crow. When he died, "two lions emerged from the depths of the wild on the run, their manes flying." Their tails brushed against the old man's body as they roared a sort of funeral prayer, after which they dug a grave with their claws and buried the body in it. Then they came "wiggling their ears and with heads lowered" to lick the feet of Saint Anthony, who watched dumbstruck and offered the beasts his blessing.

There is little to choose between Anthony and Paul as models of the anchorite life. Like Paul, Anthony spent his later years, after the age of sixty, in the mountains, living in a cave in an area described by modern explorers as particularly harsh and arid but which Athanasius's *Life* depicts as an earthly paradise. He survives on the fruits of a palm tree and a few loaves brought him by Saracens—black men, counterparts to Paul's black bird. But the early years of Anthony's life as a hermit consist of an unending struggle against visions of terrifying monsters and demons. The temptations of Saint Anthony are a "theater of shadows."

As Guillaumont writes: "The desert of the Egyptian monks appears to have been an ideal site for marvels. There the monk encounters the demon, an encounter that it must be said is all but inevitable, for the demon is at home in the desert. But the monk in his own way also finds the God for whom he has come looking."[8]

The themes of desert holiness were tirelessly reworked, multiplied, and embellished in two important anthologies of hagiography, *Conversations with the Fathers of Egypt* (early fifth century) by John Cassian, who had lived among the oriental hermits, and the *Lives of the Fathers*, a collection of anecdotes translated from the Greek that began to circulate in the West also in the early fifth century.

Western anchorites in their quest for geographical and spiritual deserts often fled to islands. At Lérins on the Mediterranean, for example, the "desert" was at times envisioned as a kind of paradise, at other times as a place of trial.[9] It was liberation for those seeking solitude (*ad solitudinum liberatem*), a "haven of salvation," a "corner of heaven" (*quasi in parte aliqua paradisi*, in the words of Caesarius of Arles).

In this incipient stage of western monasticism wilderness and city were not yet sharply distinguished. To be sure, monks who sought solitude fled the city. But monks came in such great numbers to cultivate semiarid land that they often turned deserts into cities. An expression from the *Life of Anthony* translated into Latin became a topos of monastic literature: *desertum-civitas*, or *desert-city*.[10]

Monks in the medieval West could look to the still vital cities of late antiquity as models, as Paul-Albert Février has shown. The monastery became a microcity, and the leaders of the monastic movement in the West achieved in both their lives and works a balance between desert and city. Saint Martin, for example, divided his life between the solitude of the monastery at Marmoutier and his episcopal duties in Tours; John Cassian, who experienced something like the solitude of the Egyptian deserts on the Lérins Islands, also knew the city of Marseilles; Paulinus, who had gone to be near the relics of Saint Felix near Nola, was obliged to reside in the city as its bishop.[11] A similar alternation between hermetic retirement and an urban apostolate can be found in Franciscanism.

Sometimes the wilderness was seen as a kind of paradise, whose inhabitants were commonly depicted as living on familiar terms with wild animals in the manner of Anthony and Paul. In the absence of lions in the West, bears, deer, and squirrels were cast in the role of friends and companions of eremites. Of Saint Columban it has been said that "in Luxeuil as in Bobbio he always displayed an almost Franciscan sympathy for animals." Godric (died 1170) withdrew into solitude at Finchale near Durham, where he welcomed rabbits and hares into his cell to protect them from hunters. For the wilderness was an asylum, a refuge within a refuge. Literature, neglecting the zoological facts, provided Yvain, that courtly Saint Jerome, with a lion as companion. In his *Eulogy of the Desert* (*De laude eremi*) the aristocrat Euches, who retired to Lérins between 412 and 420, recounts all the important episodes of the Old and the New Testament that took place in the desert (*eremus,* he indicates, is synonymous with *desertum*) and asserts that the monastic desert is the source of all charisma and theophany. Entering the wilderness was like a second baptism, according to Saint Jerome.

But the wilderness was also the place where one met Satan and his demons, although this theme, associated with the spirituality of the desert in the East, was not as successful in the medieval West. Euches alludes only in passing to the temptations of the Enemy, who lurks about the hermitage as the wolf lurks about the barn. By contrast, the peril that awaited the western hermit in his wilderness was acedia, or existential and metaphysical boredom.

Celtic and Nordic monks sought wilderness on islands.[12] The sea and the cold were for them what sand and sun were in the deserts of the East: "For these monks the sea replaced the Egyptian desert."[13] Saint Brendan, whose maritime wanderings were recounted in one of the most successful books of the Middle Ages, the *Navigatio Sancti Brendani,*[14] traveled from island to island encountering monsters and marvels. Avoiding the Isle of Hell, he came ultimately to the Isle of Paradise. In the late sixth-century *Life of Columban* it was said of these sea-roving monks that they "hoped to find the desert in the impassable sea" (*desertum in pilago intrasmeabili invenire obtantes*).

But these seafaring monks were far from the norm in the West, with its temperate climate and absence of vast arid wastes. Here, "desert"—meaning solitude—was quite different from what we mean by the word desert in its usual geographical sense, almost the opposite in fact: namely, the forest.

Columban, the most celebrated of the Irish monks (ca. 540–615), followed an exemplary itinerary. In 575 he set out by sea for the continent. From Armorica he traveled to Gaul. The Burgundian king Guntran offered him a place to live at Annegray in the Vosges, a place that he liked, according to his biographer Jonas of Bobbio (ca. 640), because it was in the middle of a forest: "a vast desert, a harsh solitude, a rocky terrain." But he was exiled from Annegray and the nearby monastery at Luxeuil by King Thierry II at the behest of his formidable grandmother Brunhilde. After much wandering, the elderly monk arrived in northern Italy and in 613 selected a place of solitude at Bobbio. To build his hut, the old abbot cut wood as he had done in his youth.

The history, or legend, of another Irish saint, Ronan, who settled in Brittany, incorporates many of the themes of the forest-as-wilderness. "He plunged deep . . . into the 'desert' and reached the forest of Nemet (or Nevet) in Cornwall." Working miracles, he protected the nearby population from wolves but aroused the ire of Satan, who through the diabolical peasant woman Keban finally drove him away.[15]

The history of the desert has always been compounded of both material and spiritual realities, of constant interplay between geography and symbolism, the imaginary and the economic, the social and the ideological. What was the medieval forest "really" like?

For Gaston Roupnel, the forest from neolithic times to the end of the Middle Ages was both an indispensable "extension and complement of cultivated land" and the focus of man's "legendary fears": "On this sacred and well-protected threshold the first clearers of land halted their profane enterprises once and for all."[16]

Charles Higounet has mapped the forests of the early Middle Ages.[17] Between 500 and 1200 Europe's climate was warmer than normal, encouraging an "aggressive resurgence of the forest. Among European forests, according to Higounet, the forest of the Ardennes had been since Celtic times "*the* forest par excellence." In addition to the Italian and Spanish *selva,* which perpetuated the Latin *silva,* and the German *wald,* he notes the emergence of the word *forestis* or *foresta,* which gave *forêt* in French, *Forst* in German, and *forest* in English. The earliest known occurrence of the term, in a charter granted in 648 by Sigebert III to the abbey of Stavelot-Malmédy, associates the idea of forest with that of solitude: "In our forest named Ardennes, a vast solitude in which wild animals reproduce. . . ."[18] The word no doubt comes from the expression *silva forestis,* a forest under the jurisdiction of a royal tribunal (*forum*). Originally it referred to a hunting preserve and had a legal significance. The *bellatores* or warriors, those who fulfilled the second of the three functions identified by Georges Dumézil as being common to the Indoeuropean cultures, attempted in the Middle Ages to appropriate the forest and make it their private hunting ground. But they were obliged to share it with the *oratores,* the men of the first function, whose mission was prayer and who turned the forest into a "desert" for eremites, as well as with the *laboratores,* the men of the third function, who gathered food, fuel, and honey and fed their hogs there, making it a region of supplemental economic activity. All went to the forest to behave as men of nature, fleeing the world of culture in every sense of the word.

As Higounet points out, the medieval forest served as a frontier, a refuge for pagan cults and hermits "who came looking for the 'desert' (*eremum*)" as well as for those defeated in war and those who lived on the fringes of society: fugitive serfs, murderers, soldiers of fortune, brigands. Yet it was also useful, a precious game preserve and a source of food, fuel, and honey, from which "the most common beverage in Europe" was brewed. The forest also supplied wax for candles, wood for building, materials for making glass and metals, and grazing land for domestic animals, especially pigs.

Marc Bloch long ago called attention to the two faces of the medieval forest, "which covered much more territory than today with dense woods only rarely alleviated by clearings." Men were both attracted and repelled: "Although inhospitable in many ways, the forest was far from useless."[19] The sources, Bloch tells us, refer to the "opacity" and "density" of the forest.

The medieval forest, he continues, "was far from being unexploited or devoid of men," but its denizens were a frightening lot: "A whole world of woodsmen, upon whom more sedentary folk looked with suspicion, traveled through the forest or lived in huts: hunters, charcoal burners, blacksmiths, honey and wax gatherers, ashmen employed in the fabrication of glass and soap, and bark pullers who supplied bark used in tanning leather or making rope."[20]

Of many sources that tell us something about the nature of the medieval forest, I wish to focus on three contained in a recently published book.[21] The Benedictine Lambert of Hersfeld relates in his *Annals* for the month of August 1073 an episode in Emperor Henry IV's war with the Saxons. He evoked the thick, vast (*vastissima*) German forest, so difficult to penetrate and inhospitable that Henry and his companions nearly die of hunger there. To anyone but a hunter familiar with "the secrets of the forest" it is a frightening place. In the *Life of Saint Bernard of Tiron* Geoffrey the Fat describes "the vast solitudes (*vastae solitudines*) that straddle the border of Maine and Brittany" as virtually a second Egypt (*quasi altera Ægyptus*) populated by a "multitude of hermits." One of them, named Pierre, lives on "young tree shoots" and has built himself a "small house" of "tree bark." When Bernard and others join him, he goes with baskets "into the forest that surrounds his dwelling on all sides and quickly pulls up thorny bushes and brambles and gathers nuts and other fruits from the trees." Finally, "he finds in a hollow tree a swarm of bees with wax and honey in such quantities that all these riches seemed to spring from the horn of plenty itself." The influence of early medieval monastic literature in which the desert figured as a kind of paradise is evident here. The third text that I will cite is well known. In it Suger recounts how, in looking for wood for the frame of Saint-Denis, he ignored everyone's advice and searched the forest of Yveline and "having negotiated cliffs of stone, dark thickets, and forests of thorns found trees tall and thick enough to make a dozen beams." Exploitation had reduced the outer edges of the forest to underbrush as trees were removed to meet the demand for raw materials.

There is much additional evidence that the forest was equated with the wilderness in the medieval mind. In the cartulary of Sainte-Foy of Conques for 1065, for example, there is a document stating that a community of monks had settled in a place where "there was no human habitation except for the brigands in the forests." [22]

The nascent vernacular attests to the strength of this mental association. An almost natural epithet for the forest was *gaste,* meaning devastated, empty, arid, and the nouns *gast* and *gastine,* uncultivated places or forest wastes, were almost synonymous with *forêt. Forez i a granz e gastines,* wrote the Anglo-Norman troubadour Benedict of Sainte-Maure in the twelfth century. All these words were derivatives of *vastum,* or wasteland. In addition to the triumphant *forêt* the rich vocabulary contained terms for wood with the same root as the German *Wald: galt, gant, gandine.* Dom Louis Gougaud has called attention to place names derived from the words *désert* and *ermitage* in France, *desert* in Ireland, and *peniti* in Brittany, all of which refer to places once occupied by hermits. [23] The Breton term reminds us that the desert was also a place of penitence, especially during the great penitential movement of the eleventh to thirteenth centuries.

Guibert of Nogent in his early twelfth-century autobiography relates the story of Evrard de Breteuil, viscount of Chartres, who in 1073 turned his back on the world and sought solitude and refuge in a forest where he earned his living by making charcoal. [24] Flight was common through the ages, but there were waves of enthusiasm for the "desert" between the fourth and seventh centuries, associated with the abandonment of the cities of the ancient world, and again in the eleventh and thirteenth centuries, in reaction against the renewal of urban growth: "We have abandoned everything: those are the words that have filled the forests with anchorites," exclaimed Peter Damian (died 1072) in a sermon. Nearly a century later Saint Bernard echoed this same thought, telling youths tempted by the new urban schools that "the forests will teach you more than books. The trees and rocks will teach things that the masters of science will never teach you." There is a vast literature on western eremitism. [25]

But the deeper symbolic significance of the forest must be sought in works of the imagination, including some of the greatest works of Old French literature: Béroul's *Tristan,* Chrétien de Troyes's romances, especially *Yvain* and *Perceval,* and *Aucassin et Nicolette.* The work of the Occitan troubadour Bernard Marti is also worth mentioning.

The presence of the forest-desert is also to be noted in chansons de geste, especially in the cycle of William of Orange. Initially it was depicted as a place for noble warriors to hunt, but later, in the *Moniage Guillaume,* it became a place populated with hermits in hidden "in high edges" and "in the depths of the leafy wood." Its presence is especially noteworthy in *Renaud de Montauban* (*Les Quatre Fils Aymon*) and in *Girard de Roussillon,* late twelfth-century works set partly in the forest of Ardennes, which may express the flight from the world of a warrior aristocracy threatened by a new society. In *Girard de Roussillon,* for example, the hero wandering in the forest asks a hermit if he knows a priest in the vicinity. "No," says the man of the woods, "not even a cleric." The forest is the desert as far as the ecclesiastical institution is concerned.

Thus, the Judaic and eastern tradition of the desert was joined by a "barbarian" or Celtic tradition as well as a Germanic-Scandinavian one. A good example of the latter is Snorri Sturluson's Icelandic saga of Harald Sigurdarson, near the beginning of which Harald, the future king of Norway, hides "in the isolated house of a peasant who lived in a forest." The peasant's son guides him "through the forests," and as they are riding from one virgin wood to another Harald says:

> Here I am, without glory, traveling
> From forest to forest.
> Who knows if later on my fame
> Will not spread far and wide?[26]

Here the forest is viewed as a trial.

Yet it was above all in courtly literature that the forest played an important narrative and symbolic role as the setting of the chivalric adventure story.[27] In Béroul's *Tristan* the forest is a place of refuge. Tristan and Isolde, fleeing King Mark's wrath, take refuge in the forest of the Morois, where Tristan "feels as safe as in a castle surrounded by walls." An excellent archer, he hunts for food and builds a cabin for himself and his companion, where they remain "for a long time, deep in the forest, a desert in which they remained for a long time." All the themes encountered previously recur here: the forest as refuge, the forest as desert, the association (also present in Chrétien de Troyes's *Yvain*) of the forest-desert with the bow and arrow (echoing *Genesis* and the story of Ishmael), a "savage" yet paradisaical existence despite a "harsh and bitter life."

Tristan and Isolde encounter a hermit, Ogrin, who preaches to them in vain. For a long time they continue to live in the forest, and no one comes looking for them because ordinary mortals find the woods "so frightening that no one dares to enter." Tristan perfects a bow that never misses its target and, lacking bread (the nourishment of "culture"), the couple must survive on wild game. But a forest warden, whose job it is to protect the king's rights as lord of the forest, discovers them and denounces them to Mark, who nevertheless foreswears vengeance. Knowing that they have been discovered, however, Tristan and Isolde leave the forest, which can no longer fulfill its function of refuge and hiding place.[28] This complex episode combines fear of the forest with esteem for the simple life of the wilderness, which is a place of repentance as well as asylum.

Pierre Vidal-Naquet and I have attempted to give a Lévi-Straussian interpretation of Chrétien de Troyes's *Yvain ou le Chevalier au lion,* which dates from about 1180.[29] Yvain, who, failing to keep a promise to his wife, is spurned by her, goes mad and, fleeing the court of King Arthur, takes refuge in the forest. I cannot summarize the full analysis here; interested readers may refer to our article. Here I shall focus exclusively on the theme of the forest as desert. Yvain regresses totally to the state of nature. He becomes a "hunter with bow and arrow, a naked savage, an eater of raw meat." His reintegration into society begins when he meets a man who is not entirely a savage: a hermit. This hermit has a house, or at least a hut; he practices a rudimentary form of agriculture, clearing land by burning and grubbing for roots; he buys and eats bread; he has contacts with "normal" human beings; and he cooks his food. In the same forest Yvain also encounters a "savage," a hideous, base fellow covered with hair and clad in animal skins but who gives orders to two wild bulls. Thus this savage is master of the forest and not merely a guest because he has tamed the wild beast.[30]

It should be clear, then, that neither the forest nor the desert was wholly wild or isolated. Both were places on the extreme fringes of society, where men could venture and meet other men, some of them so wild that they were mistaken at first for beasts, at least until they insisted, as the hairy savage did to Yvain, that they were men. Thus in the hermitic life, the experience of the desert, there were also degrees. The hermit remained in contact with culture, which enabled the Church to tolerate the popular belief that hermits were "holy men."

The savage was a "primitive" but already master of nature. Only a madman would have dared plunge into the depths of solitude and savagery. Ultimately, "what was 'savage' was not what was out of man's reach but what was on the fringes of human activity. The forest (*silva*) was wild (*silvatica*) not only because it was where one hunted but also because it was where some men burned charcoal and kept pigs. Between savagery and culture—asymmetrical roles—the savage, crazed hunter was an ambiguous mediator, as was the hermit after his fashion."[31]

Four characteristics of the hermit should be noted. First, he was thought of as being akin to the savage, as indicated by the fact that he wore clothing of sheepskin or goatskin. The Christian prototype was John the Baptist, the desert preacher. Second, the hermit was a popular figure. People went to him to confess their sins, to seek advice, or to obtain blessing or healing. And here I mean *popular* in the full sense of the word: of all the figures of religion, the hermit was the closest to authentic popular culture, to folklore. No place was more remote from the institutions of high culture than the "desert."[32]

Among those who sought council from hermits were kings. A tenth-century Irish poem describes a king's visit to a hermit, a "theme exploited many times in the literature of the Middle Ages."[33] This was of course a variation on the theme of the king who consults a magus, soothsayer, or prophet, but it was also a dialogue between two men of the forest. Those who went in search of holiness were obliged to visit the forest, or desert, where the king, like the lion, was in his element: "The forest was royal land not only in the sense that its resources belonged to the king but perhaps even more because it was a 'desert.'"[34]

Finally, in the forest-desert the hermit rubbed shoulders with the outlaw. According to legend he sometimes joined outlaw bands, such as Robin Hood's, for example. One English fabliau, *The Eremyte and the Outelawe*, portrays a hermit as jealous of a thief because, he says, it is too easy for the thief to make his way into heaven.

To return to Chrétien de Troyes, the forest as a place of trial and adventure figures largely in his last romance, *Perceval or the Story of the Grail*. Although Perceval is the son of the Lady of the Forest Waste and is called a "wild knave," he is not a savage in the true sense of the word.[35] But his initiation includes many trials set in the forest, as so many stages of meditation, adventure, and lonely wandering. The forest is called lonely, false, and treacherous, for it is a place of hallucinations, temptations, and ambushes, characteristic of the symbolism of the desert. At a crucial moment[36] Perceval encounters in the depths of the forest a hermit who reveals that he is Perceval's uncle and who explains the reasons for and meaning of the trials he has undergone. Penitence and revelation: this is the profound, apocalyptic Christian significance of the forest-wilderness.

The forest as a place of trial and refuge is also found in a delightful minor key in *Aucassin et Nicolette*. Nicolette flees into the immense, frightening forest: "Extending for more than thirty leagues in length and breadth, it was home to wild beasts and huge numbers of snakes. Nicolette was afraid of being eaten alive if she ventured in." Yet despite her fear she takes refuge in the forest and builds herself a "fine hut." Aucassin hastens after her, heedless of thorns and brambles, and also runs into a wild man of sorts, a fearsome-looking young peasant who has come in search of a runaway ox. Ultimately the couple emerges from the "deep wood," finds the sea, and eventually rejoins the world of men and urban civilization.

The troubadours turned the theme of the lovers' flight into the forest into an idyll, a voluntary retreat into a sylvan utopia, the desert of love. Listen to Bernard Marti: "I want to live as a hermit in the woods, provided my lady comes with me. There we shall sleep beneath a coverlet of leaves. This is where I wish to live and die. I abandon and renounce all other cares."[37]

Opposed to the forest-wilderness in the medieval Western value system was the "world," that is, organized society. In courtly romance this meant King Arthur's court. This antithesis was more complex than it may at first appear, for the king was himself a man of the forest, which he visited from time to time to hunt or consult with hermits and to renew his contact with the sources of holiness and legitimacy.

In literature, which along with art is society's primary means of symbolic expression, the antithesis is generally between the forest and the castle. But the castle also stands for the city. This was always true, despite the persistent prestige of the city. In the *commonitorium* that Vincent composed at Lérins in 434 he contrasted the solitary life of the island's monks with the crowds to be found in cities (*urbium frequentiam turbasque vitantes*).

In the Middle Ages the great contrast was not, as it had been in antiquity, between the city and the country (*urbs* and *rus,* as the Romans put it) but between nature and culture, expressed in terms of the opposition between what was built, cultivated, and inhabited (city, castle, village) and what was essentially wild (the ocean and forest, the western equivalents of the eastern desert), that is, between men who lived in groups and those who lived in solitude."[38]

In a *Summa* written in the second quarter of the thirteenth century, the Scholastic theologian William of Auvergne, bishop of Paris, states that compared with the ideal city "the rest of humanity is like a virgin forest (*quasi silva*) and all other men are like the wood of the wilderness (*quasi ligna silvatica*)." [39]

The "desert" ideal endured until the end of the Middle Ages and even experienced a revival in the second half of the fourteenth and the fifteenth century. Hermits became fashionable subjects of painting, as is evident from, among other works, the celebrated *Thebaid* by the Florentine Gherardo Starnina (born 1354, died between 1409 and 1413). [40]

The Franciscans of the Observance attempted in the fifteenth century to reverse the tide that had carried the mendicant orders into the cities. They established monasteries in the "desert," that is, in forests and on islands. [41]

In the seventeenth century the Jansenists of Port-Royal also went looking for the desert in the wooded Chevreuse Valley where five centuries earlier Suger had found wood for the beams of Saint-Denis. In the seventeenth and eighteenth centuries persecution by Church and royal authorities forced Protestants to meet in the "desert," that is, remote and isolated valleys in the Cévennes. And today ecologists are rediscovering in the mountains the ideology of the desert.

# THE PERCEPTION OF
# CHRISTENDOM BY THE ROMAN
# CURIA AND THE ORGANIZATION
# OF AN ECUMENICAL
# COUNCIL OF 1274

An essential ingredient of administrative power is the capacity to manage the distances involved in governing a geographical region. Men and information must be moved from place to place within well-defined time limits. Such a capacity requires not only a physical infrastructure of couriers, relays, information networks, and so on, but also such intellectual abilities as the capacity to make predictions.

The Roman curia in the thirteenth century is a case in point. As the vital center of all Christendom, charged with receiving church officials and dispatching envoys and orders, obliged to encompass within its own administrative networks developing royal bureaucracies, and contested by the heresies prevalent through much of the region under its jurisdiction, the curia had a pressing need to orchestrate communications over great distances.

The thirteenth century, moreover, was in many respects a calculating period. Because of the biblical story of David, whose misguided attempt to conduct a census incurred the wrath of God in the form of a devastating epidemic, census-taking had long been considered taboo, but now this taboo had begun to wane. Merchants, among whose primary activities was the exchange of currencies, attached increasing importance to the keeping of accurate accounts in an expanding monetary economy. In 1202 the Pisan Leonardo Fibonacci introduced in his *Liber Abaci* the numerals that we call Arabic (though actually of Hindu invention), as well as that capital innovation, the number zero. In the spiritual realm, new beliefs such as those associated with the

This text is a revised version of a paper delivered at the Colloquium "1274, année charnière: Mutations et Continuités," Lyons-Paris, 30 September–5 October 1974. The original version may be found in the proceedings of that colloquium (Paris: Editions du CNRS, 1977), pp. 481–89. Reprinted in the *Beihefte der Francia* published by the Institut historique allemand de Paris, vol. 9: *Histoire comparée de l'administration (IVe–XVIIIe siècle)* (Munich: Artemis Verlag, 1980), pp. 11–16.

existence of a Purgatory intermediate between Heaven and Hell led to a rationalization of the spiritual life through the calculation of indulgences. The widespread practice of confession instituted by the Fourth Lateran Council (1215) made the accounting of penances commonplace. The bureaucracies of princes and kings began to compile rudimentary budgets. As early as the twelfth century the Court of the Exchequer in England and the Renenghe in Flanders introduced systematic accounting methods in connection with the administration of state lands. The earliest known such account is the "Great Brief" of Flanders, which dates from 1187. In France accounts of receipts from royal *bailliages* and *prévôtées* date back at least as far as 1190. Ferdinand Lot and Robert Fawtier have called the accounts for 1202–1203 "the first budget of the French Monarchy," and John W. Baldwin is currently investigating the development of accounting techniques under Philip Augustus.

For the medieval Church the problems of time and space were never so urgent as when preparations were under way for an ecumenical council. Ever since the resumption of such meetings with the First Lateran Council in 1123 they had been prepared with special care and attention. We possess little information about any council prior to the Fourth Lateran in 1215, however. Innocent III sent legates throughout Christendom to plan for this meeting, and they no doubt carried with them orders from the curia. The dispatch of papal envoys not only affirmed the centralization of the Church and the preponderance within it of the Holy See but also symbolized the negation of distance, as the vastness of Christendom was effaced by the omnipresence of the Pope.

The situation was quite different in 1274 when preparations were made for the Second Council of Lyons. It is no accident that the documentary record is abundant, although there are admittedly serious gaps in that record and some questions must remain unanswered. For not only the organization but also the attitude of the curia had evolved over the years. It was now more aware than ever before of the size of the Christian world and better able to cope with the problems of transportation and communication over great distances.

## I. Preliminary Decisions

When Gregory X decided to hold the council, he had no clear idea of the limits of Christendom, but as planning proceeded it became increasingly clear that the curia's conception of the Christian realm was essentially European. For Gregory the primary purpose of the Council was to have been the provision of aid to the Holy Land, but the preparations proved that the actual frontier of Christendom lay not in Jordan but in Eastern Europe. This is clearly articulated by the author of one of the three surviving sets of documents concerned with planning for the council, Bruno, bishop of Olmütz, who, it is true, was particularly interested in the defense of that frontier. The real threat, he maintained, lay along the eastern borders of the German kingdom: in Hungary, where the Cumans remained in their heart of hearts pagans, and in Ruthenia, whose inhabitants were schismatics and under the domination of the still-pagan Tatars, Lithuanians, and Prussians. This was territory through which the Tatars had passed once and would surely return. To ignore these present dangers in favor of reconquering the Holy Land was to avoid Scylla only to confront Charybdis, and Bruno said so to the pope in no uncertain terms: *Nisi ergo vestra paterna providentia cavere voluerit periculis iam vicinis, sic studens in acquisitione Terre Sancte, quod non relinquat in periculo terras istas, volentes vitare kuribidim in cillam utique incidemus.*

Although the unity of the Church was one of the curia's principal objectives, a necessary precondition for a crusade, and therefore one of the key points of the council, preparations were carried out under conditions that implicitly denied the unique character of that portion of Christendom subject to Greek influence. The behavior of the papal legates in conducting negotiations in the East and the manner in which the Greeks were invited to Lyons reveal in opposite but complementary ways the fact that in the minds of Latin churchmen Greek Christendom was simply annexed to the region dominated by the Latin Church.

A second preliminary decision was to hold the Council outside of Rome, which necessitated moving not only the pope but the entire curia. To be sure, this was not the first lengthy journey by a medieval pope. There had even been a previous council in Lyons, in 1245, but the circumstances were extraordinary, for it had been necessary to flee Rome and the menace of Frederick II. In 1272 the choice was made deliberately and in the absence of any external threat. Holding the meeting outside Rome required that the curia take account of both the distance from Rome to any of the possible meeting places and the situation of the chosen city relative to the rest of Christendom.

The choice of Lyons was significant. There were political reasons why it was made: Lyons was an imperial city, loosely bound to the Empire yet situated at the gateway to France, whose influence the curia hoped would be favorable to its plans. There were also reasons of a material and religious order: Lyons was a city with many convents and Church buildings capable of receiving large numbers of churchmen. The Dominican monastery there was an intellectual and spiritual center of the first order, whose leader, Pierre de Tarentaise, was created cardinal and made archbishop of Lyons by Gregory X on the eve of the council. But the primary reason for the decision seems to have been geographical: Lyons was nothing less than the geographic center of European Christendom. This was a fact that the princes and prelates whom Gregory wished to attend could not fail to recognize, as he pointed out in letters sent on 13 April 1273: ". . . *ut Principum et Praelatorum eorumdem facilius habere possimus praesentiam . . . civitatem Lugdunensem, quo inibi concilium cum maiori commoditate conveniat, de ipsorum fratrum consilio duximus eligendam.*" Furthermore, "*quod ejusdem Terrae subsidium praecipue de Principum et Praelatorum pendent auxilio, quos ultra montes credimus posse commodius.*"

## II. The Preparations for the Council

Pope and curia had two main concerns: to facilitate the circulation of information and the transportation of participants. The pope in fact questioned all the prelates about the agenda he had set for the council: reconquest of the Holy Land and its two prerequisites, unity of the Latin and Greek Churches and reform of the Church and of Christendom. He set the date of the council so that there would be time for the prelates' answers to arrive and be examined before the meeting was held. Time was also necessary for high ecclesiastical officials to find replacements to run their dioceses, orders, and convents while they were away and to dispose of as much pending business as possible prior to their departure. Frequently it was necessary for the curia to reply to a response and to wait in turn for another reply. For the Italians the first obstacle to be confronted was the same that had to be surmounted in the opposite direction by all who came to Rome *ad limina:* the principal yet permeable geographical obstacle of Christendom, the Alps.

The meeting of the council was therefore put off for two years. The pope's invitations went out on 31 March 1272, and the opening of the council was set for 1 March 1274; it actually did begin on 7 May 1274. For the First Council of Lyons Innocent IV had sent invitations on 27 December 1244 for 24 June 1245, a delay of only six months, or a quarter of that provided by Gregory X. This was in part because the situation in 1244 was more urgent, in part because at Lyons I the pope imposed his decisions whereas at Lyons II he sought to engage in dialogue.

The activities of the curia during this two-year period can be divided into three phases. In the first phase, which lasted about a year, the most important event was the sending of an invitation to Emperor Michael Paleologus on 24 October 1272, six months after invitations went out to Western participants. This was an opening to Greek Christianity, a first step toward reunification of the Church.

During the second phase, the pope sent his questionnaires to participants on 11 March 1273, to be returned to the curia six months before the council, allowing six months for the drafting of replies and six months for the curia to make use of them.[1]

The third phase was for travel. On 13 April 1273 Lyons was designated as the site of the council and travel preparations could begin. The pope explicitly ordered members of the council to allow sufficient time to arrive on schedule. He wished to make all Christians aware of the importance of travel planning and to instill a rational, calculating attitude toward space and time.

He himself set a good example, planning to arrive in Lyons in about six months. (Six-month intervals were clearly an important spatial and temporal unit in contemporary minds.) This would allow six months before the opening of the council, during which he would oversee the final preparations. And in fact it was on 5 June 1273 that Gregory X left Orvieto, his residence at the time, for Lyons, which he reached on 9 or 10 November 1273. Thanks to the work of André Callebaut we are well informed about the papal journey.[2] He traveled first from Orvieto to Florence to Bologna to Milan, where on 8 October 1273 he made an official entry with a new pomp that disconcerted contemporaries, as is evident from a later account: "He came in a carriage, which in those days was not yet customary among us." From there he went to Morimond, traveling twenty-five miles in one morning by riding all out, and on to Novare and Chambéry, almost surely by way of Mount Cenis, following the same route taken by Innocent IV in 1244.

Given the lengthy preparations and travel, the brevity of the council itself is worth noting. The Second Council of Lyons was in fact exceptionally long, lasting from 7 May until 17 July with a recess while awaiting the arrival of the Greek delegation. Lateran I, II, III, and IV and Lyons I all lasted less than a month.

We have, finally, a rough idea of the number of people whose lives were disrupted over this two-year period. On the inaugural day of the council there were 1,024 prelates in attendance, and the total number of participants was perhaps 2,000. A much larger number of servants, pilgrims, and curious onlookers were drawn to Lyons for the occasion. According to the documents (J.-B. Martin, nos. 1830–1856), the number was as high as 60,000, but this seems highly exaggerated. The number of cardinals, archbishops, bishops, and mitred abbots who died during the council is said to have been 166, the most illustrious among them being Saint Bonaventure; Saint Thomas Aquinas died en route. The curia had mastered the art of dealing with space and time but not death, which found easy prey among the aged prelates in attendance.

## III. The Rational versus the Symbolic Conception of Space/Time: Toward the Avignon Papacy

The Second Council of Lyons shows, I think, that the curia recognized the value of having a capital of Christendom less eccentric than Rome in an era during which attitudes toward space and time were becoming increasingly rationalized. The Rhône was a ready-made highway. Thus Lyons II, a brilliant but ephemeral gathering, may have been the first manifestation of forces that would, three decades letter, impel the papacy to remove itself to Avignon, a move that occurred, in my view, not so much for adventitious reasons as because of a profound need for a new center of gravity in the Christian world, for a "rational" geographical center which also became, under the tax-hungry popes of Avignon, a fiscal center.

But these calculating popes forgot that space/time is not simply a rational but also a symbolic matter. Avignon was well situated from the standpoint of rational travel, but Rome remained the symbolic center of Christendom. Its geographic eccentricity proved no more of a drawback in the long run than did the eccentricity of the other two leading pilgrimage sites, Jerusalem and Santiago da Compostella. Vanquished by the power of symbolism, the papacy was compelled to return to Rome.

Thus Lyons II presaged both the success and the failure of Avignon and the brief reign of a "rational" conception of space/time in medieval Christendom.

## Principal Sources

1. Papal documents

Mansi. *Sacrorum Conciliorum nova et amplissima. Collectio XXIV*, pp. 39ff. Venice, 1780.

Martin, J.-B. *Conciles et bullaires du diocèse de Lyon.* Lyons, 1905.

Guiraud, J., and L. Cadier. *Les registres de Grégoire X (1272–1276).* Rome, 1892.

2. Preconciliar documents

Humbert of Romans. *Opus tripartitum,* ed. E. Brown, *Appendix ad fasciculum rerum expetendarum II,* pp. 185–222. London, 1690. Abridged edition, K. Michel, ed., *Das opus tripartitum des Humbertus de Romanis.* 2d ed. Graz, 1926.

Bruno de Schauenberg, bishop of Olomouc, in *MGH,* Leges, 4. 3, 589–94.

3. Conciliar documents

*Brevis nota eorum quae in secundo concilio lugdunensi generali gesta sunt,* ed. A. Franchi, *Il concilio II di Lione (1274) secondo la Ordinatio Concilii generalis Lugdunensis.* Rome, 1965.

Kuttner, S. *Conciliar Law in the Making: The Lyonese Constitutions (1274) of Gregory X* in a manuscript at Washington.

4. Studies

Gatto, L. *Il pontificato di Gregorio X (1271–1276).* Rome, 1959.

# THE TIME OF PURGATORY
# (THIRD TO THIRTEENTH CENTURY)

Purgatory as a spatial and temporal entity was formed between the third and the end of the thirteenth century. It was an elaboration of the Christian belief that certain sins could under certain conditions be redeemed after death, a belief that appeared at a quite early date. It is attested in liturgy and in funereal epigraphs (although these were frequently improperly solicited). The belief first manifested itself in certain practices: prayers for the dead and a variety of other actions taken to secure their salvation, which soon came to be known as suffrages. Only later did theologians seek textual support for these practices in the Bible. The justification of Purgatory rests on interpretations of four biblical texts that were not accepted by either medieval heretics or, later, Protestants. These were: II Maccabees 12:41–46, the story of the sacrifice ordered by Judas Maccabeus to redeem the sins of soldiers fallen in battle; Matthew 12:31–32, in which Matthew refers to the remission of sins in the other world; I Corinthians 3:11–15, which describes the purification after death of certain categories of sinners "as if by fire" (*quasi per ignem*), of all these texts the one most commented upon in the Middle Ages; and Luke 16:19–31, the story of poor Lazarus and the wicked rich man. The latter does not refer to Purgatory in the strict sense, but it is relevant for three reasons: it mentions the "bosom of Abraham," which Purgatory partially replaced or overshadowed; the other world is composed of well-defined locales to which the dead go immediately after death, without awaiting the Last Judgment; and the presence of individual persons in the other world is attested by anecdote or parable, anticipating the *exempla* that would popularize belief in Purgatory in the Middle Ages.

In theology the idea of an intermediate time and place in the other world originated with Tertullian's notion of a *refrigerium interim*. Ideas of Clement of Alexandria and Origen that might have led to Purgatory had they been developed were not pursued in the Greek Church. The Christians of late antiquity and the early Middle Ages showed

Originally published in *Le temps chrétien de la fin de l'Antiquité au Moyen Age, IIIe-XIIIe siècle* (Paris: Editions du Centre National de Recherche Scientifique, 1984), pp. 517–530.

little interest in the notion of an expanse of time intervening between death and resurrection, between the judgment of the individual and the Last Judgment of mankind. They were preoccupied by eschatological matters, with or without millenarian tendencies, which were generally regarded as heretical by the Church. As always, reflections on space and time with respect to the intermediate other world were closely linked, but they were concerned mainly with the question of *receptacula animarum,* receptacles in which souls were said to reside between death and resurrection; these reflections drew on widely read Judaic and Christian writings on the apocalypse.[1]

The true fathers of Purgatory were Saints Augustine and Gregory the Great, who established the theoretical underpinnings on which the intermediate other world was based. Augustine influenced primarily the theology of the subject, including the notion of purgatorial time, whereas Gregory contributed to the imagery of purgation, to the repertoire of apparitions and visions on which later writers drew. It is important to note, however, that Gregory believed that sins were effaced after death on earth and not in a special portion of the other world. Bede and the Celtic tradition of otherworldly visions began the process by which Purgatory acquired a tangible representation. For theologians, by contrast, purgation continued to be associated with the notion of fire, whose location in space and time was not made precise.

The second half of the twelfth century saw accelerated progress toward the definition of a place of purgatory and a time of purgation. For many the *Purgatorium Sancti Patricii* gave concreteness to the idea that Purgatory was a place, and Parisian theologians gave it a name and a definite location some time between 1170 and 1180, in the context of debates between the School of Notre-Dame and Cistercians from abbeys in eastern and northern France. Peter the Chanter and Simon of Tournai were the first theologians of Purgatory, which in the thirteenth century became a permanent fixture of Christianity: in dogma with Innocent IV's letter to his legate Eudes of Châteauroux in 1254 and the declarations of the Second Council of Lyons in 1274; in theology with the integration of Purgatory into all the great theological systems from William of Auvergne and Alexander of Hales to Bonaventure, Albert the Great, and Thomas Aquinas; and for the masses through preaching and *exempla.*[2] The birth of Purgatory altered the Christian conception of time, which was further transformed by the great changes that occurred in the West between 1150 and 1250.

## Purgatorial Time and Medieval Christianity

Once it was accepted that certain sins could be redeemed after death—some because they were minor (called *venial* in the twelfth century but previously described as slight or unimportant, *levia* or *minuta*), others because the sinner had felt contrition or, better yet, made confession but had not had time to complete his penance before death—several different notions of the time of purgation became possible.

One possible view was that purgation begins on this earth and that earthly life is the beginning if not the essence of human existence. One might refer to this pessimistic and harsh conception as one of "penitentialization" if not "infernalization" of life here below, for it usually involved the related view that life in this world is a matter of expiation through punishment. From it was derived the concept of a *purgatorium praesens,* as set forth for example in a manual for preachers written in the mid-thirteenth century by the Dominican Stephen of Bourbon, who was influenced by Augustine. Although Augustine's work was ultimately decisive in fixing the time of Purgatory between death and resurrection, the saint was for a long time full of doubts on this score. Twelfth-century theologians in their reflections on sin stressed the intentions of the sinner and stressed the new theoretical and practical definitions of confession and penance put forward by Hugh of Saint-Victor in *De sacramentis.* They tended to view Purgatory as a time of continuous penance, a view most fully elaborated by William of Auvergne at the beginning of the thirteenth century. But the great scholastics of the thirteenth century broke with this view, severing the close tie between terrestrial time and purgatorial time, a position most clearly expressed by Thomas Aquinas. A soul can no longer acquire *merit* after death, they argued, and therefore purgation is a matter not of *penance* but of *punishment.*

Another possible view was that the time of Purgatory is subsumed in the time of the Last Judgment. Some theologians held that the *day* of Judgment has some temporal "thickness," that is, that the activities of judgment have duration. In particular, according to one exegesis of the passage on purgation by fire in I Corinthians, sinners not yet purged of their sins would be obliged to endure the fire for an amount of time determined by their merits. Alcuin, for example, in *De fide Sanctae Trinitatis,* identified *ignis purgatorius* with *ignis diei judici.*

A third possible view was that purgatorial time stretches from the time of death and individual judgment to the time of resurrection and general judgment. Between death and Last Judgment anyone's sins could be redeemed. Thus Purgatory occupied a well-defined niche between terrestrial time and eternity; at the Last Judgment purgatorial time would be abolished or subsumed in eternity. Purgatorial time was the time of "first death," akin to the Judaic notion of time in *sheol*.

Latin Christendom finally settled on a fourth view: that each soul must spend a greater or lesser time in Purgatory depending on the gravity of the sins that must be expiated and the zeal of the living in offering help to the dead through their suffrages. As in earthly life a two-tiered structure of time was thus defined. From the standpoint of society Purgatory would endure until the end of the world, but from the standpoint of the individual it lasted from death until purgation was complete, just as earthly life ran from birth until death. This time was measurable, divisible, and different from individual to individual. Its definition presupposed a certain state of society and culture and had important social and cultural consequences.

## Purgatory and the Nature of Christian Time

The definitive inception of Purgatory some time between 1170 and 1220 came at a time of profound cultural and intellectual change. The most important revolution in Christian thought was an increasing interest in earthly goods, a shifting of heaven toward earth. Such a change is difficult to document, but it can be inferred from a series of convergent developments: growing prosperity, improvement in physical comforts, increased consumption of pleasure goods, growing wealth, the emergence of profane literature, the rebirth of ancient literature and revival of the theme *carpe diem,* development of an aesthetic sense based on criteria other than nobility and loftiness, the rise of "insouciance" as a literary theme, the development of legal concepts of property and associated practices, the transition from a distinction between *potens* and *pauper* (powerful and powerless) to one between rich and poor, the preeminence of avarice over pride among the deadly sins.

José Luis Romero has summed up all these changes as evidence for a shift to "feudal-bourgeois values." Not that millenarian outbursts had disappeared or that man's obsession with salvation had vanished. But for much of society, from top to bottom, the search for happiness in this world, the denial of an absolute contradiction between earthly satisfactions and eternal life, and the attribution of positive value to the world—in short, the decline of "contempt for the world" rightly stressed by Robert Bultot[3]—all these tendencies combined with the sentiment that the Last Judgment was still a long way off.

The new emphasis on earthly life is reflected in the important wave of institutionalization in the thirteenth century, quite different from the institutionalization of the earlier Carolingian period. For now it was a city of men that was being established and not a city of God on earth. Complementing this was an appreciation of duration, of the sheer expanse of time between the present and the Last Judgment. No longer was it possible to neglect the period between individual death and resurrection. Purgatorial time by human reckoning was most probably a very long time indeed. The Holy Spirit would be a long time coming.

This new idea went hand in hand with other intellectual and cultural changes. There was a new emphasis on numbers associated with the development of arithmetic and methods of calculation.[4] Improved knowledge of the geography of the earth led in turn to revisions in the geography of the hereafter, in which a multitude of *receptacula animarum* and a bipartite division of the other world into heaven and hell gave way to one of two new systems, with either three or five parts— possibly a limbo for children and a limbo for the Fathers of the Church in addition to Heaven, Hell, and Purgatory. An abundance of new ideas for thinking about and measuring time anticipated the development of clocks that divided time into many equal intervals. There was in fact an interest in intermediate categories of all kinds, as evidenced in the area of social ideology by the success of the triad *minores, mediocres, maiores*.

Thus there emerged a notion of purgatorial time as intermediate, measurable, divisible, and associated with a place whose existence was temporary and provisional. Just as the secular courts worked to fit the punishment to the crime, the Church sought to adjust the time of purgation with precision and justice. In the eleventh century, even before the emergence of a true Purgatory, Jotsuald and Peter Damian had referred to purgation as damnation for a time, *damnatio ad tempus*. But assigning to Purgatory a definite space and time was not without its problems.

## Terrestrial Time and Eschatological Time

Leaving aside the Last Judgment, the problem was to reconcile eschatological time with purgatorial time, which, like terrestrial or "historical" time was increasingly thought of as being composed of measurable and manipulable segments determined by the life history of the deceased and the quantity of suffrages intended to aid him. Initially Christianity had taken no account of the hiatus between historical time and eternity (eternal life or death). But now the linear time of the sinner was linked up with eternity in a different way. In the *Purgatorio* Dante uses a thunderbolt that shakes the mountain of Purgatory as Virgil, Dante, and Statius are climbing to symbolize the passage of a soul from Purgatory to eternal beautitude, hurdling the wall of sin.

## Purgatorial Time and Beatific Vision[5]

Theologians had long been preoccupied with a rather theoretical question: Are the saved, who are called to eternal beatitude, able to enjoy the beatific vision immediately after death and without waiting until the Last Judgment? Since this question obviously pertained primarily to saints, it caused no major difficulties in practice; little was said about souls whose fate was undecided, to be settled by God on Judgment Day. But once it was held that souls that completed their purification in Purgatory before the end of time went directly to Heaven, the problem of the beatific vision became, implicitly at least, more acute. The great thirteenth-century scholastics who incorporated Purgatory into their summas also perfected a theory of the beatific vision, whether by coincidence or out of conscious awareness of a link between the two problems we cannot say.[6] Possibly, even probably, the consideration of Purgatory figured in the background of the final sharp conflict over the beatific vision, which occurred during the pontificate of John XXII in the first half of the fourteenth century.[7] More specifically, in the exempla of Caesarius of Heisterbach's *Dialogus miraculorum* (ca. 1220) reflections on the beatific vision and reflections on Purgatory are combined. When Caesarius is asked what is the least painful purgatorial punishment, he responds that it is denial of the sight of God. Privation of the beatific vision is the "degree zero" of Purgatory.

## The Time around Death

Besides eliminating the boundary between earthly life and the afterlife, Purgatory also dramatized that period of linear, historical time that immediately precedes and follows death. The soul's destination— Heaven, Hell, or Purgatory—is determined by a sinner's entire life. It looms largest, however, at the moment of death. A soul destined to Purgatory has at least begun the process of penance through confession and sincere contrition. Hence the sinner's attitude at the moment of death takes on dramatic importance. Numerous exempla stress the gravity of a Christian's behavior *in articulo mortis*. Caesarius of Heisterbach, for example, portrays wicked individuals who by virtue of their lives and deaths seemed surely destined for Hell yet who are revealed by apparitions to be in Purgatory. Caesarius's explanation for this is that in the final moments of their lives they had begun to feel contrition, at least inwardly.

In the days, weeks, or at most months following death some souls received God's permission to leave Purgatory to solicit aid from relatives in a brief apparition. This is the period during which suffrages are most necessary and most effective. In the Dominican Thomas of Cantimpré's *Life* of Lutgarde, written shortly after the death in 1246 of the first "saint" to specialize in aid to souls in Purgatory, Lutgarde reproaches her friend James of Vitry for not having called sooner upon her intercession, even though he had to spend only four days in Purgatory.

Thus death, though no longer the definitive end it once was, made up for the loss of finality by mobilizing an anxious contingent around the transition to the afterlife, a contingent comprising not only the dying individual but also his or her friends and relatives. Purgatory enriched, complicated, and dramatized the rites of passage that marked the end of life.

## Proportionality between Time in This Life and Time in the Afterlife

In practice, then, the crucial thing as far as suffrages were concerned was that all souls were not equal: a soul's stay in Purgatory could be for a longer or shorter period of time, as Thomas Aquinas observed in a *quodlibet* at Christmastime in 1269: *utrum aequali poena puniendi in purgatorio, unus citius possit liberari quam alius*. This formulation of the question captures the problem of quantitative relations with respect to purgatorial time. Did unequal punishments correspond to unequal durations? A problem of proportion arose. Twelfth-century translations of Euclid had introduced new mathematical concepts, and the question of proportionality drew considerable attention from scholars.

The central question was the relation between time on earth and time in the afterlife. There was first of all a psychological aspect of the problem. Souls being punished in Purgatory felt that they had been there for a long time, but when they appeared to the living they discovered that they died only a short while ago. Contrast this with folklore concerning journeys in the other world: travelers who believed that they had been gone for just a few days crumbled to dust upon their return to earth, for their sojourn in the other world had exceeded their allotted

lifetime.[8] Some authorities went so far as to propose a simple arithmetic proportionality: one day in Purgatory is equivalent to one year
on earth.

Soon it became the fashion to treat purgatorial time in quantitative
terms. Attempts were made to relate the quantity of sin still to be
expiated to the time still to be spent in Purgatory. Since purgatorial
time depended in part on the suffrages of the living, relations were
computed between the quantity and duration of suffrages and the intensity and duration of purgatorial punishments. Exempla of Caesarius of
Heisterbach and Stephen of Bourbon among others depicted condemned souls in apparitions to the living that revealed in simple visible
form their progress toward liberation. Reflecting the quantity of suffrages in their behalf, their bodies were one-third or one-half white,
indicating that those who prayed for them needed to continue their
efforts for a corresponding period. In one case reported by Caesarius,
that of a usurer (who in earlier times would have been consigned to
Hell), the man's wife subjected herself to a difficult penance for twice
seven years on the strength of what her husband's soul had told her in
an apparition.

The great scholastics were wary of treating purgatorial time in this
way, because it introduced superstitious and/or pagan beliefs into religion (even if in inverted form) and diminished the spiritual significance
of the afterlife by subjecting it to base external manipulations. Yet it
was one of the first great Parisian masters of theology, Alexander of
Hales, who with the aid of Euclid proposed a subtle and nuanced theory of proportionality between terrestrial and purgatorial time. A certain relation, nonarithmetic in nature, was thus introduced between
two durations that were said to be different in nature but not utterly
dissimilar. The two were related, Alexander maintained, even though
there was no common measure between them.

By the end of the Middle Ages indulgences were being applied to
the dead, a practice inaugurated by an exceptional gesture of Boniface
VIII in connection with the Roman Jubilee in 1300. Thus, the strict
reckoning of time in the afterlife was coupled with the arithmetic of
indulgences.[9]

## Power over Purgatorial Time: The Church, Communities, and the Individual

Control of time and its measurement was an important aspect of
social and ideological conflict, and purgatorial time was caught up

in the struggle for power. In the thirteenth century three winners emerged from that struggle: the Church, the new communities, and the individual.

## The Church and Purgatorial Time

The thirteenth century was a time of trial for the Church: its power over society was diminished by the challenge of heresy, the growing independence of the civil authorities, and the estrangement of much of society from the old ideal of *contemptus mundi*. It also lost some of its power over time. Though mistress of the calendar and of church bells, it stood by while other, nonreligious ways of reckoning time gained importance. Businessmen and civic authorities kept time and rang bells for purposes of their own. In the fourteenth century the clock, a new instrument over which the Church had no control, made it possible to measure time and divide it into equal parts.[10] Yet insufficient attention has been paid to the fact that this decline in power over terrestrial time was in part compensated by the acquisition of power over time in the afterlife, specifically in Purgatory. Not only did the Church define the system of Purgatory, it also controlled an essential element of that system: the suffrages necessary for reducing the length of a soul's purgation. The principal suffrages, in order of decreasing value, were prayers, alms, and masses. The prayers of the Church were more effective than those of individuals, especially laymen, and alms were essentially controlled by the Church. Masses, too, were entirely under its jurisdiction. Accordingly, the best way for a living person to secure the suffrages necessary to rescue his or her soul from Purgatory after death was to be inscribed in the books of a community of prayer, to which in return they left a bequest in their will. Now, the Church kept the obituary lists, whose structure changed in the thirteenth century to accommodate the new belief in Purgatory.[11] Although it did not control the drafting of wills, it was of necessity the executor, if not the beneficiary, in regard to stipulations concerning Purgatory, whose content it attempted to influence. Members of the new mendicant orders, who had a good understanding of the new forms of devotion and their instruments, gained a reputation for skill at influencing the contents of wills. Purgatory in any event does not begin to be mentioned in wills until the fourteenth century, sooner in some regions, later in others.

The Church also attempted to give theoretical grounds for its power over purgatorial time. In the late twelfth and early thirteenth century canonists reinforced the earlier work of theologians. Traditionally canon law held that prior to death a Christian fell under the jurisdiction of the Church but that after death he or she came under the jurisdiction of God. But in the first half of the thirteenth century both canonists and theologians declared that souls in Purgatory fall under the *common jurisdiction* of God and the Church. Furthermore, the pope, as Bonaventure explicitly stated, was thought to have a personal right to grant indulgences to souls in Purgatory. But until the fifteenth century no pope availed of that right except for Boniface VIII, and then only in exceptional circumstances.

### Natural and Artificial Communities: Collective Memory and Purgatorial Time

Theoretically, any Christian could help a soul to escape from Purgatory more rapidly, and ultimately the true foundation of Purgatory was the communion of saints, a point made in the thirteenth century by many writers but most forcefully by Thomas Aquinas. In reality, however, responsibility for suffrages fell primarily to the relatives and friends of the deceased. We thus touch upon two of the fundamental structures of medieval society: kinship and community.

Suffrages were of concern first of all to blood relatives and spouses. The role of widows is worthy of special mention. In one of the earliest precursors of apparitions of souls from Purgatory, the father of Guibert of Nogent appears to his widow early in the twelfth century. Caesarius of Heisterbach tells of one widow from Liège, formerly married to a usurer, who reduces that great sinner's exceptionally long stay in Purgatory by doing penance by proxy for the remarkably long time of fourteen years. But the foremost practitioners of suffrages were the religious communities, who prayed for the souls of departed members of the order as well as for deceased members of families with blood and/or spiritual ties to the community. Exempla illustrate this postmortem solidarity, which clearly helped strengthen the bonds of community, especially in those orders that played an important role in the inception and diffusion of the new belief. Caesarius demonstrates this for the Cistercians in his *Dialogus miraculorum,* and Gérard Fréchet does the same for the Dominicans in his *Vitae Fratrum.* Dante, always sensitive to Purgatory in all its aspects, has the inhabitants of the mountain call upon friends, relatives, and fellow citizens for help.

The role of religious communities in suffrages was not simply an extension of their earlier role in saying prayers for the dead, perfected by Cluny in the eleventh century and afterward.[12] For new kinds of communities had emerged, exemplifying new forms of solidarity, both secular and religious: urban communities, confraternities, and the new mendicant orders. And new forms of collective memory had developed, as evidenced in the lay aristocracy by the compilation of genealogies. The solidarity of the lineage through time was emphasized by this preservation of the past.[13] Purgatorial time extended active memory beyond the moment of individual death.

## Purgatorial and Individual Time

Purgatory was one of the first signs of the increased importance attached to individual judgment in the final centuries of the Middle Ages. The purgatorial time ascribed by God to each soul at the moment of death was preeminently an individual time in the sense that, like a person's time on earth, it varied from individual to individual. What is more, its duration was in part the responsibility of the individual. While the suffrages of others mattered after death, what counted initially was each person's individual merits and demerits, virtues and vices, repentances and relapses, confessions and omissions. All of this is typical of an era in which individual traits had begun to distinguish each person from the common run and from others of similar function, rank, sex, age, profession, and order.

It is no accident that the first saint to be portrayed as having made a short stay in Purgatory was Bernard or that the first king of France to do the same was Philip Augustus. Both men were more or less contemporaneous with the birth of Purgatory. More than that, in both cases it seems possible to go beyond the topoi of hagiography and royalty to grasp for the first time the personality of a saint or king.

Thus, purgatorial time was tailored to fit each individual, its duration fixed by the behavior of the living person and, after his or her death, by the community to which he or she belonged.[14] The emphasis on individual responsibility at the time of death and on collective responsibility after death sheds light on a change in attitudes toward mortality that has I think wrongly been ascribed to the Renaissance. If the Renaissance is individualism, then as far as attitudes toward mortality are concerned it begins at the turn of the thirteenth century. If the Middle Ages are community, then the Renaissance remains profoundly medieval, for collective responsibility for the souls in Purgatory did not end, at least not in the Catholic part of Christendom. With respect to purgatorial time and in other ways, the Renaissance was but an episode in an extended Middle Ages.

# THE TIME OF THE *EXEMPLUM*
# (THIRTEENTH CENTURY)

A legacy of the Greeks and Romans, the *exemplum* was an historical anecdote employed in a rhetoric of persuasion. Used in antiquity by political and legal orators, it became in the hands of Christian moralists an instrument of edification.[1] Between the first centuries of Christianity and the central Middle Ages, however, the exemplum changed in nature and function. No longer did it revolve around the imitation of an individual: Christ had been the quintessential exemplum. Now it was a narrative, a *history,* to be taken in its entirety as an object useful for instruction and/or edification.[2]

The exemplum was associated with a new kind of preaching that came into vogue at the end of the twelfth and beginning of the thirteenth century to suit the needs of a changed society. The new society was characterized by urban needs, replacement of the old systems of orders by a new system of estates, challenges to ecclesiastical authority by heretics and lay aristocrats, and changes in thought and feeling, including new ways of thinking about, among other things, space, time, the relations between the spoken and written word, and numbers. The exemplum of the thirteenth century, the golden age of the genre, can be defined as "a brief narrative presented as truthful (that is, historical) and used in discourse (usually a sermon) to convince listeners by offering them a salutary lesson."[3]

Interest in the exemplum was connected with the vogue for narrative in literature, especially brief narrative forms such as the lay, the fabliau, and the tale. All of these forms reflect the new importance attached to narrative time, that is, historical time, a change that deserves further study from the standpoint of linguistics, *mentalités,* and social practices.

The conception of time implicit in exempla can be inferred from a study of sermons, in which three kinds of proof were used in argument: *auctoritates, rationes,* and *exempla.* The diachronic, narrative time of the exemplum, in a sense that of secular history, was combined with the retrospective and eschatological time of the auctoritates and with the atemporality of the rationes. Exemplum time must therefore be

First published in *Le temps chrétien de la fin de l'Antiquité au Moyen Age, IIIe-XIIIe siècle* (Paris: Editions du CNRS, 1984), pp. 553–56.

understood within the context of the sermon in which the exemplum occurs. The auctoritates, for the most part biblical citations, exhibit the temporal multiplicity of the Bible itself: the words are old but remain valid in the present and for the future, until the end of time and for eternal salvation. The homiletic commentary of the authorities is in the present, the timeless present of eternal truths. The rationes, on the other hand, are in the didactic present. Between the eschatological time of the Bible, brought up to date and oriented by commentary, and the eternal time of rational truths, the exemplum insinuated a segment of narrative time—historical, linear, and divisible. Thus the exemplum contains what Emile Benveniste has called the three tenses of historical utterance: aorist, imperfect, and pluperfect.

The historical roots of the exemplum are indicated by mention of the source from which it was taken by the author, preacher, or other user. Of 312 exempla in James of Vitry's *sermones vulgares* or *ad status*, 160 begin with the word *audivi*, indicating that they were obtained by hearsay, 34 with the words *memini, novi,* or *vidi*, also indicating recent acquisition, but only 73 with *legimus* (that is, taken from a book) and 45 with *dicitur* (which refers to no precise time).[4] In other words, the emphasis is on the recent past, on the time of the narrator, who insists on the contemporary character of his stories by situating them in "*nostris temporibus*."

In contrast to the auctoritates and rationes, which draw, respectively, upon the prestige of the past and of eternity, exempla derive their persuasive power from being of recent origin. Gregory the Great, the father of the medieval exemplum, had set the seal of the present upon his anecdotes, basing the apostolic succession on stories that could be verified orally by an audience that had no access to the written word or to history transmitted in writing. The use of the present time in exempla accords well with the revival in the thirteenth century of oral history, as Bernard Guénée has pointed out.[5] The time of ancient history was accessible only to specialists in memory in its written forms. By contrast, recent history was accessible to the eyes and ears: the method of Herodotus was "I saw, I heard."[6] It was no accident that the mendicant friars played an important part in popularizing both this kind of history and exempla: they were specialists in recent times.

The exemplum therefore depended on the time of memory, but memory of a particular kind: that of the spiritual and moral conscience, which was associated with a new idea of sin linked to the intentions of the sinner as well as with the new practice of auricular confession, based on introspective self-examination. The confessors'

manuals taught priests how to develop and shape that memory, aided
by the canon *omnis utriusque sexus* of the Fourth Lateran Council (1215),
which made individual confession at least once a year compulsory for
all Christians, men and women alike. The new education of the memory was part of a whole culture of the memory that developed in the
thirteenth century.[7] Preachers relied on exempla when they exhorted
the sinner to *recollere peccata sua, firmiter memorie commendare verba Dei,*
and so on. The time of the exemplum drew upon and in turn nour-
ished the time of private memory.

But the time of the exemplum was also a time of salvation. Its ultimate horizon was eschatological. A story, precisely located in recent
historical time, unfolded in narrative but invariably pointed toward
eternity—the eternity that was promised to the listener if only he
knew how to draw the lesson contained in the exemplum. First, however, a decisive event had to take place: the conversion of the listener.
The exemplum was an instrument of conversion, and conversion had
to occur immediately. Often the preacher called upon his listeners to
draw the lesson of the exemplum *hodie,* today, so that the words of
Jesus on the Cross to the thief might come true: *Hodie mecum eris in
paradiso* ("Today shalt thou be with me in paradise," Luke 23 : 43). The
historical time of the exemplum reached out from conversion in the
present toward a future of eternal happiness.

Thus the function of the exemplum was to bridge the gap between
historical reality and the eschatological unknown. Its time was caught
up in a dialectic between the time of history and that of salvation,
which was one of the major sources of tension in the central Middle
Ages (the twelfth and thirteenth centuries).

# PART THREE

# THE BODY

# BODY AND IDEOLOGY IN
# THE MEDIEVAL WEST

> A history more worthy of the name than the timid es-
> says to which we are constrained by the means
> available to us today would give proper weight to
> the vicissitudes of the body.
>
> MARC BLOCH, *Feudal Society*

## A Revolution in Regard to the Body

Among the great cultural revolutions associated with the triumph of
Christianity in the West, one of the greatest concerned the body. Even
those ancient doctrines that gave priority to the soul never conceived
of virtue or the good without reference to the mediation of the body.
The advent of Christianity caused a great upheaval in the daily life of
the ancient city by closing theaters, circuses, stadiums, and baths—
meeting places or cultural centers that in one way or another employed
or exalted the body—culminating a change in attitudes and ideas.

## Body and Soul

God's incarnation was also his humiliation. The body was an *ergastu-
lum*, a slave's prison for the soul. This was not merely a commonplace
image but a definition. Horror of the body was most acute in regard to
the sexual functions. The original sin was one of intellectual pride, intellectual defiance of God, but medieval Christianity transformed this
into a sexual sin. The height of abomination, the worst of the body
and of sexuality, was the female body. From Eve to the witch of the
late Middle Ages woman's body was the devil's stomping ground. Sex
was prohibited at certain liturgical times (Lent, vigils, holy days) but
also during periods of menstrual flow. Lepers, it was believed, were
the children of parents who violated the latter taboo. The inevitable
clash between the physiological and the sacred resulted in an effort to
deny the existence of biological man: vigils and fasting were con-

First published in Italian translation in Jacques Le Goff, *Il Meraviglioso e il quotidiano
nell'Occidente medievale* (Rome-Bari: Laterza & Figli, 1983), pp. 45–50. My remarks on
this subject were first presented in the form of a paper delivered to a colloquium on "Biological Man and Social Man" at the Centre Royaumont pour une Science de l'Homme.

ducted in denial of the need for sleep and food. Sin manifested itself in the form of physical deformity and disease. Leprosy, the ultimate symbolic and ideological malady of the Middle Ages (like cancer today) was the first and foremost an affliction of the soul. The way to spiritual perfection involved mortification of the flesh. The pauper was said to be sick and infirm, while that eminent social type, the monk, affirmed his identity by tormenting his body in ascetic discipline, and that supreme spiritual type, the saint, was never more saintly than when he (or she) sacrificed his body in martyrdom. Essential social divisions were best expressed in terms of contrasts between body types: the noble was handsome and well-built, the peasant ugly and deformed (as in *Aucassin et Nicolette,* Chrétien de Troyes's *Yvain,* and so on). Man's body was not so much dust as rot. The way of all flesh was decrepitude and putrefaction. And since the body was a favorite metaphor for society and the world, they, too, faced ineluctable decay. According to the theory of the six ages of man, the Middle Ages corresponded to old age: *mundus senescit.*

A celebrated poem of the late twelfth century attests to the ubiquity of the image of the body hastening toward destruction. Hélinand of Froimont, a Cistercian monk, wrote the *Verses on Death:*

> A well-fed body and delicate complexion
> are but a tunic of worms and fire.
> The body is vile, stinking, and withered.
> The pleasure of the flesh is by nature poisoned
>     and corrupt.

Yet salvation involved the rescue of both body and soul. The English monk who around 1180 wrote *Saint Patrick's Purgatory,* which recounts a journey in the other world, begs pardon for the fact that when it comes time to describe the tortures of the impure and the joys of the just he will speak only of things corporeal or their simulacra. Saints Augustine and Gregory are invoked to explain that corporeal punishments can be visited upon incorporeal spirits: "In corporeal and mortal man spiritual things manifest themselves only in corporeal form and appearance" (*quasi in specie et forma corporali*).

Indeed, not the least paradoxical thing about medieval Christian ideas is that the soul itself was envisioned in corporeal form. It was usually represented as a homunculus or child but sometimes assumed even more disturbing forms, as in Caesarius of Heisterbach's early thirteenth-century *Dialogus miraculorum,* in which demons toss a soul among themselves as though it were a ball.

For the men of the Middle Ages the sacred often revealed itself in such disconcerting interactions between the spiritual and the corporeal. Kings demonstrated their sacred nature by curing scrofula with their touch. The cadavers of saints revealed their sanctity by giving off a fragrant odor. Both divine revelations and diabolical acts were revealed in dreams and visions. In the twelfth century Saint Hildegarde of Bingen, one of the most original minds of the Middle Ages (sometimes diagnosed as having been an epileptic), set forth the foundations of a biological and medical science intimately related to mystical theology in her strange treatise *Causae et curae*.

## Body and Space

Is not the gesticulating man, on whom medieval clerics looked with such displeasure, reminiscent of actors in the pagan theater as well as of bodies possessed by the devil?[1] Biological man met social man in a space that was a cultural object, defined in different ways in different societies, cultures, and eras, and shaped in part by ideologies and values.

Indo-European tradition had evolved a way of interpreting space symbolically. The opposition between right and left survived in the Middle Ages, especially in representations of the Last Judgment, in which the saved were portrayed at the right hand of God, the damned at the left. But the left-right distinction seems to have been supplanted in part by high-low and inside-outside. I was astonished to discover that the Belgian psychiatrist Jacques Schotte considers this system of dualities to be fundamental for the understanding of mental illness. Therein lies a clue, perhaps, to unraveling the history of the profound but mysterious relation between biology and society.

# GESTURES IN PURGATORY

In connection with two recent studies in historical anthropology I have had occasion to look at gestures in Purgatory. Here, in honor of Maurice de Gandillac, who has long encouraged the use of new methods in medieval history and set an example with his own work, I should like to outline the results of my research.

Not long ago I completed several years of work on the birth of Purgatory.[1] From the early days of Christianity Christians have shown by their prayers for the dead that they believed in the possibility of a remission of sins after death. But the time, place, and manner of purgation for a long time remained quite vague, despite the suggested solutions to the problem put forward by Clement of Alexandria and Origen in the East, where Purgatory never took hold, and by Augustine and Gregory the Great in the West, where the location of Purgatory was never really defined before the twelfth century, in the final three decades of which the noun *purgatorium* first emerged. This veritable "birth" of Purgatory can be seen as part of a major shift in attitudes and feelings that took place around the turn of the thirteenth century, resulting in a new geography of the other world and in a new relation between the society of the living and that of the dead.

Along with Jean-Claude Schmitt and a small group of scholars associated with the Center for Historical Research at the Ecole des Hautes Etudes en Sciences Sociales, I have for some time now been investigating systems of gestures in the Middle Ages. We have been attempting to go beyond the written and spoken word to recapture the complementary dimension of gesture for serious historical research. Thus far, we have analyzed chronological changes in medieval society's attitudes toward gestures and have discovered that the Church attempted to exert its control in this area in the twelfth and thirteenth centuries. In this connection the first important theoretical text is *De eruditione novitiorum* written around 1130 by the great theologian Hugh of Saint-Victor.[2] The early medieval Church, we have concluded, looked upon gestures with great suspicion, and the word *gestus* largely drops from use between the fifth and twelfth centuries.[3] Gesticulation reminded Christians of two things they abhorred and combatted: the theater and possession by the devil. The possessed were Satan's vic-

First published in *Mélanges offerts à Maurice de Gandillac*, ed. J.-F. Lyotard and Annie Cazenave (Paris: Presses Universitaires de France, 1985), pp. 457–64.

tims, and mimes were his tool. Christ's militia was discreet and sober in its gestures, while the devil's army gesticulated visibly.

Around 1190 an English Cistercian from Saltrey wrote a treatise that played a great role in the birth and diffusion of Purgatory: *Saint Patrick's Purgatory.*[4] It was the story of an adventure, a belief, and a practice associated with Station Island in the middle of Lough Derg (Red Lake) in the northern part of what is now Ireland, near the border with Northern Ireland. The work belongs to a long tradition of visions and imaginary voyages in the other world inspired by Judeo-Christian apocalyptic literature and strongly influenced by Bede, who lived in the early eighth century, but it is the first in which Purgatory is mentioned by name and portrayed as a distinct, separate place in the other world. First written in Latin, the *Purgatorium Sancti Patricii* was soon translated into French (*L'Espurgatoire Saint Patriz*) by the celebrated poet Marie de France; in the thirteenth century it circulated in numerous versions in both Latin and the vulgar tongues.

What does the work tell us about a late twelfth-century monk's vision of gestures in Purgatory? Was gesticulation a noteworthy feature of the new afterlife? If gestures were noted, were they remarked in random fashion or incorporated into some kind of system? And what do they tell us about the place of the body in the Christian view of man's fate?

*Saint Patrick's Purgatory* tells us about the adventures of an Irish knight named Owein, adventures that form the basis for what is even today a much frequented pilgrimage site on Station Island in Lough Derg.[5] According to the story, Saint Patrick, attempting to convert the incredulous Irish, persuaded God to open a gateway to the other world at this spot. Anyone who entered this cave and spent the night there would experience the punishments of Purgatory. If he withstood the demons' torments and temptations, he would return to earth cleansed of his sins and assured of going to heaven, for, frightened and convinced by his experience, he would hasten to do penance and thereafter lead an exemplary life. But if he allowed himself to be seduced by the demons, he would never return to earth but would instead be carried off to Hell. The trial was thus an ordeal, a double-or-nothing wager on eternal salvation.

Owein had been warned that he must resist the demons' promises as well as their threats and that if he felt himself unable to hold out he should invoke, but only *in extremis,* the name of Jesus. Accompanied by demons he is conducted through various places where he witnesses men and women being subjected to a variety of terrible tortures. By invoking the name of God he avoids being dragged off to Hell and ultimately, after uttering the name of Jesus, emerges victorious from the pit, crosses a high, narrow, slippery bridge, and finds himself in the Terrestrial Paradise, from which he is able to glimpse the gates of the Heavenly Paradise. He makes the return journey easily, without danger, and emerges from the same cave mouth by which he had entered, repents of his sins, and converts to a life of piety.

The Purgatory described by the monk of Saltrey is very much like Hell. Indeed, it is a temporary hell, from which souls and visitors ultimately escape. Everything that can be seen there, including gestures, can also be seen in Hell, although in Purgatory the tortures are of a lesser degree.[6] Two other differences between Purgatory and Hell have some bearing on the question of gestures. First, Purgatory is composed of a series of places that lie at the same altitude; to cross it one need neither climb nor descend. Second, it is an open area whose boundaries cannot be seen, but from which one can escape. But *Saint Patrick's Purgatory* was very much influenced by its principal source, the *Apocalypse of Paul*. It was written, moreover, at a time (late twelfth century) before the features of Purgatory were definitively established, and certain gestures that would later become typical of the place are not yet present. Specifically, the dead do not beg visitors to alert relatives and friends upon returning to earth, so that by their suffrages they may shorten the time that the soul must spend in Purgatory, nor do they pray to God in hopes of being admitted to Heaven, to which theoretically they are destined. It appears that the inconography of Purgatory did not take shape before the fourteenth century. When it did, it was the gesture of prayer that distinguished the tortured souls in Purgatory from the damned souls in Hell.

In *Saint Patrick's Purgatory* creatures of two kinds are mobile: humans and demons. The humans include the dead of both sexes (souls, but equipped with a body of sorts that enables them to experience physical suffering) and the visitor from earth. There are also two kinds of demons: those who accompany and tempt Owein, and those who torture the dead. Their status is the same, but their mission or function is different.

The tortures endured by the dead and by Owein include physical torments, cries, shouts, unbearable wails, fetid odors, and terrifying sights. Thus they affect the entire body and all its faculties. Four of the five sense are involved: sight, smell, hearing, and touch. Only taste seems to have been left out (why?), although not entirely, for one of the tortures involves being submerged in boiling metal up to the eyebrows, *lips,* neck, chest, navel, or knees, or else in having a hand or foot immersed. Other souls have their tongues pierced and tortured. This is not the place to dwell on the system of torture, but it is worth noting that the gestures of the other world are generally incorporated in a more comprehensive system of bodily symbolism.

In Purgatory the system of gestures depends on the fact that some of the beings there manipulate others and control their actions. There are gesticulators and gesticulees, if you will: demons and humans.

Owein's actions come in three phases. As the beginning and end of his adventure, when he is free or, rather, when he is governed solely by the dictates of his human nature, subject to the influence of original sin, free will, and grace, he first descends (since Purgatory is here por-trayed as being underground), then climbs back up to the surface. In the intervening phase he neither climbs nor descends but visits a series of places situated at the same altitude.

Throughout his ordeal Owein is treated as a plaything by his escort of demons. He is pushed and pulled, dragged, assaulted. Yet he remains an earthly creature and triumphs over the demons, so his actions are rarely described in the passive voice (*missus in ignem, introductus autem domum*). He is usually the direct object of the demons' actions: *mili-tem . . .* proiecerunt, *eum . . .* torrerent, contraxerunt *militem . . . eum* traxerunt, *te . . .* ducentes, *militem* trahentes, and so on. Each time he invokes the name of Jesus he enjoys an interlude of relative indepen-dence, proceeding along his path more or less as he pleases. He comes and goes, enters and traverses this or that area of Purgatory: *pervenit, intravit, exivit,* and so on. The demons who compel him to retrace his steps allude to his eventual return with verbs that express the freedom of action and movement that he will then enjoy: *revertaris, reverti volue-ris,* etc. *Standing,* the most polysemic of bodily gestures, is the word used to describe his posture in the most difficult situations. Having been ejected from the pit of Hell, for example, he stands next to it for a moment (*iuxta puteum solus aliquandiu stetit*), then moves away, but he is unsure which way to turn (*cumque se ab ore putei subtrahens stetisset ignoransque quo se verteret*), and strange demons emerge from the pit and ask what he is doing (*quid ibi stas?*). The expression is obviously meant to be symbolic of his situation (and his choice) between salva-tion and damnation. By contrast, faced with the ultimate trial, the bridge to be crossed, he regains the initiative. Liberated by the inter-vention of Jesus, whose name he has invoked (*cogitans . . . de quantis eum* liberavit *advocatus eius piissimus*), he cautiously moves toward the bridge, steps up onto it, moves forward (*coepit pedetentim . . . incedere,*

*incedebat, ascendit, incedebat, securus . . . procedens*). Here it is the demons who are not allowed to proceed (*qui hucusque* perduxerant, *ul-
terius* progredi non valentes, *ad pedem pontis* steterunt), and henceforth
they are powerless to manipulate him (*videntes* eum libere transire).

Owein crosses a dark meadow, four fields, and an area occupied by
a huge wheel of fire; he passes a bath house and a mountain swept by
high winds and washed by a glacial river. He then descends toward a
bridge over a river of fire, beneath which lies the pit of Hell. In all of
these places he sees souls being tortured. For present purposes it is unimportant that these images of Purgatory can all be traced back to earliest antiquity. Note simply that everything is on a level, except near
the mouth of Hell, to which Owein descends, and the bridge to
Heaven, toward which he climbs. Most interesting of all, the spaces he
traverses are immense. The first region is *vasta,* and in leaving it
Owein passes through a very broad valley (*per vallem latissimam*). The
first field is long and large (*latissimum et longissimum*), so long that the
knight cannot see its end (*finis autem illius campi prae nimia longitudine
non potuit a milite videri*). The second field also stretches out into the
distance, and Owein crosses it, as he did the first, on a diagonal (*in
transversum enim campos pertransivit*). Nothing is said about the size of
the next two fields, but the house is so large that Owein cannot see its
extremities (*ut illius non potuisset ultima videre*). By contrast, the pit of
Hell broadens out only as Owein falls farther and farther down into it,
and similarly the bridge widens the farther he progresses along it. It
may be that the components of Purgatory are portrayed as immense in
order to impress both hero and reader (or listener), but I read the description as a sign of the author's uncertainty as to the geography of
Purgatory and of his desire to allow the traveler a certain latitude in his
gestures and movements in these apparently boundless spaces.

The tortured have no initiative as far as their own gestures are concerned. Either they are in passive postures or situations or they are objects of attack by demons. Among the passive postures are lying
stretched out on the ground (*in terra* jacentibus, ventre *ad terram verso
illorum ventres, istorum dorsa* terrae haerebant, *in terra* extendebantur, *in
terram* iacebant) or hanging (*suspendebantur, pendebant, pendentes*) or
held fixed, usually by hooks or nails (*defixis, fixis, fixi, transfixi, infixi*),
or submerged in a liquid of some sort (imersi, *utriusque sexus et aetatis*
mergebatur *hominum multitudo*). Souls attacked by demons or monsters (dragons, serpents, toads) passively respond with gestures of
pain: *inter eos et super eos discurrere et caedere, super alios sedebant et quasi
comedentes eos dentibus ignitis lacerabant, capita sua pectoribus miserorum im-*

*primentes flagris eos cruciabant, flagris daemonum cruciabantur, cremabantur, urebantur, assabantur, eos immerserunt,* etc.

The demons are free to move and attack both Owein and the tortured souls as they please. Their freedom is conveyed by words like *irruere, egredientes, euntes venissent, discurrere, transcurrentes, transeuntes, pervenerunt, vertunt discurrentes, procedentes, recedentes, currentes,* and *approximantes.* Most of these words convey excessive agitation, thought to be characteristic of diabolic gesticulation. The aggressiveness of the demons was expressed with words like *proiecerunt, traxerunt, torrerent, contraxerunt, proiicere, praecipitaverunt se trahentes secum militem,* and so on, most indicating dragging or hurling.

It would be useful to classify all action words in this way and subject them to statistical analysis. I have done this in a limited way for chapters six through fifteen of the Mall edition of *Purgatorium Sancti Patricii* (pp. 160–177) and count 166 verbs or expressions pertaining to gestures, movements, and postures. Of these, 76 pertain to the demons, 58 to Owein, and 32 to the tortured souls. There is clearly a hierarchy of gesticulation: demons gesticulate freely and Owein retains some measure of independence, while the tortured are entirely passive. Of the 32 words and expressions pertaining to the latter, 16 are passive, 9 are quasi-passive (*iacere, pendere,* and the like), 3 are negative, and 3 express a failed effort.

To conclude, let me propose two hypotheses that are supported by the research of other members of my group. First, indications of spatial orientation are important. In the Middle Ages the most important oppositions were up/down and inside/outside, correlative to the actions climb/descend and enter/exit (sometimes enter/traverse/exit).[7] In medieval Christian ideology positive value was ascribed to high and inside. Ascent and internalization constituted an ideal. Here the narrative unfolds entirely in the other world, a new other world that held out a prospect of hope, of enhanced likelihood of salvation thanks to a purgative and punitive ordeal. The visitor descends, moves laterally, then ascends.[8] Here the goal is to escape from an evil interior; the visitor enters, traverses, and exits.

A second hypothesis is that the system of gestures in a narrative is also important. Every gesture is part of a larger system of actions and reactions. In Purgatory progress is indicated by freedom of gesture. A soul must cease to be passive and regain the human freedom to gesticulate on its own initiative, to move upward, inward, and toward greater moderation, steps on the way to the great return, the *redditus* of God.[9]

In a text like *Saint Patrick's Purgatory* references to the prevailing Christian system of gestures are of course overdetermined, for what is really at stake is man's salvation. The gestures of Purgatory are merely the gestures of man on earth writ large. The knight Owein is a sinner in *via*, a *viator*, whose gestures are encompassed in a system in which the stakes are eternal life (or death).

# THE REPUDIATION OF PLEASURE

I love the horror of being virgin.
MALLARMÉ

A widely held opinion has it that a major change in Western sexual practices and thinking about sexuality occurred in late antiquity. Previously, it is said, the Greeks and Romans placed a positive value on the pleasures of the flesh and enjoyed substantial sexual freedom, but now sexuality was broadly condemned and strictly regulated. The principal agent in this reversal is supposed to have been Christianity.

Recently Paul Veyne and Michel Foucault have argued that a major change of this sort did take place but well before the triumph of Christianity, in the first and second centuries of the Common Era.[1] Among the pagan Romans, they further maintain, there existed a "virile puritanism."

Christian attitudes toward sexuality, these authors argue, were influenced by Jewish, Greek, Latin, and Gnostic traditions as well as by the spirit of the times. The first four centuries of the Christian era were a time of economic, social, and ideological upheaval, of which Christianity was (as so often happens in history) both cause and effect. Its role was crucial, however.

As Paul Veyne says, Christianity, through its interpretation of Genesis and original sin and the teachings of Saint Paul and the Church Fathers, provided a transcendent biblical and theological justification of the new sexual attitudes. At the same time it transformed a minority tendency into a majority norm applicable at least to the dominant classes, the aristocracy and the urban elite. It provided a conceptual framework for the new sexuality, complete with its own vocabulary, definitions, classifications, and distinctions. The Church and, following its lead, the secular authorities established rigorous ideological and social controls. Finally, in the monasteries the Church created living examples of the new sexual ideal.

Beyond whatever reasons the pagan Romans may have had for moving toward greater chastity, confining sexuality to marriage, condemning abortion, disapproving "amorous passion," and discrediting bisexuality, Christians added a new and urgent motive: the impending end of the world, with its concomitant requirement of purity. Saint

Originally published as "L'amour et la sexualite," *L'Histoire* 63 (1984):52–59.

Paul had issued a warning: "But this I say, brethren, the time is short:
it remaineth, that both they that have wives be as though they had
none" (I Corinthians 7:29). Certain extremists of purity even cas-
trated themselves, like Origen: "And there be eunuchs which have
made themselves eunuchs for the kingdom of heaven's sake," observed
Matthew 19:12.

## The Sinful Flesh

One Christian innovation was the establishment of a connection between sin and the flesh. Not that the expression "sins of the flesh" was
common in the Middle Ages. But throughout the medieval period the
Bible was interpreted in such a way as to justify the repression of most
sexual practices. "And the Word was made flesh" (John 1:14), and
Jesus at the Last Supper spoke of his flesh as the bread of eternal life: "I
am the living bread. . . . Except ye eat the flesh of the Son of man, and
drink his blood, ye have no life in you. Whoso eateth my flesh, and
drinketh my blood, hath eternal life" (John 6:51–54). But John already distinguishes between the spirit and the flesh: "It is the spirt that
quickeneth; the flesh profiteth nothing" (John 6:63). Paul, too, introduces a subtle shift in meaning: "God sending his own Son in the like-
ness of sinful flesh, and for sin, condemned sin in the flesh. . . . For to
be carnally minded is death. . . . For if ye live after the flesh, ye shall
die" (Romans 8:3–13). Early in the seventh century Gregory the
Great was quite unambiguous: "What is sulfur but food for the fire?
What therefore feeds the fire so that it gives off such a powerful
stench? What do we mean by sulfur, therefore, but the sin of the flesh"
(*Moralia in Job* 14:19).

Early Christians spoke more commonly of *sins* in the flesh (in the
plural) than of a sin of the flesh (in the singular), however. Three notions were central to the condemnation of sexuality. One was fornication. The commandment "Thou shalt not commit adultery" and the
condemnation of fornication in the New Testament were used in the
thirteenth century to condemn all illegitimate sexual practices (even
within marriage). The second central notion was concupiscence, frequently mentioned by the Church Fathers and seen as the source of
sexuality. And the third notion was lust, which encompassed all sins
of the flesh in the system of deadly sins that was constructed between
the fifth and twelfth centuries.

The biblical heritage did not burden Christian doctrine with a
heavy baggage of sexual repression. The Old Testament, often indul-

gent of sexual behavior, concentrated its repression of sexuality in the ritual taboos enumerated in Leviticus 15 and 18, primarily pertaining to incest, nudity, homosexuality and sodomy, and intercourse during menstruation. These prohibitions were taken up by the early medieval Church. Ecclesiasticus was highly antifeminist: "Of the woman came the beginnings of sin, and through her we all die" (Ecclesiasticus 25: 24). By contrast, the Song of Songs is a hymn to conjugal love, palpitating with amorous and even erotic fervor. But the Church, following one line of Jewish tradition, hastened to provide an allegorical interpretation. Where Jews had seen the union of Yahweh with Israel, Christians saw that of God with the soul of the believer and of Christ with the Church. In the twelfth century, which saw the revival of Ovid and the birth of courtly love, people again turned to the Song of Songs, and no other book of the Bible attracted more commentary; but the church, with Saint Bernard in the forefront, insisted that the only valid interpretation was an allegorical and spiritual one.

The Gospels of the New Testament are very discreet on the subject of sexuality. They praise marriage provided it is monogamous and indissoluble. Accordingly, adultery is denounced in Matthew 5:28, and divorce is assimilated to adultery in Matthew 19:2–12, Mark 10:2–12, and Luke 16:18. Mary remains a virgin in marriage, however, and Christ remains a bachelor. These "models" figured prominently in the medieval case against matrimony, which rested primarily on Paulian texts. To be sure, Paul did not identify the flesh with sinful sexual activity; at bottom the flesh is nothing but a metaphor for human nature, as in the Gospel of John. But Paul lays stress on the opposition between flesh and spirit. He sees the former as the principal source of sin and tolerates marriage as a lesser evil best avoided if possible: "It is good for a man not to touch a woman. [Note the antifeminism.] Nevertheless, to avoid fornication, let every man have his own wife, and let every woman have her own husband. Let the husband render unto the wife due benevolence: and likewise also the wife unto the husband. . . . I say therefore to the unmarried and widows, It is good for them if they abide even as I. But if they cannot contain, let them marry: for it is better to marry than to burn (*melius est enim nubere quam uri*). . . .Art thou bound unto a wife? seek not to be loosed. Art thou loosed from a wife? seek not a wife" (I Corinthians 7). and further: "I have also told you in time past, that they which do such things [of the flesh] shall not inherit the kingdom of God" (Galatians 5:21).

For Paul, this counsel of virginity and continence was based on respect for the human body, "tabernacle of the Holy Spirit." By contrast, the Middle Ages saw the flesh and the body as diabolical, as something akin to a place of debauch. Castigated as the source of sin, the body was deprived of all dignity.

## Original Sin and Sex

Saint Paul's views ultimately became the basis for a social hierarchy based on sexuality. The Church set forth its own unsubstantiated interpretation of the parable of the sower (Matthew 13:8 and 23 and Mark 4:8 and 20) whose seed produced either a hundredfold or sixtyfold or thirtyfold depending on the quality of the ground onto which it was cast; the Church classified men and women as virgins (*virgines,* producing a hundredfold), continent (*continentes,* producing sixtyfold), or married (*conjugati,* producing thirtyfold). Saint Ambrose in the fourth century characterized this hierarchy in these terms: "There are three forms of chastity: marriage, widowhood, virginity" (*On Widows,* 4:23).

Between the time of the Gospels and the triumph of Christianity in the fourth century two series of occurrences ensured the success of the new sexual ethic: theologians developed new concepts of flesh, fornication, concupiscence, and sexualization of the original sin, while in practice the status of virgin became an accepted social position and the idea of chastity was realized in the monasticism of the "desert."

The distinction between flesh and spirit became absolute. The meaning of *caro,* flesh, underwent a change. No longer did it refer to the human form assumed by Christ in the Incarnation; rather, it denoted weak flesh, corruptible flesh. Carnal came to mean sexual. Thus the metaphorical use of *caro* to refer to human nature soon came to connote the sexual aspects of that nature. Just as in pagan ethics there developed a notion of "sin against nature," which in the Middle Ages resulted in an expansion of the idea of sodomy to include not just homosexual sodomy but rear entry, anal intercourse, and positions in which the woman lay above the man, all of which were proscribed.

Fornication was condemned in the Bible, in particular in the New Testament (I Corinthians 6:19–20, for instance). The experience of monks eventually led to distinguishing three forms of "fornication": illicit sexual union, masturbation, and involuntary erections and ejaculations (John Cassian, *Collations,* 12:3). Saint Augustine was the first to give prominence to the concept of concupiscence, sexual desire, although the word (in the plural) can be found in Saint Paul: "Let not sin therefore reign in your mortal body, that ye should obey it in the *lusts* thereof" (Romans 6:12).

More important was the lengthy evolution that ultimately led to the identification of original sin with sin of the flesh. In Genesis the original sin is a sin of the spirit, a matter of conceiving an appetite for knowledge that leads to disobedience of God's will. In the Gospels Christ has nothing to say about original sin. Clement of Alexandria (ca. 150–215) was the first to relate original sin to the sexual act. To be sure, the principal consequences of the original sin according to Genesis were loss of closeness to God, concupiscence, suffering (in toil for men and childbirth for women), and death. It was Augustine who definitively linked original sin to sexuality via concupiscence. Three times between 395 and 430 he asserted that concupiscence transmits original sin. Through the children of Adam and Eve original sin was bequeathed to mankind through sex. By the twelfth century this view was accepted by nearly everyone except Abelard and his disciples. In the vulgar version promulgated by preachers, confessors, and authors of moral treatises, the original sin was simply said to be sexual. Humankind was engendered in the sin that is an inextricable part of the sexual act because of the concupiscence that necessarily manifests itself in copulation.

In the mean time virginity was exalted by an important current of opinion that affected both theory and practice. Tertullian (early third century) and Cyprian produced the first in a series of works that, beginning with the *Method of Olympus* in the second half of the third century, became genuine treatises on virginity. Consecrated virgins, who lived in special houses set apart from the rest of the community, were considered brides of Christ. As Aline Rousselle points out, the powerful movement toward asceticism in Christianity began with women who had vowed to live as virgins; not until the end of the third century did it involve men who vowed only to remain continent.

The great flight into the wilderness was more a quest for sexual purity than for solitude. In the beginning it often ended in failure, notably in the form of homosexual behavior among young men who had followed a parent or master into the "desert." Accounts of the desert life were long filled with the common images of sexual temptations (the temptations of Saint Anthony). The sexual appetite was not the only one vanquished. From the first Desert Fathers down to the end of the Middle Ages battle was waged against concupiscence in the form of hunger and thirst (*crapula, gastrimargia*) as well as sexual desire.

During the fifth century, when monks compiled lists of deadly sins, lust (*luxuria*) and gluttony (*gula*) were often linked. Lust, it was said, was frequently the result of excess food and drink. According to Aline Rousselle, the battle against concupiscence, waged on two fronts, often ended in impotence for men and frigidity for women, the culmination and ultimate success of ascetic discipline.

## Augustine's Conversion

The new sexual ethic was only the most visible and common form of the Stoic repudiation of pleasure, which Christianity adopted as its own and imposed on the West, according to J.-L. Flandrin, "for eighteen centuries." Any serious historical study is sufficient to point up the inadequacy of Max Weber's notion that sexual repression lies at the root of western economic growth.

There is no better account of the way in which the new ideal imposed itself on the converts of late antiquity than Augustine's *Confessions*. The future saint admits that women, especially the woman with whom he was living, had been the final obstacle to his conversion. His mother, Monica, had always associated the conversion she so fervently desired for her son with his abandonment of sexual activity. Two important passages of the work are devoted to matters of the flesh, the most interesting being book eight. Not yet converted, Augustine conceives a hatred of the flesh as the locus of wicked desires and habits: "The law of sin is the violence of custom, whereby the mind is drawn and holden, even against its will" (8.5.12, Pusey translation). Thus the repression of sexual desire was but one form of the exaltation of the will characteristic of the new man, pagan as well as Christian. In the warrior society of the Middle Ages abstinence would be evidence of the highest prowess.

In adolescence chastity was desired but still feared: "Give me chastity and continency, only not yet" (8.7.17). Success is almost at hand: "For on that side whither I had set my face, and whither I trembled to go, there appeared unto me the chaste dignity of Continency, serene, yet not relaxedly gay, honestly alluring me to come, and doubt not. . . . And she again seemed to say, 'Stop thine ears against those thy unclean members of the earth'" (8.11.27). Finally he hears a voice command him to take up the book of the apostle and read, and what he reads is this: "Not in rioting and drunkenness, not in chambering and wantonness, not in strife and envying: but put ye on the Lord Jesus Christ, and make not provision for the flesh, in concupiscence"

(8.12.29). The conversion episode ends with an evocation of Monica's joy, "in a much more precious and purer way than she erst required, by having grandchildren of my body" (8.12.30).

The primary victim of the new sexual ethic was marriage. Lesser evil though it was, it still bore the mark of sin, of the concupiscence that accompanied the sexual act. Augustine's contemporary Saint Jerome, the author of a violent attack on marriage in *Adversus Jovinianum* (a text that was widely read in the twelfth century, at which time it was even used to justify extramarital courtly love), drew on the work of Sextus Empiricus, a philosopher who antedated him by two centuries, in arguing that "overly ardent love of one's wife is also adulterous." Gregory the Great (pope from 590 to 604) in a letter to Saint Augustine of Canterbury spoke of the taint of conjugal love: sexuality in marriage could thus be transformed into fornication. In the first half of the twelfth century the great Paris theologian Hugh of Saint-Victor said that "since the coupling of the parents does not take place without carnal desire (*libido*), the conception of children is not without sin." It was as hard for the married man or woman to please God in the Middle Ages as it was for the merchant.

The Middle Ages increasingly objectified the sins of the flesh and made them subject to an ever more elaborate system of definitions, taboos, and sanctions. Men of the Church, often Irish monks, extremists in asceticism, composed penitentials, lists of sins and penances, which in spirit resembled barbarian legal codes. They were much taken up with sins of the flesh, reflecting the ideals and fantasies of monkish militants. With its contempt for the world and humiliation of the flesh the monastic model exerted a tremendous influence on western mores and attitudes. Benedictine discipline, while it eliminated some of the extremes of the eastern desert tradition, perpetuated some of its attitudes and practices in the forest and island monasteries that were the western equivalent of the desert wastes.

## The Repudiation of Pleasure

Burchard of Worms, a German specialist in canon law whose *Decretum* was widely read, has left the following text on the "abuse of marriage," an heir to the tradition described above and to the taboos in Leviticus:

> Have you, with your wife or any other woman, coupled from behind in the manner of dogs? If so, you shall do penance of ten days on bread and water.

Have you had intercourse with your wife during her period? If so, you shall do penance of ten days on bread and water. If your wife entered the church after childbirth but before being purified of her blood, she shall do penance of as many days as she ought to have stayed away from church. And if you copulated with her during that time, you shall do penance on bread and water for twenty days.

Did you copulate with your wife after a child was moving in her uterus? Or less than forty days before the birth? If so, you shall do penance of twenty days on bread and water.

Did you have intercourse with your wife after a conception was apparent? You shall do penance of ten days on bread and water.

Did you sully yourself with your wife during Lent? You must do penance of forty days on bread and water or give twenty-six sous in alms. If it happened while you were drunk, you will do penance of twenty days on bread and water. You shall maintain chastity for twenty days before Christmas, and every Sunday, and during all the fasts fixed by law, and for the birthdays of the apostles, and on the principal holy days, and in public places. If you fail to do so, you shall do penance of forty days on bread and water.[2]

These controls on the sex life of married couples affected the majority of men and women in their daily lives. The rules had consequences of many kinds: on population, relations between the sexes, and popular attitudes, to name three. Jean-Louis Flandrin has minutely analyzed the "antinatural" requirements of the Church's calendar. In the eighth century the restrictions would have allowed "devout couples" to have sex only 91–93 days per year, not counting times during which the female was considered to be impure (menstruation, pregnancy, postpartum). Flandrin thinks it more plausible that couples refrained from sex only on weekends. He also finds that the continent periods were redefined over time. The total number of taboo days remained more or less constant, but their distribution changed: instead of three long chaste periods around Christmas, Easter, and Pentecost there were numerous shorter periods of fasting, abstinence, and continence.

## Love and Leprosy

Between the prescriptions and the practice the gap was no doubt wide. The fact that Saint Louis's confessor insisted—as a proof of sanctity—on scrupulous (and even exaggerated) respect for the rules of conjugal continence is evidence that such respect was rare. In Flandrin's view, however, the Church's prescriptions reinforced certain deepseated tendencies in the culture and attitudes of the masses: a notion of sacred time (evident in peasant calenders), a consciousness of impurity, and respect for taboos. In other words, there was a convergence of the ethics of the learned with the culture of the multitude. Yet the realm of sexuality also reveals a social and cultural cleavage (evident to the feudal Church at any rate) between clergy and laity (including the nobility) as well as between clergy and knights taken together and workers. This cleavage emerges most clearly in the common medieval explanation of leprosy. Certain theologians saw a connection between the supposed origin of leprosy in sin and differences in sexual behavior between dominant and dominated strata of society. Was there in fact a sexuality of the elite as opposed to a sexuality of the common folk? Be that as it may, contempt for the lowborn was fueled by sexual suspicion. In the first half of the sixth century, Caesarius, bishop of Arles, delivered a sermon in which he warned that incontinent couples would have "leprous or epileptic, perhaps even demoniacal, children. . . . In sum, lepers are generally born not to learned men who preserve their chastity on forbidden days and during festivities but to common peasants who cannot control themselves."

Leprosy, with its supposed sexual origin, was a disease that haunted the people of the Middle Ages and filled them with guilt. In the fourteenth century it was supplanted in part by the plague. But until then it was regarded as a visible sign of fornication in the flesh, including (especially perhaps) "fornication" between man and wife. Since the original sin was transmitted in the flesh, moreover, the children paid for their parents' misdeeds. The literate were also obsessed with the supposed sexual excesses of the illiterate: paupers and peasants. It is no accident that serfdom was believed in the Middle Ages to have been a consequence of original sin. Slaves of the flesh more than other men, serfs deserved to be enslaved to their lords. In this distortion of the ideal of willpower, resistance, and spiritual struggle inherited from late antiquity, the oppressed strata of society were portrayed as weak, insatiable, and intemperate but also devoid of willpower. In a world of warriors, peasants were viewed as near beasts governed by wicked desires.

## Sex and Damnation

The new sexual ethic dominated the West for centuries. Only in relatively recent times has it begun to lose its grip, as passion has become an accepted part of sexual relations and marriage. Throughout the Middle Ages the new ethic reigned supreme, though not without change. It was affected by three major events between the tenth and fourteenth centuries, a period of dramatic advances in the West: the Gregorian reform and the introduction of a sexual division between clergy and laity; the triumph of indissoluble, monogamous, exogamous marriage; and the conceptual unification of the sins of the flesh under the head lust (*luxuria*) in the list of seven deadly sins.

What is known as the Gregorian reform was actually an effort of modernization initiated and carried out by the Church from about 1050 until 1215 (the year of the Fourth Lateran Council). The reform first of all established the independence of the Church from secular society. And what better barrier could have been erected between clergy and laity than that of sexuality? Marriage became the property of lay men and women; virginity, celibacy, and/or continence became the property of priests, monks, and nuns. A wall separated the pure from the impure. Impure liquids were banished from the realm of the pure: the clergy was not allowed to spill sperm or blood and not permitted to perpetuate original sin through procreation. But in the realm of the impure the flow was not stanched, only regulated. The Church became a society of bachelors, which imprisoned lay society in marriage. As Georges Duby has demonstrated, the Church imposed its model of indissoluble, monogamous marriage according to the gospel in the twelfth century.

In the confessors' manuals that replaced the old penitentials in the thirteenth century, incorporating the new notion that penance should reflect the intentions of the sinner, matrimonial sins were usually treated in a special chapter on marriage. Although the casuistry of marriage became more sophisticated in both theory and practice, marriage was generally excluded from the process of diversification and adaptation that affected religious life as society evolved. As Michel Sot has shown, Christian marriage was a new fact to be reckoned with in the thirteenth century.

Marriage was not the only target of sexual repression, however. As John Boswell has shown, the Church up to the twelfth century had been rather indulgent toward homosexuality, at least in practice. A gay culture had been able to flourish in the shadow of the Church if not in its very bosom. But in the thirteenth century this tolerant attitude for the most part ended. Sodomy was linked to heresy and combatted as a redoubtable enemy. Sexual sinners were condemned in the great operation of exclusion that took place in the thirteenth century. Indeed, few of them were even offered the benefit of Purgatory. Sexual misdeeds were punished in Hell.

With the establishment of seven deadly sins, the sins of the flesh were at last unified under the head of lust. To be sure, lust was rarely at the head of the list, an honor disputed by pride (*superbia*) and avarice (*avaritia*). Lust enjoyed another kind of supremacy, however. It was common to personify the sins as "daughters of the devil," each of whom was married by Satan to a particular class of society. But lust remained a prostitute, whom Satan "offers to all." It may have enjoyed the tolerance that the Church and public authorities, especially in the cities, now demonstrated toward prostitutes. The straitjacket of marriage encouraged the proliferation of bordellos and bathhouses. The sins of the flesh had their place on earth as in Hell. The image of lust on the tympanum of Moissac—a naked woman whose breasts and genitals are gnawed by snakes—would haunt the western sexual imagination for a long time to come.

## Select Bibliography

Ariès, Philippe. "Saint Paul et la chair." *Communications* 35 (1982): 34–36.

Boswell, John. *Christianity, Social Tolerance, and Homosexuality*. Chicago: University of Chicago Press, 1980.

Bugge, J. *Virginitas: An Essay in the History of a Medieval Ideal*. The Hague: Martinus Nijhoff, 1975.

Chiovaro, F. "XI–XIIIe. siècle: Le mariage chrétien en Occident." *Histoire vécue du peuple chrétien*, ed. Jean Delumeau. Vol. 1, pp. 225–255. Toulouse: Privat, 1979.

Duby, Georges. *Le Chevalier, la femme et le pretre: Le mariage dans la France féodale*. Paris: Hachette, 1981.

Flandrin, J.-L. *Le Sexe et l'Occident: Evolution des attitudes et des comportements*. Paris: Editions du Seuil, 1981.

Foucault, Michel. "Le combat de la chasteté." *Communications* 35 (1982): 15–33.

Noonan, J.-T. *Contraception: A History of Its Treatment by the Catholic Theologians and Canonists* (Cambridge: Harvard University Press, 1986).

Rousselle, Aline. *Porneia: De la maîtrise du corps à la privation sensorielle (IIe–IVe siècle de l'ère chrétienne)*. Paris: Presses Universitaires de France, 1983.

Veyne, Paul. "La famille et l'amour sous le Haut-Empire romain." *Annales ESC* (1978), pp. 35–68.

———. "Les noces du couple romain." *L'Histoire* 63 (1984): 47–51.

# PART FOUR

# LITERATURE AND IMAGINATION

# LÉVI-STRAUSS IN BROCELIANDE

# A BRIEF ANALYSIS

# OF A COURTLY ROMANCE

The episode that we have chosen for comment[1] is taken from Chrétien de Troyes's *Yvain ou le Chevalier au lion,* written some time around 1180.[2] Yvain, a knight in King Arthur's court, following a series of adventures about which we shall have more to say in a moment, obtains the permission of his wife Laudine to leave her for a year "in order to accompany the king and go to tournaments" (lines 2561–2562). Should he remain away for more than the allotted time by so much as a single day he will forfeit his wife's love. Inevitably—for this is a fantastic tale, in which conditions are set only to be transgressed[3]—Yvain allows the deadline to pass. A damsel from his wife's household (*mesnie*), riding a symbolic black palfrey, comes to tell him that all is lost and that he must never attempt to see his wife again. Yvain, losing his wits at this news, flees the court and heads for the forest.

A word needs to be said about the setting of the action. Like other of Chrétien's works (most notably *Perceval* and *Erec et Enide*) and many other courtly romances, the story unfolds in two series of episodes of radically different, even opposite, meaning (or *sen,* as one would have said in twelfth-century French).[4] The narrative opens with the story of a failure, a bungled "adventure." Calogrenant, another knight in Arthur's court and a cousin of Yvain, is unable to defeat Esclados le Roux, the guardian of a magic fountain in the heart of Broceliande. Yvain follows the same route and succeeds everywhere where Calogrenant has failed. Not only does he defeat and slay the lord of the fountain, but he also marries the man's widow and, like the king of Nemi studied by Frazer, replaces him on the throne. Yvain's feats are what might be called gratuitous adventures, exploits for exploits' sake, in which the magical interventions of Lunette, maid to the lady of the fountain, were of crucial assistance.

> Mes or est mes sire Yvain sire,                    2166
> Et li morz est toz obliez

This essay was written in collaboration with Pierre Vidal-Naquet and first published in abbreviated form in *Critique* 325 (1974): 543–571. The more complete version reprinted here first appeared in *Claude Lévi-Strauss* (Paris: Gallimard, 1979), pp. 265–319.

> Cil qui l'ocist est mariez;
> Sa fame a, et ensanble gisent. . . .

[Now Sir Yvain is lord and the dead man is completely forgotten. His murderer has married and taken his wife, and now they sleep together.]

The poet, who is not an adventurous knight but most probably a clergyman, does not disguise his feelings about the matter. Indeed, subsequent to Yvain's madness, the episode that chiefly interests us here, the knight ceases to make conquests for himself and works only on behalf of others, as a defender of widows and orphans. Having legitimated his lordship, he regains his wife's love.

The episode that is most important for our purposes occupies lines 2783–2883:

> Yvain was beside himself. Everything he heard upset him, and everything he saw tormented him. He wished he were far away in a land so wild that no one would know where to look for him, and that neither man nor woman would know more of him than if he were at the bottom of an abyss. His trouble mounted. He hated nothing so much as himself, and he knew not where to seek consolation. He saw that he was responsible for his own disgrace, that he had ruined himself. Rather than fail to take vengeance against himself for the theft of his happiness, he preferred to lose his mind. He parted without a word, so afraid was he of raving in the presence of the barons. The latter paid no heed. They allowed him to wander off on his own. Their words and their concerns, they believed, would be of little interest to him.
>
> Soon he was far from their tents. Madness took hold of his mind. He flayed himself and shredded his garments and fled across fields and furrows. His worried companions looked for him everywhere, among the tents, in the hedges, and through the orchards, but they did not find him.
>
> Yvain ran like a madman until near a park he encountered a boy with a bow and very broad and sharp barbed arrows. He had just enough sense to take them away from the youth. He lost all memory of what he had done until then. He lay in wait in the woods, slew whatever animals happened by, and ate their meat raw.
>
> He wandered among the hedgerows like a frenzied man of the wild until he came to a small, low house. There lived a hermit who was out grubbing for roots. When the hermit saw the naked figure of a man, he realized that the fellow had lost his wits and ran into his house to hide. But out of charity the good man placed some bread and water out through the window.
>
> The madman drew near and, his appetite whetted, took the bread

and ate. Never had he tasted such bad-tasting stale bread. The flour from which it was made had cost no more than five sous per measure, for it contained barley with the straw mixed in and was more bitter than yeast and mildewed and dry as bark. But hunger tormented him, and the bread seemed good, for hunger is sauce for any dish well prepared and well preserved. He ate all the bread and drank the cold water from the pot.

When he was finished he fled into the woods in search of stags and does. And the good man under his roof when he saw him run away prayed to God to protect him but never to allow him to stray again into that part of the woods. But nothing could prevent the lunatic, witless though he was, from returning to a place where someone had done him a good turn.

Thereafter, as long as his madness lasted, not a day went by when he did not bring some wild beast back to the hermit's hut. He spent his time hunting, and the good man spent his skinning and cooking the game, and every day there was bread and water in the window for the wild man. He had to eat venison without salt or pepper and drink cold water from the fountain. And the good man took it upon himself to sell the skins and buy oat or barley bread of which the other man ate his fill. This continued until one day when a lady and two damsels from her household found the madman sleeping in the forest.

The lady and one of the damsels then healed Yvain's madness with a magic ointment that the lady had previously obtained from the fairy Morgue (Morgan).

We shall have much more to say about Yvain's reintegration into the human world, for a lot more was involved than the damsel with the magic ointment. The "wild man theme" was a common topos of medieval Latin literature. The prototype can be found in a well-known episode of the *Vita Merlini* (1148–1149) by Geoffroy of Monmouth, a text that draws heavily upon ancient Celtic tradition.[5] Responsible for a battle in which two of his brothers die, Merlin takes to the woods (*fit silvester homo,* line 80), where he leads a miserable life but acquires prophetic powers. The theme occurs frequently in courtly romance,[6] and brilliant use was made of it by Ariosto in *Orlando furioso* (which is why Frappier would call the episode in question "Yvain furioso").[7] Our goal, however, is to comment on the text in detail, avoiding facile "psychological" explanations in which Chrétien appears to have been almost a psychiatrist: "All the details, all the precise little indications, suggest that in describing his character's madness Chrétien did not allow himself to diverge very far from certain observed facts."[8] That Chrétien transformed courtly romance into a kind of psychologization

of mythology is not without importance, to be sure, but the significance of this particular episode lies elsewhere, and no matter how fine
an observer he was, Chrétien undoubtedly met very few madmen in
the forest of Broceliande. Yvain was not just any madman, moreover:
he was neither the mad Heracles of Euripides nor the mad Orestes of
Racine; nor was he a client of Charcot's.[9]

It is useful to reread this episode with an eye to what structural analysis
can reveal.[10] Yvain first abandons his companions, the "barons," who
stand for all society and mankind. He crosses cultivated fields and is
soon beyond the limits of the region in which the knights of King
Arthur's court search for him (among tents, orchards, and hedgerows).
His madness is situated in the forest,[11] a more complex place than it
first appears. In the medieval West the forest was the equivalent of
what the desert was in the East: a refuge, a hunting ground, a place of
adventure, impenetrable to those who lived in cities and villages or
worked in fields.[12] In England or at any rate in "Britain" it was even
more: a place where in a sense the hierarchy of feudal society broke
down. Offenses committed in the forest did not fall under the jurisdiction of the regular courts. The laws of the forest issued "not from the
common law of the kingdom but from the will of the prince, so that it
was said that what was done according to those laws was just not in an
absolute sense but according to the law of the forest."[13] Henry II, king
of England and Anjou, in 1184 prohibited "bows, arrows, or dogs in
his Forests to anyone without surety."[14] The forest was royal property
not only because of the resources it supplied but perhaps even more
because it was a "desert." Here Yvain ceases to be a knight and becomes a hunter-predator:

> Les bestes par le bois agueite                    2826
> Si les ocit; et se manjue
> La venison trestote crue.

[In the woods he lay in wait for beasts and killed them, and he ate the
venison raw.]

He strips his body of its clothing and his mind of its memory. He is
naked and without memory. Yet between the world of men and that of
wild beasts Chrétien has provided a rather curious mediation: a "park,"
that is, an enclosed area for grazing,[15] a place for raising livestock (and
thus different from both the world of agriculture and that of gathering). There he finds a "boy," that is, a servant, a person who stands at

the bottom of the social scale.[16] No sooner does the lad appear than he is robbed of his bow and arrows:

> Un arc                                    2818
> Et cinq saietes barbelées
> Qui molt erent tranchanz et lées.

[A bow and five barbed arrows, broad and sharp.]

Now, bow and arrow are the weapons of a hunter, not of a knight in battle or tournament. To digress for a moment, there was a time long before the twelfth century when a contrast was drawn between the fully-equipped warrior and the isolated and even savage archer, namely, in archaic and classical Greece. In Euripides' *Heracles* the king of Argos contrasts the archer of the title to a valiant hoplite and finds him wanting: "a nullity of a man who fought with apparent bravery in his contests with animals but was incapable of any other prowess. He never held a shield on his left arm or confronted a lance. Carrying a bow, the most cowardly of weapons, he was always ready to flee. For a warrior the test of courage is not firing arrows but standing at his post and watching, without averting his eyes, as a whole field of raised lances runs toward him, always steadfast in his rank."[17] From the time of Homer until the end of the fifth century the bow was the weapon of bastards, traitors (such as Teucros and Pandaros in the *Iliad*), and foreigners (such as the Scythians in Athens)—in a word, of subwarriors (in the sense in which one speaks of "subproletarians"). Yet it was also the weapon of the superwarriors, in particular of Heracles, whom only a tragedian influenced by the sophists could have portrayed as a second-class fighter. For it was Heracles who passed on to Philoctetes, the lonely hero, the weapon that would decide the fate of Troy, and it was Ulysses who, wielding his bow at Ithaca, affirmed his sovereignty.

The distinction between the "heavy" and the "light" warrior, between the solitary, wily hunter and the soldier who fights as part of a unit, predates archaic Greece. To confine our attention to Indoeuropean sources, Georges Dumézil has found it in an Indian epic, the *Mahabharata,* certain elements of which date from Vedic times. Here, however, the bow is the sign not of the isolated hunter but of the armed combatant: "As a warrior, Arjuna was different from Bhima [two of the five brothers who are heroes of the Indian epic]. He fights not naked but clad in breastplate and mail and armed, indeed 'super-armed': he wields a huge bow. . . . He is not like Bhima a solitary warrior, an advance guard."[18] In other words, the bow is a sign whose value is determined solely by its *position* in a system, obviously a fact that calls for comment in any Lévi-Straussian analysis of the work.

Let us return, however, to the twelfth-century works with which we are primarily concerned. In Béroul's *Roman de Tristan*,[19] roughly contemporary with Chrétien's *Yvain,* the hero, about to plunge into the forest with Isolde, obtains a bow from a forest warden along with "two feathered, barbed arrows" (lines 1283–1284), which he uses to hunt game to keep himself and his companion alive. Later in the Morois forest episode, he fabricates a new "bow" (or, more precisely, an infallible trap for wild animals):

> Trova Tristan l'arc Qui ne faut                1752
> En tel manière el bois le fist
> Riens ne trove qu'il n'oceïst.

[Tristan made the Unerring Bow of wood in such a way that there was nothing that it failed to kill.]

In line 1338 of Béroul's poem the "laburnum" bow is also the emblematic arm of Tristan's prince and Isolde's husband, King Mark— emblematic because, unlike Tristan, Mark does not make use of his bow,[20] any more than Charlemagne does of the emblematic bow that he gives to Roland as a sign of his mission in the *Chanson de Roland* (lines 767ff.). Thus the bow can be a royal symbol (as for Ulysses), or it can be the emblem of a solitary hunter. In the Middle Ages it was predominantly the latter. If further proof is needed, it can be found in the late thirteenth-century anthology of *Merlin's Prophecies*,[21] in which two knights, Galeholt the Brown and Hector the Brown[22] land on a desert island teeming with wild animals and in a sense reinvent civilization at its most primitive level. Their first act is to make a bow.[23] Thus the bow is an ambiguous symbol, capable of signifying either a lapse from civilization or a revival of civilization. What is more, the "unerring bow" made famous by Béroul's poem[24] was also the name applied to the weapon used by the traitor Eadric to assassinate Edmund II (The Ironside), king of Wessex, according to the Anglo-Norman historian Geffrei Gaimar's *Estoire des Engleis*.[25] A weapon like Tristan's, though a legitimate arm when used against wild animals in the Morois forest or against the criminal lords at King Mark's court who drove the hero into exile, became illegitimate in knightly combat.

The text cited above is not isolated. It is easy to cite similar examples in chronicles, chansons de geste, and church documents. For example, the Latin chronicle of the murder (on 2 March 1127) of Charles the Good, count of Flanders, written by the notary Galbert of Bruges tells us about the knife-wielding Benkin *in sagittando sagax et velox.*[26] Many other documents portray archers among brigands and other "wild men" living on the fringes of society and engaged in inferior forms of military activity.[27] As for chansons de geste, consider Bertrand of Bar's *Girard de Vienne,* whose hero shouts: "A hundred curses among which archers are first. They are cowards, they dare not draw near." For the knight, to be an archer is to become a "shepherd boy."[28] In 1139 the Second Lateran Council anathematized in its twenty-ninth canon "the murderous art, hated by God, of crossbowmen and archers. We forbid the use of this art against Christians and Catholics."[29] This text is particularly interesting in that it was not the product of knights and their entourage: the ninth canon of the same council prohibited tournaments, but in a rather different tone. Courtly romance encoded this prohibition by likening the archer to a wild animal or even a centaur, the sign of Sagittarius. In the *Roman de Troie,* for example, Benedict of Sainte-Maure describes one of Priam's allies as an infamous criminal yet an infallible archer: "Whatever he aims at he strikes at once. His body, his arms, his head were like ours, but he was not at all handsome. He never wore cloth for he was as hairy as a beast. . . . He carried a bow that was made not of laburnum but of boiled leather joined together by a strange technique."[30]

Thus far we have concentrated primarily on French and Anglo-Norman sources. In other words, we have been looking at a sector in which chivalric norms and values, ways of life and forms of thought predominated. But just as what was true of Greece was not true of India, what was true of France and England was not true of Wales, where the bow was a noble weapon. Now, it so happens that we possess a Welsh version of Yvain's adventures, similar in some ways to Chrétien's version but different in others. It is highly unlikely that the two versions are directly related.[31] Yet the Welsh version is far from being utterly alien to the civilization of French chivalry. A book has even been written on the influence of chivalric culture on Welsh tales.[32] Nevertheless, the Welsh resisted the French denigration of the bow as a weapon of war. The episode that corresponds to Yvain's madness does not involve the theft of a bow and its use against wild animals. In the fortress where in the French version first Calogrenant and later Yvain encounter a vavasor and a girl familiar with the weapons used by knights, the Welsh storyteller has his heroes meet two youths practicing archery with ivory bows.[33] Similarly, in the *Gest of Asdiwal* the concrete details of the myth change in a manner reflecting the local ecology and customs but without altering the myth's structure.[34]

But let us get back to our archer, a naked savage and eater of raw meat.[35] No sooner is his metamorphosis complete than his reintegration into society begins. Yvain "finds" a man who is living at a primitive level of civilized technology: he has a "house" and engages in a rudimentary form of agriculture. A conquest of the wild by civilization is clearly implied. The man "grubs for roots," in other words, he gathers food from land that had been cleared by burning. He also purchases bread. The hermit thus belongs to an intermediate status between the constituted orders of society and the chaos of barbarism. He recoils and hides from Yvain, whose naked body marks him as a savage.[36] He barricades himself inside his hut. At this point the hermit and the knight-made-savage enter into a form of commerce motivated, according to the Christian interpretation, by the hermit's charity. The hermit offers the madman bread and cooked venison, at the bottom of the scale in terms of food preparation. Yvain has never tasted bread so bad or stale, eating it dry rather than in a kind of porridge, the basic dietary staple of the Middle Ages. Water is served in a pitcher, but it is very cold spring water, that is, "natural" water. The venison is cooked but served without salt or pepper. Thus the poet implicitly or explicitly points out a series of absences: of porridge, wine, salt and spices, and table manners. Yvain eats alone, in a sense clandestinely. In exchange the savage brings the hermit stags, does, and other wild beasts. This commerce even gives rise to a surplus, which allows this de facto society to enter into trade with others. The hermit skins the animals, sells their hides, and with the profits buys unleavened barley and rye bread to satisfy Yvain's needs. The arrangement between the two men is one of silent barter, with contact between them reduced to a bare minimum: the mad knight hurls his prey in front of the hermit's door, and the hermit sets bread, water, and cooked meat in the hut's narrow window. Communication between the world of the hunt and the world of agriculture, the raw and the cooked, thus takes place at the lowest possible level.

The opposition is apparent at two levels: between Yvain and the hermit, who represents an enclave of "culture" in the midst of "nature," and between Yvain and the environment in which he moved prior to entering the forest. Yvain has chosen nature in the wild, that is, the forest and what it has to offer. Nudity replaces clothing. Raw foods replace prepared and especially cooked foods. Impulsive behavior and repetitive actions supplant memory. Yvain has abandoned culture. He has fled organized society with its economic system en-compassing plowed fields and orchards surrounded by hedgerows. He has abandoned tents, houses, and military camps for open-air camp-sites. And he has given up agriculture in favor of hunting with bow and arrow.

Yvain and the hermit are guests of the forest. Both lead solitary and frugal lives. But the hermit leaves the forest occasionally to sell hides and buy bread in transactions with "civilized" men. Although the hut in which he lives is rudimentary, it is nevertheless a product of human construction. He wears clothing and is shocked by Yvain's nakedness. And he barters hides for bread. He lives by basic dietary rules. Al-though we are not told how he cooks the venison that Yvain supplies, there is little doubt that the meat is roasted. In Béroul's *Tristan* the lovers, with help from Gouvernal the squire, live on venison roasted directly over the fire without milk or salt.[37] Thus we see here what Lévi-Strauss has called the "culinary triangle," with roast meat in the mediating role, though boiled meat is present only metaphorically.[38] In other words, the meeting between Yvain and the hermit is possible because the former stands at the upper limit of "nature" (whose lower levels comprise the forest flora and fauna) while the latter stands at the lower limit of "culture" (the upper levels of which are represented by the court and its knights, whose superiority is called into question, as we shall see).

In making provisional use of the concepts of "nature" and "culture" here, we do not mean to suggest that they were clearly and con-sciously distinguished in Chrétien's mind.[39] The oppositions we have identified are all based on a further opposition, between the dominant world of humans and the dominated world of animals (dominated by hunting as well as domestication). The "wild" is not what is beyond the reach of man but what is on the fringes of human activity. The forest (*silva*) is wild (*silvatica*) not only because it is the place where one hunts for animals but also because it is the haunt of charcoal burn-ers and swineherds.[40] Between the asymmetric extremes of savagery and culture the mad and savage hunter is an ambiguous mediator, as is the hermit, but in a different way.

Twelfth-century thinkers reflected a good deal on the concept of na-ture, largely stripping it of its sacred qualities. Figurative art accom-plished much the same thing, as with the sculpture of Eve in the flesh at Autun.[41] The concepts wildness, matter, and nature, though they had many points in common, were not identical.[42] When Chrétien played on the opposition between *Nature* and *Norreture* (which Greek called *paideia*) he did not mean to oppose culture to wildness, for there were good "natures" (like Yvain's) as well as bad.[43] Nature is not the same as animality. In courtly literature, moreover, the juxtaposition of madman or savage (they were not always the same) with hermit was commonplace, one couple among others deserving systematic study: the knight and the shepherdess, the knight and the female savage,[44] the lady and the leper (an instance of which can be found in Béroul). The list could be extended. Courtly romance contains numerous examples. In Béroul, for instance, the lovers' sojourn in the forest of Morois (after they have been driven mad by a potion) is framed by two dialogues with the hermit Ogrin, the very person who facilitates Isolde's return to the court of King Mark. In Chrétien de Troyes's *Conte du Graal* Perceval "has lost his memory so completely that it no longer reminds him of God."[45] Not until he meets in the forest a hermit who turns out to be his uncle does his adventure begin to take on a meaning.[46]

A romance written after Chrétien's time, *Li Estoire del Chevalier au Cisne (The Story of the Knight with the Swan),*[47] describes a man who is much more fully a savage than Yvain, for he exhibits all the traits of the savage of folklore: he is as hairy as an animal, he meets a hermit with certain Christian characteristics, and he attains the summit of knightly glory. In *Valentine and Orson,* a romance that enjoyed immense popularity in the late Middle Ages and beyond,[48] we find a variant of the theme in which Orson, the reeducated savage, himself becomes a hermit.[49] Again it would be worthwhile to study systematically the savage-civilizer couple (in which the civilizer himself lives a half-savage life), in this case a noteworthy variation on the theme of Yvain and the hermit.[50]

In the thirteenth-century allegorical romance *Quête du Graal,*[51] certain of the characters are in essence enlightened interpreters of God. As Tzvetan Todorov has observed, the "possessors of meaning are a distinct group among the characters. They are "wise men," hermits, abbots, and recluses. Just as the knights could not know, these men could not act. None of them takes part in any episode except those involving interpretation. The two functions (action and interpretation) are strictly divided between the two classes of characters."[52] Twelfth-century romances were "symbolic" in the sense that their authors discussed the hidden significance (*sen*) of their poems. By symbol we mean here simply "the attribution by any literary means of an intellectual value to a physical reality (object, place, gesture, etc.)

that does not attach to that reality in normal language and usage."[53] In this sense the encounter between the savage and the hermit is indeed "symbolic," but it does not exhaust the *sen* of the romance or even of an episode whose significance extends far beyond. The admirable ambiguity of the text is perhaps that this encounter is pure action, that the exchange is at no time cast in dialogue form.

It is not easy to define precisely what the notion of "wild man" involves and how the mad knight relates to that notion. Societies in fact define their relations to alien beings by way of their representations of wild men. Indeed, historical societies were not interested in the wild man as such. In both written documents and images and even with respect to institutions the whole interest is in the relations between the wild man and his "cultivated" brother. Every culture has its own way or ways of classifying aliens, whether by viewing them as radically different, interchangeable, or in terms of a series of intermediaries. From Enkidu, the wild brother of Gilgamesh, the Mesopotamian king of Uruk, to Tarzan and the Yeti, to say nothing of Polyphemus the Cyclops and Caliban, literature has defined man in relation to the gods, the animals, and other men. Depending on the period and person, this definition has been either exclusive or inclusive.[54] Societies also define their relation to the proximate and remote environment and explicate the concept of seasonal time through the wild man theme.[55]

The same theme might also be worth studying in folklore. Its significance is ambiguous, for the wild man is classified in thematic indices both as a "supernatural helper" (in which case he is generally destined to rejoin society) and as a dangerous adversary, perhaps an ogre, of which Homer's Polyphemus is one example among others.[56]

There were moments in western history when things were relatively simple. The men who interpreted the age of discovery classified the "new men" in one of two fundamental ways, either as domesticable animals or as wild animals.[57] The former were to be converted to Christianity and put to work, the latter to be exterminated. Such is the conclusion that emerges from a reading of travel literature, although it should be noted that Montaigne in the *Essays* and Shakespeare in *The Tempest* gave a critical reading whose ambiguity must be respected—and saluted: Caliban is neither a mere animal nor a simple colonial rebel.[58]

The Middle Ages in their way are far more complex. Medieval classifications were more commonly series than discrete entities. (The tympanums of Vézelay and Autun, for example, portray monsters as capable of understanding the divine word.) Yet even near neighbors could be cast as devils: women, shepherds, Jews, foreigners.[59] Medieval forests were populated not only by hermits but also by demons. Wild men in the forests could therefore appear as innocents of the golden age, as in the *Estoire del Chevalier au Cisne,* which portrays men who

> Rachinetes manjuent et feuilles de pumier          329
> Ne savent que vins est ne nus autres daintiés.

[eat tiny roots and leaves of apple trees; they know nothing of wine or any other sophisticated refreshment.]

But they could also appear as minions of Satan.

We do not intend to explore systematically this vast domain but are simply making a modest attempt to understand, with the aid of structural analysis, the text with which we began by restoring the context from which we extracted it,[60] and, further, to show how this kind of analysis, which originated in the study of so-called cold societies, can be incorporated into historical research as such.[61]

The story of Calogrenant at the beginning of Chrétien's romance is something like a dress rehearsal (albeit ending in failure) for the first part of Yvain's adventures, which culminates in his marriage to Laudine. Wherever his predecessor went Yvain too will go, but he will succeed where Calogrenant failed. The world into which Calogrenant ventures "alone like a peasant, seeking adventure . . . armed with all armors as every knight should be" (lines 174–177) is, in a spatial sense, oddly laid out and curiously populated. As in any chivalric romance the setting is the forest, Broceliande, portrayed as the wilderness par excellence.[62] It is an abstract forest, not a tree of which is described.

> Et tornai mon chemin à destre          177
> Parmi une forest espesse
> Molt i ot voie felenesse
> De ronces et d'espinnes plainne.

[Mounted on my charger I followed my path through a thick forest, along trails thick with thorns and brambles.]

The knight takes his bearings and chooses the right-hand path, the "good" direction.[63] Yvain's adventure would take him down the same path but with a redundancy heavily stressed by the poet:

> Erra, chascun jor, tant          762
> Par montaignes et par valées,
> Et par forez longues et lées

> Par leus estranges et salvages
> Et passa mainz félons passages
> Et maint péril et maint destroit
> Tant qu'il vint au santier estroit
> Plain de ronces et d'oscurtez

[He wandered every day through mountains and valleys and through forests long and broad, through strange and wild places and through many a difficult passage, and braved many perils and straits, until he came to a narrow path, dark and full of brambles.]

The *félons passages,* the characteristic treachery of the forest, thus give way to an incipient order symbolized by the path. By way of the forest the knight gains access to another very different kind of place, having nothing to do with either the culture symbolized by court and fields or savage nature. It is a kind of moor (line 188), an "other world" of sorts, in which the hero encounters at a castle gate a vavasor (minor noble) who holds a goshawk in his hand, indicating the he is a hunter, but a cultivated one.

In courtly romance the vavasor is the traditional host, and it is in the role of hosts that he and his daughter, "a beautiful and gentle virgin" (line 225) greet the knights-errant whom they welcome into their fortress. Hosts and not guides: the vavasor confirms that the route taken was the right one (lines 204–205) but gives no indication as to how to proceed. Here the thread of the plot is interrupted. The signs of otherworldliness are discreet but incontrovertible. Although this is a warrior's castle, no object is made of iron. Everything is copper, a metal of superior value:

> Il n'i avoit ne fer ne fust                                213
> Ne rien qui de cuivre ne fust.

[There was nothing of iron, Nothing that was not made of copper.][64]

And there is also an orchard (or, more precisely, a walled garden or meadow), an unambiguous sign for anyone familiar with the symbolism of "Breton" romance:

> El plus bel praelet del monde.                             237
> Clos de bas mur à la reonde.

[The most beautiful meadow in the world, Enclosed by a low wall.]

An "enclosed place, separate from the rest of the world, in which all connections with normal social life and its concomitant responsibilities are broken,"[65] the otherworldly quality of the place is also signified by sexual temptation: the hero is attracted by the presence of the young maiden and does not wish to leave (lines 241–243).

The return to the forest leads the knight[66] to a place that is the antithesis of the one he has just left. In the midst of the forest, "in a clearing," he comes upon "terrifying wild bulls" that "were fighting among themselves and making so much noise, with such pride and ferocity," (lines 277–281) that the narrator backs off.[67] These bulls have a master, a "peasant who looks like a Moor,"[68] a giant and an authentic wild man in the sense that he is not just a man who has returned to the wild but one whose features and body and clothing are all borrowed from the animal world: "His head was larger than that of a horse or any other animal, and he had bushy hair, a broad, hairless forehead more than two hands wide, large, soft ears like those of an elephant, enormous brows, a flat face, owlish eyes, a cat's nose, a cleft mouth like a wolf's, sharp, reddish teeth like a boar's, a black beard, a curly moustache; his chin touched his chest, and his backbone was long, humpbacked, and twisted. He leaned on a club and was clad in a strange outfit that was made not of linen or wool but of two pieces of cowhide attached to his neck" (lines 293–311).[69] Unlike the vavasor, who is only a host, this savage "peasant," this "anti-knight," is a guide,[70] of the sort known to specialists in medieval folktales as a "helper," in this case a human (as opposed to a supernatural) helper. He is called upon to identify himself and explain how he is able to control beasts that *appear* to be totally wild: "By Saint Peter of Rome, they know nothing of man. I do not believe that it is possible in plain or hedgerow to keep a wild animal unless it is tied up or penned in" (lines 333–338). Whereupon he demonstrates his mastery and explains himself in such a way that his humanity is evident: "And he told me that he was a man" (line 328). "I am the sire of my beasts" (line 334). Indeed, he is a lord who can not only question the knight as an equal but also guide him on the road to discovery, showing him the way to the magic fountain that guards the castle whose lady is Laudine. He gives a meaning to the forest:

> Ci près troveras or en droit             375
> Un santier qui là te manra
> Tote la droite voie va,
> Se bien viax tex pas anploier
> Que tost porroies desvoier:
> Il i a d'autres voies mout.

[Nearby you will find on the right a path that will take you there. Follow the right hand if you wish to avoid going astray. There are many other ways.]

This guardian is therefore an ambiguous figure. He possesses most of the features typical of the medieval wild man as we know him from art and literature,[71] but certain details seem out of place: his technical (rather than magical) mastery over the wild animals and the fact that his animals, while ferocious, belong to a species domesticated by man,[72] The wild man is not merely a guest of the forest but its master. The knight is searching for an "adventure or marvel" (line 366), but the peasant "knows nothing about adventure" (line 368). He does know something about a marvel, however, namely, a magical country, which brings us to a new theme in *Yvain*.

This new thematic space encompasses all three spaces already traversed—culture, nature, and the other world of hospitality and femininity—but at a higher level, thanks to magic. At its center is a fortress adjacent to a town and surrounded by cultivated fields whose defense in case of enemy attack poses a number of problems.[73] The food eaten here is of course cooked, and Yvain can eat roast capon and good wine served on a white tablecloth. This feudal domain, graced by the same institutions as King Arthur's court (a seneschal, numerous knights, and so on), is guarded by a magic fountain adjacent to a chapel. The fountain is a most artful work, described by the savage as made of iron but actually of gold (lines 386 and 420) with stairs of emeralds and rubies. The water in it is cold yet boiling, and when poured it creates a terrifying tempest.

But access to this courtly society is via a supernatural wilderness. The peasant tells Calogrenant: "You will see this fountain, which is boiling yet colder than marble. The most beautiful tree ever shaped by Nature covers it with its shadow" (lines 380–383).[74] When combat begins between Esclados la Roux, the defender of the fountain, and Yvain, Chrétien resorts to animal imagery that he never uses in clashes between two knights of equal rank. Esclados attacks Yvain "as if he were hunting a rutting stag" (line 814), and Yvain is compared to a gyrfalcon stalking cranes (line 882).

Finally, once Yvain has killed the knight this world is predominantly female, and Laudine's beauty, like that of the tree beside the fountain, is supernatural: "Yes, I swear that Nature could not dispense such beauty, it was beyond all measure. Perhaps Nature had nothing to do with it! How could that be? Where did such great beauty come from? God created it with his own hands for Nature to ponder. No matter how much time it took to counterfeit such a work, it would never succeed. Even God, were he to apply himself to the task, could never with all his efforts produce its like" (lines 1494–1510). Here, sexual temptation, previously encountered at the vavasor's, is so present that Yvain, after being threatened with death and saved by the ring given him by Lunette, marries Esclados's widow and becomes master of the castle.

Thus this is a world with three aspects: savagery, culture, and courtliness. But from another point of view it is also a divided world, as Chrétien continually emphasizes. The approaches to the fountain are, successively and alternatively, paradisal and infernal. The marvelous singing of the birds gives way to the terrifying tempest. Yvain himself describes the ambiguity of the situation:

> Ce qu'Amors vialt doi je amer          1457
> Et doit me elle ami clamer?
> Oïl, voir, par ce que je l'aim
> Et je m'anemie la claim
> Qu'ele me het, si n'a pas tort
> Que ce qu'ele amoit li ai mort
> Donques sui ge ses anemis?
> Nel sui, certes, mes ses amis.[75]

[She, whom Cupid wants me to love, must she call me friend? Yes, surely, because I love her. And I call her my enemy, because she hates me, and with good reason, because I killed the man she loved. Am I therefore her enemy? Surely not, because I love her.]

What takes place inside the fortress can be classed under the head of courtly spirit, refined love, and culpable ruse. Lunette brings Yvain and Laudine together through a series of lies. The feminine world is itself divided, for servant and mistress in a sense share roles.

Yvain's madness marks the severance of the hero's ties with both Arthur's court and the world just described. The bulk of the text (from line 2884 to the end, line 6808) is taken up with describing the stages of Yvain's return: cured of his madness, he regains the love of his wife and legitimate possession of his estate. To make sense of the previous interpretation we must examine the stages of this return. The madness episode is indeed of crucial importance. Previously the savage world is represented by the forest, the scene of adventure and initiatory exploits. But madness turns Yvain himself into a savage and simultaneously makes the status of the forest seem more complex. In terms of structural analysis, there is no forest as such. Even within the context of a single work the forest exists only in relation to that which is not forest. Oppositions come into play even within what appeared to be simple.[76]

When Yvain, healed by the magic ointment given him by the Lady
of Noroison, reawakens,

> Si se vest                                    3029
> Et regarde par la forest
> S'il verroit nul home venir.

[He dressed and looked into the forest to see if anyone was coming.]

the forest effectively becomes populated. The very presence of the
lady is a sign that a castle is nearby, "so near that it was no more than a
half league away, just a short walk, according to the measurement of
leagues in that country, two of whose leagues equal one of ours, and
four, two" (lines 2953–2957). It is as though the spaces that are so
carefully distinguished in the first part of the text have ceased to be
separate. The forest, the moor with its orchard, the court, and the
magic fountain are no longer isolated from one another. Laudine's estate has been integrated into Arthur's court,[77] and the characters go
from one space to the other without the aid of mysterious guides and
without submitting to rites of passage. To be sure, the forest still exists, and a maiden comes close to losing herself in it:

> Si pooit estre an grant esmai              4842
> Pucele au bois, et sanz conduit
> Pas mal tans, et par noire nuit,
> Si noire qu'ele ne veoit
> Le cheval sor qu'ele seoit.

[With great emotion the damsel took to the woods without a guide, in
bad weather and in the dark of night, so dark that she could not see the
horse on which she was sitting.]

But the maiden, who calls upon God and her friends "to rescue her
from this bad pass and guide her toward some inhabited place" (lines
4851–4852) is in fact guided by Yvain, who uses exclusively human
means (one of his helpers is Lunette, who makes no use of magic), and
it is on "flat and level terrain" (line 5031) that she ultimately encounters the knight who will rescue her.

The forest is no more than an element—a humanized element[78]—of
the landscape, but the savage wilderness still exists, and Yvain's sojourn in it is not without consequences. After his recovery, he enters
the service of the lady of Noroison and does battle against the knights
who have pillaged Count Allier. Chrétien compares him to a falcon
hunting ducks and to a "lion tormented and pursued by hunger loosed
among the deer" (lines 3191 and 3199–3200). This is the last animal

metaphor used in connection with Yvain.[79] The metaphorical lion is made flesh. Yvain, again traveling through the forest, sees locked in struggle two creatures of the wild, a lion and a serpent, the latter in fact almost a dragon, for it breathes fire (line 3347).[80] The lion is about to succumb. If Yvain saves it, he risks death himself. But Yvain does not hesitate for a moment between the "venomous and criminal" animal (line 3351) whose vices are well known to readers of Genesis[81] and the noble beast depicted in the *Roman de Renart* as the king of the wild, "the frank and gentle beast" (line 3371). As it happens, however, the lion loses the tip of his tail—a rather obvious symbol of castration or at least domestication—to the knight's sword. The grateful lion renders a vassal's homage to Yvain and subsequently becomes his companion and even his pet (line 3435). Yvain is henceforth the "knight with lion."[82] The lion took part in his battles, at least in those in which the rules of chivalry, which prescribe combat between equals, are not respected.[83] The striking fact, not yet taken seriously by any commentator, is that the relations that are established between Yvain and the lion from the outset reproduced the relations established between the hermit and Yvain during his madness. But in this case it is obviously Yvain who plays the human role.[84] The lion *hunts* on behalf of Yvain. He detects the scent of a kid within a *bowshot* (line 3439), a word that calls to mind the bow of Yvain the hunter. But now it is Yvain who slits the animal's hide, roasts it on a spit (roasting is explicitly mentioned in lines 3457–3460), and shares the meat with the animal (who receives the surplus). The absence of "table manners" and in this case of bread (there being no commerce involved, in contrast to the situation with the hermit) is emphasized, but it is of course Yvain and not the lion who complains about the savage nature of the repast: "This meal gave him little pleasure, for he had no bread or wine or salt or tablecloth or knife or other utensil" (lines 3462–3464).

In fact Yvain's encounter with the lion and the elimination of the serpent remove the ambiguities associated with the savage world in the first part of the romance. From this point on Yvain will confront only wild creatures about which there is no ambivalence.[85]

He first saves a damsel threatened with being delivered into prostitution by a "giant criminal" (line 3850) named Harpin of the Mountain, who possesses certain characteristic traits of the savage.[86] He is armed not with a sword but with a pike (lines 4086–4098), he has a hairy chest (line 4217), and he is covered with a bearskin (line 4191). He is compared to a bull (line 4222) and goes down "like a felled oak" (line 4238), but this time the connotation is entirely diabolical. The battle with the Maufé [the Evil One] takes place not in the forest but in the plain under the sign of God, Christ, the Virgin, and the angels (line 4106).[87] Yvain has heard mass (line 4025), which is mentioned for the first time.

In the château de Pême-Aventure (the Worst Adventure), which in some respects resembles the residence of the hospitable vavasor,[88] Yvain comes upon a group of captive girls forced to work with silk. Here Yvain, accompanied by his lion, does battle not with a metaphorical devil but "with two sons of the devil, and this is no fable, for they were born of a woman and of one Netun" (lines 5265–5267).[89] The fight with these "hideous and black" creatures (line 5506) is a struggle against diabolical savagery.[90] Yvain the victor will finally be able to return to the castle by the fountain. His fight with his peer Gawain so that he may return home is strictly a knightly combat in which there is neither victor nor vanquished. Nor is any low trick used in securing his return to the good graces of Laudine, which is negotiated, without the aid of magic, by Lunette. Laudine agrees to help the knight with the lion to return to his lady, unaware that he and Yvain are one and the same. There is no deception involved, only a play on the hero's two identities.

The lion, which is inseparable from Yvain as he makes his return to humanity and which is gladly welcomed by Laudine, is simply merged with Yvain when his itinerary is complete and disappears from the story.

Let us therefore review the characters that populate the wild in Chrétien's tale.[91] At the two extremes are the lion and the serpent, and in between is a whole range of other figures. The helpful hermit may be paired with the giant ogre Harpin of the Mountain and the two sons of diabolical Netun.[92] A central figure, monstrous but human, is the "peasant who looks like a Moor," about whom Yvain asks "how nature could have done such foolish work, so ugly and common" (line 798); this is the savage in the strict sense. Yvain himself traverses all the degrees of the scale, confronting his enemies and helped by his helpers. At a critical moment in his adventure he himself becomes a savage, thus assimilating that aspect of the wild needed by the perfect knight.

Certain of the codes that underlie Chrétien's tale have emerged in the course of the analysis. But we owe it to readers of *Yvain* to sketch out more fully than we have done thus far the relations between the tale and the society from which it issued and to which it returned. To be sure, we have already had occasion to make extensive reference to twelfth-century society. Such references were an expository convenience, permitting us to shorten the argument and to verify certain points. But narrative elements such as the bow, the hermit, the savage, the lion, the serpent, God, and the Devil could have been decoded without reference to the outside world. Yet that world did exist, and in the final analysis it is what interests historians.[93]

The question is made more complex by the fact that an image of the world of chivalry is available in two very different sorts of twelfth-century literary works—different in terms of both the audience addressed and the underlying ideology. The chanson de geste appeared somewhat earlier than the courtly romance,[94] but in the twelfth century the two genres were mutual influences and rivals.[95] For the positivist historians of the last century (who have more than one imitator today) it was essential to choose between the two. Thus Léon Gautier, in his celebrated work on chivalry, stated authoritatively that "the romances of the Round Table, which to biased or hasty judges seem so profoundly chivalric, actually number among the works that hastened the end of chivalry."[96] Having made this judgment, he can then tranquilly and with admirable knowledge of the texts trace the life of the knight from birth to death using evidence drawn almost exclusively from chansons de geste without once asking himself whether those sources were indeed written for the purpose of providing positivist historians with data and footnotes. Historians nowadays are less confident; we know that we are mortal, and that our errors will be as transparent to our successors as those of our predecessors are to us. But at least we have learned that fiction, like myth, and indeed like society, cannot be treated as though it were a thing.

"The relation of the myth to the idea is definite, but it is not one of *re-presentation*. It is dialectical in nature, and the institutions described in myths may be the inverse of the real institutions. Indeed that may always be the case when the myth seeks to express a negative truth. . . . Mythological speculations seek in the final analysis not to portray reality but to justify its rather rough construction, since extreme positions are *imagined* only in order to show that they are *untenable*."[97] What is true of myth is even more true of the literary work, whose complex texture must be respected. We must not seek to decompose literature into primary components to which the narrator adds an ideological dimension and a set of personal choices.[98] There is admittedly a kind of literature that is nothing but a degraded form of myth, as Lévi-Strauss has said of the serialized novel.[99] To be sure, some courtly romance resembles the serialized novel, but taking a broader view the whole genre attests to a comprehensive ideological project. That project, which has been described in great detail by Erich Köhler,[100] concerned what Marc Bloch has called the "second age of feudalism," in which the nobility transformed itself from a de facto into a de jure class. Threatened by the rise of royal authority and by urban development, the new class aimed to restore an order that was subject to continual challenge. Romances were written as works intended to be read; as such, they deliberately excluded the mixed public that listened to the chansons de geste. Only the two major orders, knights and clergy, were consumers of courtly romance,[101] as was stated in these well-known verses by the author of the *Roman de Thèbes:*[102]

> Or s'en tesent de cest mestier,                    13
> Se ne sont clerc ou chevalier
> Car aussi pueent escouter
> Comme li asnes al harper
> Ne parlerai de peletiers
> Ne de vilains, ne de berchiers.

[Nothing will be said here about those whose trade is not that of cleric or knight, for if asses can listen to the harp, so can they. I shall not speak of furriers or peasants or shepherds.]

Clergy and knights were not on the same plane, however. The ideal of adventure was held out to the knight, not to the cleric. This was to be sure a complex ideal, ambiguous by nature and subject to a variety of internal tensions: think of Chrétien's critique of *Tristan* in *Cligès.*[103] Köhler, however, has summed up its intentions quite well: "Adventure was a way of overcoming the contradiction that had come to exist between the ideal life and the real life. Romance idealized adventure and thus conferred upon it a moral value. Adventure was dissociated from its concrete origins and situated in the center of an imaginary feudal world in which a community of interests among the various strata of the nobility, already a thing of the past, still seemed possible to achieve."[104] Courtly love, a "precious and holy thing" (*Yvain,* line 6044), was at once the point of departure and the point of return for an adventure that left the feudal court for the wild only to prepare the way for a triumphant return. In the meantime, the hero secured his salvation in accordance with the wishes of the clergy, saving himself by saving others. At the center of Chrétien's romance the hermit preserves Yvain's humanity and the lady of Noroison begins his return to chivalry. But medieval ideology reduced all the diversity of society to just three functions (enumerated most recently by Georges Dumézil, after so many others). Besides the clergy, who prayed, and the knights, who fought, there were those who worked. This third function is represented in the romance by the peasant: his humanity is acknowledged, but his hideous appearance marks him as a member of his class.

To further our knowledge of an imaginary world, recognized as imaginary by courtly writers themselves,[105] we must proceed by investigating what Freud called displacements and condensations, as well as by examining the extensions and inversions introduced by the poets. Consider, for example, the problem of initiation. As has been known for some time, dubbing, the ceremony by which young men were inducted into knighthood, was an initiatory rite comparable to similar rituals found in many societies.[106] It is clear, moreover, that courtly romances can readily be interpreted as revealing an initiatory pattern, with a departure followed by a return.[107] Yet it is striking that the dubbing rite experienced by so many aspiring knights on the battlefield or on the night of Pentecost plays but a limited role in Chrétien's romances, among others.[108] It is not mentioned in *Yvain,* and although it is present in *Perceval* and *Cligès* it is in no sense a turning point of the story. The knights who head into the "forest of adventure" are already dubbed. The theme of childhood, so important in the chansons de geste, is of relatively minor interest in courtly romance. Compared with "real" initiation, therefore, the initiation described in the romances is disproportionately extended in time and space.

In an important article Georges Duby has suggested another comparison.[109] Duby calls attention to the existence of a special class in twelfth-century aristocratic society: the youths (*juvenes*). Duby writes: "A 'youth' was in fact a grown man, an adult. He was admitted to a group of warriors, given arms, and dubbed; in other words, he became a knight. . . . Youth can therefore be defined as that part of life comprised between dubbing and fatherhood,"[110] which could be a very long time indeed. Youths were footloose, vagabond, and violent. They were the "leading element in feudal aggressiveness."[111] And their long, adventurous quest—"a long sojourn shames a young man"—had a purpose: to find a rich mate. "The intention of marrying seems to have governed all of a young man's actions, impelling him to cut a brilliant figure in combat and to show his prowess in athletic matches."[112] Marriage was made more difficult by the proscriptions of the Church, which often made it impossible to find a bride close to home. Duby himself has noted the inescapable parallel between this situation and that described in courtly literature: "The presence of such a group at the heart of aristocratic society fostered certain attitudes, certain collective images, certain myths, of which one finds both reflections and models in literary works written in the twelfth century for the aristocracy and in the exemplary figures that those works proposed, which encouraged, perpetuated, and stylized spontaneous emotional and intellectual reactions."[113] Indeed, Yvain, husband of the wealthy widow Laudine of Landuc, accords rather well with the model proposed by Duby.

Let us take a closer look, however. Note first that in *Yvain* as well as *Erec et Enide* marriage takes place not *after* but *before* the great adventure that demonstrates the hero's mettle. Among the reasons for youthful restlessness suggested by Duby are certain inevitable conflicts: between father and son and especially between younger brother and older brother (and heir). Many "youths" were younger sons who became knights-errant because of their position in the family. Yet such conflicts are apparently absent in Chrétien's romances.[114] What is more, it is as if *all the poet's heroes* were only sons: this is true of Yvain, Cligès, Lancelot, Perceval, and Erec.[115] Brothers and sisters belong to the *previous generation*. Yvain and Calogrenant are first cousins. Erec, Enide, and Perceval discover uncles and aunts in the course of their adventures. Cligès becomes the rival of his paternal uncle for possession of Fenice, daughter of the emperor of Germany.[116] The adventures of the youths are collective, moreover. The chroniclers portray bands of *juvenes* furnishing the "best contingents for all remote expeditions."[117] Yet adventure in courtly as opposed to epic literature is always individual.[118] Thus it would appear that the courtly writers refracted the social facts in such a way that their interpretation often amounts to an inversion of reality. The mechanisms employed to accomplish this deserve further study: shift from the present to the past, from the plural to the singular, from the masculine to the feminine.

Yet much of the real economic and social evolution of the twelfth century is present in *Yvain*, but at an unconscious level: the transformation of the rural landscape and of seigneurial and clerical revenues, and the changes in peasant life that resulted from vast efforts to clear the land begun in the tenth century and apparently culminating in the twelfth.[119]

Shortly before *Yvain* was written the Norman poet Wace in the *Roman de Rou* described the magic fountain of Broceliande, which plays so central a part in Chrétien's story, as a thing of the distant past:[120]

Mais jo ne sai par quel raison                          6386
Là sueut l'en les fées véeir
Se li Breton nos dïent veir
E altres merveilles plusors
Aires i selt aveir d'ostors
E de grans cers mult grant plenté
Mais vilain ont tot désesrté
Là alai jo merveilles querre
Vi la forest e vi la terre
Merveilles quis, mais nes trovai
Fol m'en revinc, fol i alai,
Fol i alai, fol m'en revinc
Folie quis, pour fol me tinc.

[I do not know, however, why people were in the habit of seeing fairies there. If the Bretons tell of these and other marvels, there were buzzards and lots of huge stags, but the peasants soon left. I went in search of marvels and saw forest and earth but of marvels found none. Mad I came back and mad I went, mad I went and mad I came back. What I was asking was mad, and I consider myself mad.]

Obviously we cannot prove that Chrétien read this text, which so eloquently bears witness to the disenchantment of the forest as it was cut down to make way for new fields. Instead we shall turn to *Yvain* itself, for the text of the romance provides us with our best argument.

In interpreting *Yvain* we have stressed the importance of the hero's three encounters in the forest: [121] with the savage who gives him directions, with the hermit who saves him and restores his humanity, and with the lion that he tames. Now, the meeting with the peasant takes place on cleared land (Lines 277, 708, 793) as does the meeting with the lion (line 3344); the hermit is grubbing for roots on cleared land (line 2833). [122] Finally, the encounter with Harpin of the Mountain takes place after the poet has described him "galloping through the woods" (line 4096), "before the gate," to be sure," but "in the middle of a *plain*" (line 4106), where the word *plain* was commonly used at the time to refer to recently cleared land. The only encounter that does not take place on cleared land is that with the sons of diabolical Netun, but this is not situated in any concrete location. [123] Turning now from the savage world to the magical world, we find, as J. Györy has observed, that one consequence of the use of the fountain is the destruction of the estate's trees despite their admirable, almost paradisal qualities: "But if I could, sir vassal, I would shift to you the suffering caused me by the obvious injury of which proof surrounds me, in my wood that has been cut down" (lines 497–501). The theme disappears, however, after the Calogrenant story. The magical world—and perhaps the interests of the lords, not all of whom benefited from the clearing of land—is here in contradiction with the savage world.

The peasant and the lion were both encountered in clearings, then, but only the hermit is actively clearing land and modifying space. The three characters are therefore both similar and different.[124] The active role ascribed to the hermit is not particularly surprising since it corresponded to reality: hermits played a far greater role than the monks of the great abbeys in the major episodes of land-clearing.[125] Admittedly peasants played no less important a role, but the ideology of the clergy was opposed to acknowledging this fact, deplored by Wace, in the marvelous world into which Chrétien introduces us.[126]

Yvain's itinerary, as we have reconstructed it with the aid of structural analysis, intersects with and sheds light on several historical schemata. The key space, the clearing, corresponds to a very important economic phenomenon of the twelfth century, the clearing of land. Yvain's adventure follows in the footsteps of the groups of "youths" identified by Georges Duby, whose contradictory relations with the rest of society have been analyzed by Erich Köhler. Finally, the Christian atmosphere of the time is present in the very texture of the analysis, in the implicit judgment on chivalric behavior, and, more specifically, at critical transitional stages in Yvain's trajectory: a chapel watches over the stairs, the pine, and the magic fountain where everything begins; a hermit preserves Yvain's humanity; and Yvain's rehabilitation is accomplished through a confrontation with the world of the devil. In order to return to the world of culture Yvain himself must first be Christianized, and even the forest is marked by Christian signs.

We hope that the reader will forgive us for ending our analysis here. In order to carry it further we would have to move to another plane, one explored by Chrétien himself in *Perceval*.[127]

# VESTIMENTARY AND ALIMENTARY CODES IN *EREC ET ENIDE*

Vestimentary and alimentary codes are important features of a society's culture. It is not enough to study their role in social practices. We can better understand their function by examining their place in works of the imagination.

In feudal society these codes were particularly effective because they played an essential role in the system of values and social status. Through them appearances were forcefully expressed.

In literary works dress and diet were used to indicate the social status of the characters, to symbolize plot situations, and to underscore significant moments in the story. Chrétien de Troyes employed these devices with his customary genius.

In this brief essay in honor of René Louis, who understood and demonstrated the value of literary works as historical sources in the broadest sense, I shall limit myself to examining the function of vestimentary and alimentary codes in *Erec et Enide*. I have used the Mario Roques edition and, based on it, the fine [modern French] translation by the teacher in whose honor this essay is written.

In my compilation I have not included passages concerning men's military garb. By doing so I have neglected an important aspect of the interplay between male and female roles. To repair this omission would require a more comprehensive and ambitious study.

Dress first comes into the romance through its hero, Erec. Although he probably shared the doubts of other knights (expressed by Gawain) concerning King Arthur's decision to restore the white stag costume, his behavior reconciled obedience to Arthur, the code of courtesy, and his personal situation. He does participate in the hunt, but as a knight serving Queen Guinevere he remains aloof. He chooses a costume intermediate between formal and battle attire yet sufficiently costly to indicate his rank: that of a king's son and renowned knight of the Round Table.

Originally published as "Quelques remarques sur les codes vestimentaire et alimentaire dans *Erec et Enide,*" *La Chanson de geste et le mythe carolingien, Mélanges René Louis,* vol. 2, (1982), pp. 1243–58. References are to Chrétien de Troyes, *Erec et Enide,* translated from the Old French by René Louis, based on the edition by Mario Roques (Paris: Librairie Honoré Champion, 1977).

> Sor un destrier estoit montez,
> afublez d'un mantel hermin . . .
> S'ot cote d'un dïapre noble
> qui fu fez an Costantinoble;
> chauces de paile avoit chauciees,
> molt bien fetes et bien taillies;
> et fu es estriés afichiez,
> un esperons a or chauciez;
> n'ot avoec lui arme aportée
> fors que tant seulemant s'espée.
> (lines 94–104)

[Riding a charger, he was dressed in an ermine mantle. He wore a costly diapered tunic woven in Constantinople, and well-made, well-cut silk breeches. Firmly braced in his stirrups, he wore gold spurs but carried no other arm than his sword.]

Here clothing is a code for status and situation.

Clothing figures next in an episode involving the appearance of the heroine of the tale, Enide. In pursuit of the knight, damsel, and midget who have offended the queen, Erec accepts the hospitality of an aged vavasor. Chrétien's objective in this episode is to show not only the nobility of rank and spirit but also the poverty of the vavasor and his family (a wife and a daughter). Erec will in fact marry Enide. For him a *mésalliance* is impossible, yet courtesy requires that he note the position of the family into which he will marry.

Enide appears dressed in a refined but not sumptuous manner, wearing only a chemise and a blouse with sleeves (*chainse*). Her clothes are white and the chemise is finely made, but there are holes in the elbows of the blouse:

> La dame s'an est hors issue
> et sa fille, qui fu vestue
> d'une chemise par panz lee,
> deliee, blanche et ridee;
> un blanc cheinse ot vestu desus,
> n'avoit robe ne mains ne plus,
> et tant estoit li chainses viez
> que as costez estoit perciez
> povre estoit la robe dehors,
> mes desoz estoit biax li cors.
> (lines 401–410)

[The lady came out with her daughter, who was wearing a chemise with fine, broad tails, white and pleated. Over this she had put a white blouse, and that was all she wore. The blouse was so worn, moreover, that there were holes in the elbows. The clothing was poor outside, but underneath the body was beautiful.]

Erec then takes Enide to watch the fight for the sparrow hawk, which is also the occasion for vengeance on the wicked knight. She follows him, still poorly dressed and riding a poor horse. She wears neither a belt nor a cloak.

> La sele fu mise et li frains;
> desliee et desafublee
> est la pucelle sus montee.
> (lines 738–740)

[The horse was fitted with saddle and reins. Without belt or cloak the damsel mounted.]

After his victory, Erec, having asked for and obtained the hand of Enide, prepares to take her to the court of King Arthur, where they will marry. He details for his future inlaws the dowry (*Morgengabe*) that he will give to his wife and of which they will be the beneficiaries, for they will then be elevated to an estate worthy of their rank and of the rank about to be bestowed on their daughter. Among the gifts are châteaux and *clothing*:

> Einz que troi jor soient passez
> vos avrai anvoie assez
> or et argent et veir et gris
> et dras de soie et de chier pris
> por vos vestir et vostre fame.
> (lines 1325–1329)

[Within three days I shall have sent you quantities of gold and silver, vair and squirrel, costly silk fabrics for your clothing, for you and your wife who is my dear, sweet lady.]

He then announces his decision to take Enide dressed as she is. The queen will give her clothing worthy of her when they arrive at court.

> Demain droit à l'aube del jor,
> an tel robe et an tel ator,
> an manrai vostre fille a cort:
> je voel que ma dame l'atort
> de la soe robe demainne,
> qui est de soie tainte an grainne.
> (lines 1331–1336)

[Tomorrow at dawn's first light I shall take your daughter to court in the gown and accoutrement she is wearing. I shall ask my lady the queen to dress her in a formal gown of dyed silk.]

This decision shocks not Enide's father and mother, anxious not to contradict their future son-in-law, but her cousin and her uncle, who is a wealthy count. They want to give Enide a beautiful gown:

> "Sire, fet ele, molt grant honte
> Sera a vos, plus qu'a autrui
> se cist sires an mainne a lui
> vostre niece, si povrement
> atornee de vestemant."
> Et li cuens respont: "Je vos pri,
> ma dolce niece, donez li
> de voz robes que vos avez
> la mellor que vos i avez."
> (lines 1344–1352)

["Sire, it will be a great shame, for you more than for any other, if this lord takes your niece with him so poorly attired." The count answered: "I beg you, my dear niece, give her from your own gowns the one you consider most beautiful."]

Whereupon Erec becomes angry. The queen will dress Enide:

> "Sire, n'an parlez mie.
> Une chose sachiez vos bien:
> ne voldroie por nule rien
> qu'ele eüst d'autre robe point
> tant que la reine li doint."
> (lines 1354–1358)

["Sire, do not speak of that. Know one thing: I do not wish her to have any gown until the queen has given her one."]

Enide therefore leaves for the court "el blanc chainse et an la chemise" ("in the white blouse and chemise," line 1362).

Many commentators on the text have been troubled by Erec's stubborn insistence on taking Enide to court in her poor clothing. Their explanations, often psychological, seem to me inadequate and even out of place. Erec's decision, I think, is the result of a conjunction of two systems. One is that of marriage, which is a rite of passage. The episode in question is the first stage of that rite, the stage of separation. The future bride leaves her parents' home, but in other respects her estate is to remain unchanged. The wedding is to mark not only a passage from celibacy to marriage, from one family to another, from one house to another, but also a transition to a higher status, from poverty to wealth. The material embodiment of this change in status, as marked by dress, is to come only at the next stage of the rite, as in what Van Gennep called "marginal rites" (*rites de marge*). One of the key themes of the romance, moreover, is that of the couple's status. For Chrétien there is supposed to be equality between husband and wife, but this equality must be compatible with a certain superiority of the man over the woman, in order to preserve medieval Christian concepts of marriage and the couple. Chrétien on many occasions insists on the equality of Erec and Enide. Eventually equality is sanctioned by marriage and, at the end of the story, by the joint coronation of the pair, but earlier it is expressed through equality with respect to the preeminent values of the aristocratic system: courtesy, beauty, generosity, wisdom, and courage:

> Molt estoient igal et per
> de corteisie et de biauté
> et de grant deboneretré.
> Si estoient d'une meniere,
> d'unes mors et d'une matière,
> que nus qui le voir volsist dire
> n'an poïst le meillor eslire
> ne le plus bel ne le plus sage.
> Molt estoient d'igal corage
> et molt avenoient ansamble.
> (lines 1484–1493)

[They were equals and peers in courtesy, beauty, and generosity. They resembled one another so much in manner, education, and character that no man resolved to tell the truth could have decided which was better, handsomer, or wiser. Their hearts were identical and perfectly suited to each other.]

Erec's superiority over Enide stems primarily from the fact that he is a warrior, a high-ranking knight and the son of a king. To become a knight he had previously been dubbed. (At the time of the story he is twenty-five years of age.) Enide is also to be raised to a higher rank. When Erec and Enide marry, moreover, Arthur is to make knights of one hundred youths. Guinevere is to give Enide new and splendid clothes, which for her represents a kind of dubbing. In other words, the queen's gift of clothing is a female equivalent of dubbing.

In the mean time, the cortege that accompanies Erec and Enide to court is expected to dress formally:

> N'i remaint chevalier ne dame
> qui ne s'atort por convoier
> la pucele et le chevalier.
> (lines 1416–1418)

[Not one knight or lady did not don the utmost finery to accompany the damsel and the knight.]

When they arrive at court, Erec explains to the queen what he expects of her:

> "Povretez li a fet user
> ce blanc chainse tant que as cotes
> an sont andeus les manches rotes.
> Et ne por quant, se moi pleüst,
> boenes robes asez eüst,
> c'une pucele, sa cosine,
> li volt doner robe d'ermine
> de dras de soie, veire ou grise;
> mes ne volsisse an nule guise
> que d'autre robe fust vestue
> tant que vos l'eüssiez veüe.
> Ma douce dame, or an pansez,
> car mestier a, bien le veez,
> d'une belle robe avenant."
> (lines 1548–1561)

["Poverty has caused her to wear out this white blouse to the point where both sleeves have holes in the elbows. And yet, had it pleased me, she would not have lacked for fine gowns, for a damsel, her cousin, wanted to give her a robe of ermine and silk, vair and squirrel. But I would never have agreed for anything in the world that she wear another robe until you had seen her. My sweet lady, think about it now, for as you see she needs a fine and handsome gown."]

Guinevere immediately acquiesces and announces that she will give one of her gowns ("good and beautiful . . . fresh and new," lines 1563–1566) to Enide. She takes Enide into her principal chamber and sees to it that she is given a new *bliaut* and a cloak as well as a gown that she had had tailored for herself. Guinevere, respecting the code of courtesy that forbids her to give Enide used clothing, treats her as though she were another self, giving her clothing that is not only new but personal. Dress thus becomes a symbol of identification.

The dubbing of Enide via the queen's new clothes is described at length by Chrétien in one of the bravura pieces of his work (lines 1572–1652). Historians of medieval costume regard this as one of the most precise descriptions we have of de luxe female attire. Abundant details create a portrait of the ultimate in dress: rare furs, silks, gold, precious gems, vivid colors, belt, jewels, and diverse ornaments are combined to raise Enide to the pinnacle of luxury in costume.

Shortly before the wedding, Erec keeps his promise to his in-laws. Precious metals and rich clothing are loaded on five beasts of burden escorted by ten knights and ten sergeants:

> Cinq somiers sejornez et gras,
> chargiez de robes et de dras,
> de boqueranz et d'excarlates
> de mars d'or et d'argent an plates,
> de veir, de gris, de sebelins,
> et de porpres et d'osterins.
> (lines 1805–1810)

[Five beasts of burden, well rested and well fed, laden with clothing and fabric, with buckram and scarlet, with gold marks and silver plate, with vair, with squirrel, with sable, and fabric of purple and *osterin*.]

Thus clothing, previously depicted in its function as dowry and gift, here serves as a sign of celebration and ceremony.

Among the resplendent guests at Erec and Enide's wedding are many kings. The first to arrive is "Gavras of Cork, a king of proud mien," with five hundred richly dressed knights in train:

> Gavraz, uns rois de Corques fiers,
> i vint a.vc. chevaliers
> vestuz de paisle et de cendax,
> mantiax et chauces et bliax.
> (lines 1913–1916)

[Gavras of Cork, a king of proud bearing, came with five hundred knights clad in paile and sendal, cloaks, breeches, and tunics.]

When Arthur dubs the hundred youths, he gives each a handsome item of clothing, chosen by the recipient. Thus the initiate is gratified with a gift of clothing: the new knight is allowed to exercise choice, like an adult warrior. The gift of clothing is here a dubbing rite.

The jongleurs who entertain the invited guests also receive handsome gifts, clothing first of all:

> Et molt bel don donné lor furent:
> robes de veir et d'erminetes,
> de conins et de violetes,
> d'escarlate grise ou de soie.
> (lines 2058–2061)

[And many beautiful gifts were offered: clothes of vair and erminette, *connins* and violet, gray scarlet or silk.]

The cortege that accompanies Erec and Enide—especially Enide—to their new home, inaugurating the final phase in the rite of passage that is marriage, is of course nobly clad:

> Erec ne volt plus sejorner:
> sa fame comande atorner
> des qu'il ot le congié del roi,
> et si reçut a son conroi
> .L.X. chevaliers de pris
> a chevax, a veir et a gris.
> (lines 2237–2242)

[Erec was willing to wait no longer. He ordered his wife to prepare herself as soon as he received the king's leave. For an escort he took sixty valiant knights with their horses and fur of vair and squirrel.]

Upon arriving in Erec's country, Enide performs several rites to complete the marriage ritual. God and religion are of little concern in this romance, being mentioned, one is tempted to say, only for the sake of decency. When the Christian setting needs to be underscored, Enide performs various religious acts. She places, for example, a magnificent chasuble on the altar of the Virgin, to whom she has prayed that she be granted an heir to perpetuate the dynasty. Originally, however, this chasuble was a sumptuous, "marvelously elegant" garment of gold and silk, made for her friend by the fairy Morgan and obtained by ruse by Queen Guinevere with the assistance of Emperor Gassa. Guinevere had it made into a chasuble, which she kept in her chapel, and gave it to Enide when the latter left King Arthur's court. Thus this magical or "marvelous" garment is here Christianized and transformed into a treasure that enhances Guinevere's magnificence in Enide's eyes and strengthens the bond between the two women.

Finally, when Erec out of love for Enide neglects the tournaments, he sends his knights in his stead and maintains his rank by dressing them lavishly:

> Mes ainz por ce moins ne donnoit
> de rien nule a ses chevaliers
> armes ne robes ne deniers:
> nul leu n'avoit tornoiemant
> nes anveast, molt richemant
> apareilliez et atornez.
> (lines 2446–2451)

[But his gifts to the knights were no less generous in arms, clothing, and coins. There was no tourney to which he did not send them magnificently attired and equipped.]

At this point the second part of the story begins: following the marriage comes the couple's ordeal. In Enide's arms Erec forgets the duties of knighthood. Upset by rumors critical of her husband's behavior, Enide contrives to warn him of the danger. Erec comes to his senses but hardens his heart against his wife. He orders her to follow him in the adventures upon which, as a good knight, he is about to embark. What is more, he imposes upon her a trial, a prohibition: she is never to speak to him without first being spoken to. Here I am omitting discussion of the folkloric background not only of this romance but of all of Chrétien's work. I see Erec's attitude as an attempt to perfect his marriage with Enide. On the one hand he wants to raise her even more toward his level, toward equality. Her inferiority stems from her not having embarked upon an adventure, not having shared the dangerous life of the knight. Erec therefore proposes that Enide join him and share the risks of knightly wandering. Since she is incapable of fighting, moreover, she must submit to another kind of trial: silence. Yet despite the fantasies of courtly love, no woman could really achieve equality with a man; this was what the Church taught and the aristocracy practiced. In some respects, therefore, Enide was destined to remain Erec's inferior, his subject.

Situations of inequality within equality were perfectly in keeping with the medieval mentality and the logic of medieval institutions such as vassalage.[1] Enide had nearly reduced Erec to a state of inferiority in two ways. First, in spite of herself, she caused him to forget his knightly duties, restraining him by her love. Second, she attempted to instruct him about his duties, albeit in covert and indirect fashion. Erec feels the need to reassert his authority over his wife, but at the same time he invites her to join him in the fulfillment of their destiny, which is knightly adventure.

In this part of the romance the vestimentary code has less of a role to play. It could hardly be otherwise, since the action is now set in the usual locale of knightly adventure, the forest, where ostentatious dress would hardly be appropriate. In any case, the costume that is most important here is that of the warrior, which I have deliberately excluded from consideration in this essay.

Nevertheless, certain manifestations of the vestimentary code are not without interest. When Erec decides to set forth again on the road of adventure, he orders a sorrowful Enide to put on her finest gown:

Levez de ci, si vos vestez
de vostre robe la plus bele
sor vostre meillor palefroi.
(lines 2576–2578)

[Get up, put on the finest of your gowns, and saddle your best palfrey.]

Enide fails to grasp the meaning of this command. Erec, having decided that his wife should accompany him, wants her to take her finest clothing with her, just as he will take his finest arms (lines 2632–2657). In these preparations for adventure there is apparent equality.

The first consequence of Erec's decision is that the sight of this sumptuously dressed lady arouses the desire of a knight-brigand (line 2805). For the remainder of the adventure Enide's beauty will be her only vestment.

The next point at which the vestimentary code makes its influence felt is after the lovers have been reconciled and survived all their trials and Erec lies recovering from his wounds at the home of Guivret, who offers splendid garments to both him and Enide:

Quant il pot aler et venir
Guivreaz ot fet deux robes feire,
l'une d'ermine et l'autre veire,
de deux dras de soie divers.
L'une fu d'un osterin pers
et l'autre d'un bofu roié
qu'au presant li ot anvoié
d'Escoce une soe cousine.
Enide ot la robe d'ermine
et l'osterin qui molt chiers fu,
Erec la veire o le bofu,
qui ne revaloit mie mains.
(lines 5184–5195)

[When he was able to come and go, Guivret ordered two robes to be made, one lined with ermine, the other of vair. Both were made of a variety of silks. One was of sea-green *osterin*, the other of striped *bofu*, which a cousin of his had sent from Scotland as a gift. Enide received the robe of precious *osterin* lined with ermine, Eric the no less valuable garment of *bofu* lined with vair.]

At Guivret's the couple find not only gifts of clothing but signs of a twofold healing: physical and social. Their return to social life will be interrupted, however, in the third part of the romance, which contains their greatest adventure and supreme trial, the Joy of the Court.

With Erec victorious, the couple proceeds toward its ultimate triumph. Three episodes mark this apotheosis, in which the vestimentary code again plays a key role. The first of these is the return to Arthur's court, the center of all values and symbol of order and civilization. Before being received by Arthur, Erec, Enide, and Guivret change into their finest attire:

> As ostex vienent, si s'aeisent,
> si ne desvestent et atornent,
> de lor beles robes s'atornent;
> et quant il furent atorné,
> a la cort s'an sont retorné.
> (lines 6402–6406)

[They went to their hôtels, made themselves comfortable, undressed, and then dressed in their finest robes. When all preparations had been completed, they left for the court.]

Note the significant coupling of return and attire.

The second episode is the death of King Lake, Erec's father. Now the couple dress in mourning garb, the sign of another passage: death for the late king, accession to the throne for the son and his wife. Here the clergy return to the scene, and with them the paupers, beneficiaries of the distribution of clothing that marks the occasion:

> Molt fist bienc ce que fere dut:
> povres mesaeisiez eslut
> plus de cent et .LX.IX.
> si les revesti tot de nuef;
> as povres clers et as provoires
> dona, que droiz fu, chapes noires
> et chaudes pelices desoz.
> (lines 6475–6481)

[He did very well what he was supposed to do. He chose more than 169 paupers in distress and clothed them in new garments. To the poor clerics and priests he gave, as was proper, black capes with warm fur linings.]

The ultimate triumph of the vestimentary code comes with the coronation of Erec and Enide by Arthur and Guinevere. For this occasion Arthur shows himself more generous even than Alexander and Caesar, and once again gifts of clothing are of central importance:

> Chevax dona a chascun trois,
> et robes a chascun trois peire,
> por ce que sa corz mialz apeire.

Molt fu li rois puissanz et larges:
ne donna pas mantiax de sarges,
ne de conins ne de brunetes,
mes de samiz et d'erminetes,
de veir antier et de diapres,
listez d'orfrois roides et aspres.
(lines 6602–6610)

[They gave each one three horses and three pairs of robes to add brilliance to the court. The king was very powerful and generous. He did not give coats of serge or rabbit fur or *brunette* but of samite and ermine, of vair in one piece and diapered, bordered with hard, rigid orphreys.]

Once again recipients are free to choose which items among the abundant gifts they wish for themselves:

Li mantel furent estandu
a bandon par totes les sales;
tuit furent gitié hors des males,
s'an prist qui vost, sanz contrediz.
(lines 6624–6627)

[The coats were laid out in all the rooms. They were taken from the chests and given to whoever wanted them, without restriction.]

In this division of roles by sex, it is once again Guinevere who dresses Enide:

Quanque pot, d'Enide attillier
se fut la reine penee.
(lines 6762–6763)

[The queen took pains to show Enide at her best.]

This time, however, in inverse symmetry with the wedding scene, it is Erec's robe that receives the lengthy description, for the young king is the principal hero of the ceremony. Extraordinary and marvelous, this robe is the work of four fairies and was described by Macrobius. It is also a program for wisdom, for the fairies represent the four sciences of the quadrivium: geometry, arithmetic, music, and astronomy. It is decorated with fur from Indian monsters called *berbiolettes:*

La pane qui i fu cosue
fu d'unes contrefetes bestes
qui ont totes blondes les testes
et les cors noirs com une more,
et les dos ont vermauz desore,

les vantres noirs et la coe inde;
itex bestes neissent en Inde,
si ont berbïoletes non,
ne manjüent se poissons non,
quenele et girofle novel.
(lines 6732–6741)

[The fur sewn into it came from monstrous beasts with fair heads and
bodies black as mulberries, with crimson backs, black stomachs, and
dark blue tails. These animals come from India and are called berbiolettes. They eat only fish, cinnamon, and new cloves.]

The robe was complemented by a cloak with clasps of precious gems
set in gold.

Erec, a king with almost supernatural powers, is crowned by another king, Arthur, whose legitimacy derives from magic transmitted
by the kiss of the white stag. Along with Enide, Erec is to become the
center of another model society, like the court of King Arthur, and
with his crown and scepter he dons a marvelous garment that completes his magical investiture before the bishop, by anointing him,
completes his Christian investiture.

The alimentary code in *Erec et Enide* is less rich than the vestimentary
code. At times the two operate in concert, at other times separately.

At the vavasor's castle the alimentary code is part of the symbolism
of rank and situation. The elderly vavasor offers Erec a meal that,
while modest because of the vavasor's poverty, is nevertheless emblematic of the minor noble's effort of generosity and worthy of his
guest's rank. The only servant in the household is an excellent cook. In
the absence of large game, he prepares the meat in the two appropriate
forms, boiled and roasted, and serves small birds:[2]

Cil atornoit an la cuisine
por le soper char et oisiax.
De l'atorner fut molt isniax,
bien sot apareillier et tost
char cuire et an eve et an rost.
(lines 488–492)

[For supper the servant prepared meat and fowl in the kitchen. He prepared the meal quickly, being well versed in the preparation and rapid
cooking of meat, whether boiled or roasted.]

The decor is that of a courtly meal, with tables, tablecloths, and
basins:

> Quant ot le mangier atorné
> tel con l'an li ot comandé,
> l'eve lor done an deus bacins;
> tables et nappes et bacins,
> fu tost apareillié et mis,
> et cil sont au mangier asis;
> trestot quanque mestiers lor fu
> ont a lor volanté eü.
> (lines 493–500)

[When the meal was prepared as ordered, he brought out water in two bowls. He quickly laid the tables with cloths and bowls. They sat down. Whatever they needed they had aplenty.]

> Li rois Artus ne fu pas chiches:
> bien comanda as penetiers
> et as queuz et aus botelliers
> qu'il livrassent a grant planté,
> chascun selonc sa volanté,
> et pain et vin et veneison;
> nus ne demanda livreison
> de rien nule que que ce fust
> qu'a sa volanté ne l'eüst.
> (lines 2006–2014)

[King Arthur was not stingy. He ordered his pantlers, cooks, and butlers to serve in abundance, to each man as much as he pleased of bread, wine, and venison. No one asked for anything without his wish being granted.]

Indispensable accoutrements of the noble banquet, venison and wine were of course available in abundance.

In the middle part of the romance, which is taken up with the adventures of Erec and Enide, there are four instances in which an alimentary code is evident. The first occurs in the forest. After the battle with the five knights, Erec and Enide, having gone without food or drink since the previous evening, at noon encounter a squire accompanied by two valets carrying bread, wine, and five rich cheeses. The squire, realizing that he has run into a knight and a lady, offers this food to the hungry couple.

> De cest blanc gastel vos revest,
> s'il vost plest un po a mangier.
> Nel di pas por vos losangier:
> li gastiax est de boen fromant
> ne rien nule ne vos demant;

>  boen vin ai et fromage gras,
>  blanche toaille et biax henas.
>  (lines 3140–3146)

[I make you a gift of this white cake, if you care to eat a little. I do not do so to win your good graces. The cake is of good wheat, but I ask nothing of you. I have good wine and rich cheeses, white napkins and beautiful goblets.]

A picnic is prepared, and in keeping with the aristocratic code of table manners, the squire serves Erec and Enide:

>  Puis a devant ax estandue
>  la toaille sor l'erbe drue;
>  le gastel et le vin lor baille
>  un fromage lor pere et taille;
>  cil mangièrent qui fain avoient,
>  et del vin volantiers bevoient;
>  li escuiers devant ax sert,
>  qui son servise pas ne pert.
>  (lines 3165–3172)

[On the thick grass in front of them he laid a white cloth. He gave them the cake and the wine, prepared and cut them cheese. They ate with a healthy appetite and eagerly drank wine. The squire serving them did not waste his efforts.]

This is a quality meal, with wheat bread, wine, cheese, a white table-cloth, beautiful goblets, and service by the squire, but since it takes place in a forest in which Erec and Enide have returned to nature, the meal is itself natural yet not "savage."

The wanderings of Erec and Enide are interrupted by a brief so-journ at the court of King Arthur, but their adventures are not over. There can be no feast, only a Saturday supper, a meatless vigil. Arthur and his guests eat fish and fruits, but this being a civilized place Chrétien makes clear that the food is both raw and cooked:

>  Ce fu un samedi a nuit
>  qu'il mangièrent poissons et fruit,
>  luz et perches, saumons et truites,
>  et puis poires crües et cuites.
>  Après souper ne tardent gaire;
>  comandent les napes a traire.
>  (lines 4237–4242)

[It was a Saturday night. They ate fish and fruit, pike and perch, salmon and trout, followed by pears raw and cooked. After supper they did not tarry; the tablecloths were ordered removed.]

The third occasion on which food is mentioned is quite special. Enide, who believes that Erec is dead, has been forced to marry a count, and an attempt is made to force her to eat as well. The count's men "have placed the table before her" (line 4750). But she refuses to eat and drink if Erec, who she thinks is lying dead but who in reality is in a prolonged state of unconsciousness, cannot eat with her:

> Sire, ja tant con je vivrai,
> ne mangerai ne ne bevrai,
> si je voi mangier einçois
> mon seignor, qui gist sor ce dois.
> (lines 4777–4780)

[Sire, as long as I live I will neither eat nor drink until I see my lord eating, he who is stretched out on that round table.]

In other words, with the couple apparently dissolved, the alimentary code ceases to function for the surviving member.

But Erec regains consciousness, kills the count, and goes to his friend Guivret's to convalesce. The restored couple resumes eating, but only to a limited extent, following a convalescent's diet. Guivret invites Erec and Enide to eat a cold pâté and drink wine mixed with water:

> Et puis li ont un cofre overt,
> s'an fist hors traire trois pastez;
> "Amis, fet il, or an tastez
> un petit de ces pastez froiz
> vin a eve meslé avroiz;
> j'en ai de boen set barriez pleins
> mes li purs ne vos est pas sains."
> (lines 5104–5110)

[Then a coffer was opened, and Guivret ordered that three pâtés be taken from it: "Friends," he said, "taste a little of these cold pâtés for me now. You shall drink wine mixed with water. I have a good vintage, seven barrels' worth, but unwatered wine would not be good for you."]

Guivret presses them:

> Biax dolz amis, or essaiez
> a mangier, que bien vos fera;
> et ma dame aussi mangera . . . .
> Eschappez estes, or mangiez,
> et je mangerai, biax amis.
> (lines 5112–5119)

[Handsome, gentle friend, try to eat, it will do you good; and my lady, your wife, will eat too. . . . You have made a handsome escape. Now you are out of danger. Eat, then, fine friends, and I shall eat with you.]

Enide allows herself to be persuaded, but Erec eats only half his portion, as though he were ill, and cuts his wine with water:

> Andui de mangier le sermonent;
> vin et eve boivre li donent,
> car li purs li estoit trop rudes.
> (lines 5123–5125)

[Both pleaded with Erec to eat. They gave him wine and water, because uncut wine was too strong for him.]

Guivret's sisters care for the injured knight, washing and dressing his wounds. They give him food and drink, but it is a convalescent's diet, without spices:

> Chascun jor catre foiz ou plus
> le feisoient mangier et boivre,
> sel gardoient d'ail et de poivre.
> (lines 5164–5166)

[Four times a day or more, they made him eat and drink, but they did not allow him to eat either garlic or pepper.]

In the third and final phase of the romance, before and after the great adventure of the Joy of the Court, alimentary rules are again in evidence. King Evrain, in whose territory the adventure takes place, first stages a banquet in honor of Erec and Enide that is a *summum* of aristocratic dining, with birds, venison, fruits, and wine:

> Li rois comanda aprester
> le souper, quant tans fu et ore. . . .
> Quanque cuers et boche covoite
> orent plenieremant la nuit,
> oisiax et venison et fruit
> et vin de diverse menière.
> (lines 5532–5539)

[The king ordered that supper be prepared at the proper time. . . . Whatever the heart and palate might desire, they had in abundance that night: venison, fruit, and wine of various vintages.]

But Erec cuts short the meal because he is thinking of the Joy of the Court:

> Molt furent servi lieemant,
> tant qu'Erec estrosseemant
> leissa le mangier et le boivre,
> et comança a ramantoivre
> ce que au cuer plus li tenoit.
> (lines 5543–5547)

[But above all a fine welcome, for of all dishes the finest is a warm welcome and a handsome face. They were served happily until suddenly Erec stopped eating and drinking and began talking of what weighed most heavily on his mind.]

The Joy of the Court is framed by two brief allusions to food, in both cases of a "marvelous" variety. Like the vestimentary code, the alimentary code is here touched by magic.

When Erec enters the magic orchard in which he is to face his supreme trial, he discovers that there are magical fruits growing there that remain ripe all year long but cannot be eaten inside the garden:

> Et tot esté et tot yver
> y avoit flors et fruit maür;
> et li fruiz avoit sel eür
> que leanz se lessoit mangier
> mes au porter hors fet dongier;
> car qui point an volsist porter
> ne s'an seüst ja mes raler
> car a l'issue ne venist
> tant qu'an son leu le remïst.
> (lines 5696–5704)

[All summer and all winter there were flowers and ripe fruits. The fruits were under a spell, so that they could be eaten in the garden but not taken outside. Anyone who tried to take fruit out would never have found the way out until the fruit had been put back in its place.]

When, at the end of the romance, Erec for his coronation dons the extraordinary robe I described earlier, Chrétien points out that the monstrous berbiolettes of India whose fur embellishes the garment "eat only fish, cinnamon, and new clove" (lines 6740–6741).

In the finale of the coronation, both the alimentary and the vestimentary code achieve their highest degree of perfection. After the coronation mass preparations are made for a banquet with five hundred guests, filling five dining rooms. A king, a duke, or a count presides over each table, at which a hundred knights are seated. "A thousand knights serve the bread, a thousand others the wine, and a thousand others the dishes, all clad in fresh ermine" (lines 6872–6874). But just as the dishes are about to be described, Chrétien stops short and ends with a pirouette, leaving the listener (or reader) with mouth watering but still hungry.

> De mes divers don sont servi,
> ne por quant se ge nel vos di,
> vos savroie bien reison randre;
> mes il m'estuet a el antendre.
> (lines 6875–6878)

[As for the various dishes that were served, if I do not list them all, I owe you a description, but I must apply myself to another task.]

To sum up, we have been able, with the help of the vestimentary code, to shed light on certain key structures and moments in the story of Erec and Enide: relations between spouses, rites of marriage and death, royal function, departure for adventure, return to social life. The vestimentary code is a fundamental symbolic reference.

The role of the alimentary code is more discreet. Elsewhere, however, Chrétien de Troyes makes full use of it, as in *Yvain* in the episode of Yvain's madness. The contrast between the raw and the cooked is significant in Yvain's regression to the savage state and in his relations with the hermit.[3] To determine which is the rule and which the exception, an analysis of the kind outlined here would have to be extended to the whole of Chrétien's work. It would then be possible to say whether the use of vestimentary and alimentary codes is determined primarily by the work and the situation or by the obsessions of the poet.[4]

# WARRIORS AND CONQUERING
# BOURGEOIS: THE IMAGE OF
# THE CITY IN TWELFTH-CENTURY
# FRENCH LITERATURE

The twelfth century was the great period of urban development in the Christian West. In literary works written in the still young literatures of the vulgar tongue, the city was portrayed in a variety of guises, with varying significations and degrees of importance. In the *langue d'oïl* (spoken in northern France) we find representations of the city in the chansons de geste of the William of Orange cycle, *Le Charroi de Nîmes* and *La Prise d'Orange;* in four of the twelve *Lays* of Marie de France (*Lanval, Yonec, Laüstic,* and *Eliduc*); and in a romance by Chrétien de Troyes, *Perceval ou le Conte du Graal.*[1]

In *Le Charroi de Nîmes,* William, having helped Charlemagne's son Louis gain the crown and obtain coronation in Rome after killing the giant Corsolt "below the walls of Rome, in the meadow"[2] (as described in the *Couronnement de Louis*), returns to France to go hunting in a forest and later enters Paris by way of the Petit Pont.[3] His nephew Bertrand informs him that in his absence Louis has distributed fiefs to his barons and that in this distribution he has forgotten William and Bertrand. To the others he has given land or a castle or a city or town.

Furious, William goes looking for Louis in his palace and bitterly reminds the emperor of all that he owes him. He had defeated Louis's three greatest enemies: Richard the Norman, who had been delivered to the emperor at his court in Paris; Guy the German, who had demanded that Louis surrender his crown and the city of Laon and whom William had killed; and Otto, whom he had captured below the walls of Rome where Louis had made camp at the place called Nero's Park and where William himself had pitched the king's tent and served him excellent venison.

Disconcerted, Louis offers William a quarter of his kingdom: one fourth of France, one abbey in four, one market in four, one city in four, and one archbishopric in four. William proudly refuses this offer

First published in *Mélanges en l'honneur de Charles Morazé* (Toulouse: Privat, 1979), pp. 113–36.

on the grounds that the king must not diminish his power. In a violent rage William leaves Louis and encounters his nephew Bertrand, who calms him down and suggests that he ask Louis for something to conquer: "Ask him for the kingdom of Spain, Tortolouse and Portpaillart-by-the-sea, and then for Nîmes, the powerful city, and also for Orange, which is so deserving of praise."[4]

Delighted with this idea, William returns to Louis who, doubling his offer, proposes to give him half his kingdom, including whatever he might wish in the way of "castle, city, burg, or town, donjon or fortress." William dismisses this offer with laughter and insists that he be given Spain and the cities that are its jewels: "Valsore the great," "Nîmes and its solid fortification," "Nîmes with its high pointed towers," and "Orange the redoutable city." Louis hesitates to make a gift of land that is not his. He reiterates his offer of half his kingdom: "Let us divide our cities into two equal parts. You shall have Chartres and leave me Orléans."[5]

Finally Louis agrees and with his glove invests William as lord of Spain, which he is given as a fief of the king. William then climbs onto a table and recruits "poor bachelors" by promising them "money, estates, castles, lands, donjons, fortresses."

Before setting out on his expedition William commends to God "France and Aix-la-Chapelle, Paris, Chartres, and all the rest of the country." Crossing Auvergne, William and his companions skirt Clermont and Montferrand (the city known today as Clermont-Ferrand) "on the right hand": "They avoid the city and its opulent residences, for they wish to do no harm to the townspeople."

Following the Regordane road, used by both pilgrims and merchants, William and his companions pass Le Puy and some time later encounter a Muslim peasant hauling a barrel of salt from Saint-Gilles in the hope of earning a good profit. William questions this peasant about the city that is his obsession: "Have you been to Nîmes, the powerful and well-stocked city?" A significant misunderstanding arises (line 904) over the word *garnie*. The peasant, taking the word to mean well-stocked, replies that prices are low there, much to William's annoyance: "Idiot, that is not what I am asking." He wants information about the garrison of pagan troops. One man speaks the language of economics, the other of war. About military matters the peasant knows nothing. But one of William's knights has an idea. The peasant's cargo suggests a ruse, an updated version of the Trojan horse. Why not hide a thousand armed knights in barrels pierced with holes and introduce them into Nîmes as merchandise? William agrees, and wagons and oxen are requisitioned along with peasants, who are set to work making barrels with hatchets and broadaxes. Woe unto anyone who dares protest: "Whoever cursed soon repented, for he lost his sight and was hanged by the neck" (lines 962–963).

William and his knights disguise themselves as wagon drivers. Pretending to be merchants, they carry large purses for making change. The count wears a sackcloth tunic and large breeches tucked into cowhide boots, with a belt like that worn by the bourgeois of the region, from which hangs a knife in a handsome sheath. He rides a worn-out mare; his stirrups and spurs are old, and he wears a felt hat. After passing "Lavardi," the quarry from which the stones used to build the towers of Nîmes had been taken, the French convoy arrives at Nîmes and enters the city gates. News of the arrival of rich merchants reaches even the palace, and the Saracen king Otranto and his brother Harpin, governors of "the good city," hasten to the market with an escort of two hundred pagan soldiers.

Here the author of the chanson addresses his readers, asserting the truth of the tale and the reality of the city of Nîmes where, he says, there now stands a church dedicated to the Virgin where people once had worshipped Mohammed and his idols.

William tells Otranto and Harpin that he is a merchant "from Canterbury, a rich city" in powerful England, and he lists the items that his barrels are supposed to contain: fabrics, weapons, spices, skins, and furs. He also describes his itinerary from Scotland to France, Germany, Hungary, Italy, Spain, and Palestine, with a stop in Venice to exchange currency. He orders that the wagons proceed to "broad squares" to be unloaded.

Otranto is dazzled and benevolent, but Harpin is insulting and provocative, whereupon William reveals himself, renounces his merchant's guise, and in a show of physical strength kills King Harpin. He then sounds the trumpet, and knights leap from the barrels shouting "Monjoie." A great battle ensues, terrifying in its intensity. Fierce and bold in combat, the French, protected by strong, stout shields, strike their enemies with swords and pikes. Defeated, Otranto and his companions refuse to convert to Christianity and are pitched from windows: "Now that the French have liberated the city with its high towers and tiled rooms, they have found wine and wheat in abundance. There should be no famine for seven years, and no one should be able to take the city or weaken its defenses" (lines 1463–1467).

The warriors who had previously been left in camp now go to Nîmes. Meanwhile, the peasants reclaim their wagons and oxen, and the knights, exuberant in victory, not only allow the peasants to leave but offer them extra payment. Word of the exploit even reaches France: "Count William has liberated Nîmes. The story was told to Louis."

What does the chanson tell us about the warriors' attitudes toward the city? In the first place we are reminded that a warrior's way of life was different from a citydweller's. The warrior's natural haunt was the forest, where he lived in a tent and hunted game. Physical strength and ardor in combat were highly valued. Citydwellers, on the other hand, ate not game but bread: "We saw two large breads sold there for a denarius," reports the peasant with the barrel of salt, speaking of Nîmes. They traveled not for war but for business, in search of profit, and were contemptuous of ostentation. When the barons and knights disguise themselves as merchants, we are treated to an account of the contrast in appearance, costume, mounts, and armament between the warrior and the bourgeois. The contrast applies particularly to barons and knights; kings, whether Christian or Muslim, are already rather urbanized, for they live in palaces located in cities.

The strongest social contrast, however, is not that between warrior and bourgeois. The bourgeois of Clermont-Ferrand are not disturbed in their urbanity, which is praised. The real contrast is between warrior and peasant. Although the warriors, euphoric over their victory, are relatively indulgent toward the peasants whose services they have used, they are contemptuous of peasant labor and indeed of the peasant way of life. Much is made of the contrast between weapon and tool, between prowess and labor.

It is important to note that positive images of the city predominate in the chanson. The first remarkable thing is the quality of information concerning urban life and economic realities. The central mechanisms of markets and commerce are accurately described: merchandise, roads, tariffs and tolls, profits, currency, and exchange. William, referring to the Crac des Chevaliers (lines 1200–1201), describes it as the site of a very old market.

It is clear, moreover, that these warriors are truly fascinated by the city. In the descriptions of itineraries and countries cities play a major role. And when Louis evokes the kingdom of France, he virtually equates his kingdom with its cities.

In speaking of cities the epithets that come naturally to the lips of William and his companions are *bonne, belle,* and *forte,* good, beautiful, and strong. A city is pleasant to look at and better still to capture. It is a handsome prey, a desirable prize. When William attempts to entice other warriors to follow him to Spain, he promises them money,

estates, castles, lands, donjons, and fortresses, but for himself he re-
serves Nîmes, the city.

In describing Nîmes, the author of the chanson constructs a medieval urban stereotype by combining some real details with imaginary
elements, thus giving the fictional city another level of reality. Among
these elements are walls and gates and especially towers—high, pointed
towers—building materials such as stone, and the grid of streets and
squares. Palaces and churches are also mentioned. But the central element of the city, the real and symbolic site of its principal and essential
activity, is the marketplace, where the Muslim kings and their escort—the power that is about to die—confront William and his companions—the power that is about to be born.

I shall have more to say about the significance, from my point of
view, of the warriors' recourse to ruse and disguise. This rapid review
of the *Charroi de Nîmes* can perhaps best be summarized by saying that
the heroine of the chanson is the city of Nîmes.

*La Prise d'Orange* is the sequel to the *Charroi de Nîmes,* although the
version that has survived is that of a "modernizer" who worked from
a version that no doubt predates both the *Charroi* and the *Couronnement de Louis.* The chanson begins with a recap of the conquest of
Nîmes and a description of the city: "All have sung the city of Nîmes,
which William holds in his possession, with its high walls and halls of
stone and its palace and castellanies" (lines 13–16). Immediately, however, William is seized with a violent desire to take yet another city,
Orange: "But God! he did not yet possess Orange."

Orange, as it happens, belongs to King Tibaut of Africa (line 27) or
Persia (line 35), who is married to "the noble and sage Orable" (line
34). The action begins in the month of May in a setting that is half-
urban, half-sylvan, that is, part bourgeois, part knightly. William,
standing at the great window of the palace of Nîmes, is looking at the
newly planted grass and roses (a mixture of nature and culture). He is
melancholy. In Nîmes he has what he needs for conquest—war-horses
and weapons (hauberks, helmets, swords, shields, lances)—as well as
abundant supplies of the kinds of foods that are eaten in cities and that
William has begun to eat himself: bread, wine, salted meat, cereals.
Yet three essential ingredients of the martial (or noble) life are lacking: artistic distractions (harpists and jongleurs), amorous distractions
(damsels to divert "our persons"),[6] and above all war. The Saracens
are unfortunately passive.

Still standing at the palace window, which also penetrates the wall
of the city (line 105), William sees emerge from the Rhône a Christian

who has escaped from the Saracens. This person enters the good city of Nîmes through the gate. He finds William in the feudal (and courtly) surroundings that he has managed with some difficulty to recreate in at least part of the city: the count is standing beneath a spreading pine with a number of renowned knights listening to a jongleur sing a very ancient chanson. William apparently recognizes the man as one of his own class, for he orders that he be served not only bread and wine but food and drink appropriate to a warrior: "spicy drinks, light wine, cranes, wild geese, peacocks with pepper sauce" (lines 172–173).

When questioned, Guillebert reveals that he is in fact the son of Guy, duke of Ardenne, Artois, and Vermandois. The Saracens had taken him prisoner at Lyons and brought him to Orange. He then adds to William's temptation by describing Orange and the Saracens' fear:

> There is no fortress like it between here and the Jordan River. The walls are high, the tower tall and wide, as are the palace and its dependencies. Inside are twenty thousand pagans armed with lances, and one hundred and forty Turks with prize banners, who stand watchful guard over this [famous] city of Orange, for they are much afraid that Louis and you, handsome sire, and the barons of France may take it.

He adds yet another enticement:

> With the king Aragon, son of Tibaut of Spain, there is Lady Orable, a gracious queen. There is none so beautiful short of the Orient. Her body is well proportioned, slender, and pretty. Her skin is as white as the flower on a tree.

Finally, combining the salvation of the soul with the blandishments of the flesh, he says: "God! What good are her beauty[7] and youth, since she does not believe in God, the omnipotent Father!" Once more we encounter repetition of the sort already discussed in connection with the *Charroi,* but more skillfully integrated into the logic of the narrative and the psychology of the characters. William is insistent: "Is Orange as you have described it?" Guillebert replies: "Why, it is even better still! If you could only see how high the princely palace is, and fortified all around!" He also emphasizes the city's other attraction:

> There you could contemplate the noble Orable, the wife of Sir Tibaut l'Escler; no other such beauty can be found in all Christendom or in pagan lands. Her body is graceful, slender, and shapely, her eyes as brilliant as those of a molted falcon. What good is her great beauty,[8] since she does not believe in God or his goodness?

And William, succumbing to temptation, utters the key words of the chanson: "I shall set down my lance and shield if I cannot make the lady and the city mine."[9]

*La Prise d'Orange* is the story of the gratification of a double desire: to seize both a woman and a city. The one is as desirable as the other; indeed, the two desires coincide. The "modernizer" of the chanson is hardly the clumsy workman he has been accused of being. On the contrary, he was clever enough to link the conquest of Orable to that of Orange and, coupling psychological with historical verisimilitude, to combine a courtly romance with an epic poem.

For form's sake and for the benefit of the chanson's listeners, William repeats his question: "Is Orange so rich?"[10] Guillebert embroiders on what he said before:

> If only you could see the palace of the city, entirely made of vaults and decorated with mosaics! . . . Not a flower grows between here and Pavia that is not artfully represented in gold. Inside is Queen Orable, wife of King Tibaut of Africa. No equal beauty exists in any pagan land. Her neck is elegant. She is thin and slender. Her skin is as white as the hawthorn blossom. Her eyes are brilliant and clear and always laughing.

"No count or king owns such a city," William concludes from this description. He decides to renounce food until he "has seen Orange and Gloriette, the famous marble tower, and Lady Orable, the noble queen."

To carry out his designs William again resorts to ruse and disguise. This time, however, he goes only with his nephew Guïelin and with Guillebert. In order to make themselves look like Saracens, the three men blacken their faces, chests, and feet. Orange, like Nîmes, is well worth a masquerade.

> They left Nîmes, crossed the Rhône at Beaucaire, passed Avignon,
> heading straight for Orange, with its walls and moats,
> its high halls and its palace trimmed with mosaics,
> its gilt orbs and eagles.
> . . . . . . . . . . . . . . . . . . . . . . . . . . . . . . . . . . . . . . . . . . . . . . . . . . . . . . .
> "God," said William, "you who caused me to be born,
> what an admirable city this is!
> How powerful is he who is charged with governing it!"
> And they went up to the city gates.
> Pretending to be Turks, they went to the palace,
> its pillars and walls made of marble

and its windows decorated with silver,
and the golden eagle gleamed and sparkled;
not a ray of sunshine, not a breath of wind.

The three warriors are far from familiar nature, in the thick of a world of artifice: "Everything here dazzled them and seemed more beautiful than in Nîmes, the strong and powerful city."[11] The Saracen king Aragon receives them courteously and orders that they be served, in addition to bread and wine, dishes worthy of noble warriors: "cranes, wild geese, and tender roast peacock." The three men are then granted the privilege of being taken to see Queen Orable in Gloriette Palace, in the shadow of a magical pine tree (this being a traditional feature of the marvelous tale, here urbanized in a manner much in vogue in the twelfth century).[12]

There follows a series of digressions, courtly episodes interspersed with battles. Orable falls in love with William and vows to aid the three Christians, who have revealed their identity. The three barons seize Gloriette and barricade themselves inside, but the Saracens enter by way of an underground passage and take them prisoner. Orable delivers them from prison, however, and all four again barricade themselves inside Gloriette, where they are immediately surprised by the Saracens. William, Guïelin, and Orable are thrown into prison, while Guillebert, the eternal escapee, somehow manages to get away. Taken from prison and led before Aragon, William and his nephew engage in desperate battle against the pagans and perform a thousand exploits but apparently only to stave off the inevitable, even though they manage once again to barricade themselves inside Gloriette.

In these thousand lines of the poem (lines 738–1654) the urban theme is a leitmotif. Orange and Gloriette are repeatedly praised:

Here is the palace and the tower of Gloriette,
made of stone to the very top.
(lines 1121–1122)

Here is Gloriette, the principal palace,
constructed of stones as hard as rock.
(1132–1133)

Here is Gloriette, the famous marble tower,
a stone edifice in the midst of a meadow.
(1160–1161)

In Orange, this famous and rich city.
(line 1282)

In the powerful city of Orange.
(line 1319)

For he [Tibaut] will lose his strong and opulent city
and his wife Orable of the slender body.
(lines 1322–1323)

Also mentioned repeatedly are Nîmes and Narbonne, the two cities taken from the Saracens by William and his nephews:

William Fierebrace
who took Nîmes, its palace and its halls.
(lines 722–723)

The count had made him prisoner in the city of Nîmes
(line 748)

. . . in the city of Nîmes
(758)

. . . whom we left previously in Nîmes
(1097)

As he had taken Nîmes
(1284)

. . . Narbonne, the great
(1074)

. . . Narbonne, the powerful
(1281)

The names of other cities, both Christian and Saracen, are also mentioned: Reims and Laon (line 801), Rome (lines 962 and 1628), Aix-la-Chapelle (line 1420), Barcelona (line 969), and Babylon (line 972), as well as various unidentified cities such as Valsonne (line 976), Valdonne (line 977), Voirecombe (line 978), Valsone (line 983), and Vaudon (line 1247).[13]

Meanwhile, Guillebert succeeds in returning to Nîmes, where he alerts William's nephew Bertrand, who had been unwilling to follow William to Orange. Tortured by remorse and then galvanized by Guillebert's report, Bertrand, too, succumbs to the fascination of Orange. After alluding to the "gold of ten cities" (line 1692) he declares: "I shall not fail to go to Orange, even if I lose my limbs." When Guillebert tells him that the prisoners are held "inside Orange, the opulent city, in Gloriette, the famous marble tower," Bertrand asks: "Shall we attack the city of Orange? Shall we break those ramparts and halls of stone? . . . Shall we attack the powerful city of Orange?

Shall we break those walls and high fortifications?" (lines 1761–1762, 1768–1769). To spur him on Guillebert says: "Never in your life will you take that city."

Furious, Bertrand rallies 13,000 Frenchmen, enters Gloriette, and delivers William and Guïelin. Together they then march on Orange proper:

> They went to the gates of the powerful city and opened them at once. Those who were outside entered the city. They shouted Montjoie fore and rear.

The chanson ends with the baptism of Orable, who becomes the Christian woman Guibourc and marries William, a logical consequence of the capture of a city which is also the capture of a woman: "Once the city was captured by force, he ordered that a great tub be prepared and filled with clear water" (lines 1863–1865). In the end William reconciles love, possession, and war. He fights on for thirty more years, an eternity for a man of the twelfth century. The final three lines (1886–1888) read:

> Count William married the lady;
> thereafter he remained in Orange for thirty years,
> and never stopped fighting for one day.

*La Prise d'Orange* confirms some of what we have learned from the *Charroi de Nîmes* and adds a good deal more. Positive images of the city are here even more numerous than in the latter chanson, and they are given greater prominence. The fascination of warriors with the city becomes a veritable obsession.[14]

The emphasis on the city is particularly apparent in the epithets that accompany city names, particularly that of Orange and to a lesser degree Nîmes and Narbonne—urban prey. Among these are *bonne* (good, line 135), *riche* (or magnificent, line 267), *mirable* (admirable, line 417), *fort* (strong, line 482), *vaillant* (powerful, line 482), *grant* (great, line 641), *garnie* (opulent, line 1282), and *bele* (beautiful, applied to Gloriette in line of 1419). It is also evident in the descriptions of the components of cities—walls, gates, palaces, towers, halls, monuments, and ornaments—as well as in such "marvels" as mosaics, gilt orbs and eagles, and magic pines (*esperiment,* line 652), and in such materials as stone, marble, silver, and gold.

But the clearest indication that the attraction of the city intensified between the time of *Charroi* and that of *La Prise* lies in two innovations: In the latter work we do not, to be sure, find a bourgeoisie that is at once respected and despised, a world of markets, merchants, and merchandise. All the characters are kings, barons, and knights, whether Saracen or Christian, vaguely surrounded by lower-ranking soldiers, valets, and porters. Yet a compromise, indeed a marriage, is effected between the warrior life and city life, symbolized by the wedding of William and Orable. Nature and culture, chivalry and courtesy are reconciled. One can live as a warrior in the city, which no longer symbolizes a renunciation of the life of the military noble.

Of particular importance is the fact that the capture of Orange is inextricably associated with the capture of Orable, whose beautiful, slender body is not just comparable to the tall towers of the city but is the very incarnation of the city's desirability. For these warriors the city is a woman, and in this world of rapine, where cities and women are taken by force, the conquest of a city is also a conquest in love. At this point the reader may object that this view is exaggerated, that I have been misled by the courtly aspects of a work that has been described as a "masterpiece of humor," an almost "heroicomic" work.[15] In my view, however, the modernizer of *La Prise d'Orange* has masterfully achieved the aims implicit in the prototypical chanson de geste, *La chanson de Roland*. Lines 703–704 of that work tell how Charlemagne ravaged Spain: "The castles taken, *the cities violated*." The theme of the city as woman, to be looked at, admired, feared (for woman is also Eve, a creature of the devil), and ultimately taken, is at the heart of warrior ideology as expressed from the very beginning in the chansons de geste.

The atmosphere in the *Lays* of Marie de France appears quite different. Among the causes of that difference is the fact that the lay imposes a form, a style, and to some extent an ideology quite alien to those of the chanson de geste. How is the city treated?

Let me lose no time in saying that the city plays a far more modest role in the *Lays* than in the two chansons just analyzed. Cities are mentioned in only four of the twelve surviving lays, and they appear as backdrops rather than as heroines.

Lanval is a young knight who has served King Arthur well yet received nothing but ingratitude in return. During a walk near a river he comes to a castle in which there lives a very beautiful and mysterious young lady. He becomes her lover and she gives him the power to satisfy all his needs of generosity provided he keep their love secret. But Lanval subsequently rejects the queen's advances and, accused by her, is ordered put on trial by the king. Just as the verdict is about to be handed down, the damsel arrives on a white horse and takes Lanval to Avalon. He is never heard of again.

In this story, which describes a Melusina-like figure, the only detail of interest for present purposes is the dialectic between city and nature (or city and forest). Arthur shuttles between the city in which he lives (Kardoel, or Carlisle, line 5) and the forest, and Lanval alternates between his residence in town and the meadows outside. By contrast, the marvelous damsel never leaves the solitude of her tent (*tref,* line 80) except to rescue her lover from the men of the city, while the wicked queen never leaves her urban palace, perhaps not even her chamber, except to witness the judgment of Lanval.

At the beginning of the lay, Lanval leaves the city: "Fors de la vilë est eissuz" (line 43). After his adventure he returns to his urban residence: "Il est a sun ostel venuz" (line 201): "Alez s'en est a sun ostel" (line 406).

At the end he flees with his mysterious lover to a very beautiful island: "En un isle ki mut est beaus" (line 643).[16]

Within this system of spatial ideology, Marie de France seems to insist on one fact: that knights live in cities. In line 205 she says: "N'ot en ville chevalier (ki de surjur ait grand mestier)."

In *Yonec,* the lay that devotes more space than any other to the marvelous, two countries are contrasted, one real, the other magical. In the first lives the wicked hero. The second is the birthplace of a marvelous prince, who returns there to die. That prince is the father of Yonec, a handsome knight who changes into a bird in order to find his beloved. (*Yonec* is the oldest known version of *The Blue Bird.*)

In each of these countries there is a city. In Brittany is the city where the jealous old lord of Caerwent resides between hunts: "La citez siet dur Duëlas / Jadis i ot de nes trespas" (lines 15–16). Situated on the Duëlas River and once a haven for passing ships, this city is the northern version of such fictional southern ports as Porpaillart-sur-Mer, Royaumont-sur-Mer, and Sorgremont-sur-Mer, which are mentioned in *Le Charroi de Nîmes* and *La Prise d'Orange.*

The bird-prince's lover follows his trail of blood through a tunnel in a hillside that opens onto a beautiful meadow, whereupon she catches sight of a city. "Quite nearby there stood a city, with walls all around. There was not a house or hall or tower that did not appear to be made entirely of silver. The buildings were quite splendid. On the town side were swamps and forests and enclosed fields. On the other side, toward the donjon, a river skirted the city. Ships landed here, and there were more than three hundred masts. The downstream gate was open, and the lady entered, still following the trail of fresh blood. She crossed the town and headed toward the castle. There was not a soul to talk to, man or woman. She entered the tiled hall of the palace, which she found filled with blood."

This is a realistic description of a medieval city, hedged about by protective nature, divided between *cité* (castle or cathedral) and *bourg* (the town proper), and dominated by the castle. Such a city was an economic center but also a city of the dead, a folkloric version of the afterlife.

The woman returns to the other side of the hill, where she lives for a long time with her husband, the murderer of her lover, and their son Yonec, who is actually the bird-prince's child. In the year that Yonec receives his knightly arms, the story comes to a climax, and blood again flows in an urban setting: "The feast of Saint Aaron was celebrated at Caerleon and in several other cities, and the lord had been invited to attend with his friends, according to the custom of the country, and to bring with him his wife and son, a splendid entourage. And so it came to pass, and they went, but whither they did not know. With them was a young man who led them to a fortified city,[17] the most beautiful in the world."

They find the bird-prince's tomb in an abbey in this city. The lady reveals to Yonec the secret of his birth and then drops dead. Yonec decapitates his stepfather. The people of the city bury the lady in great pomp in the same coffin as her beloved, and they make Yonec their lord.

*Laüstic* is a charming story about a nightingale that falls victim to a love affair and whose body is carried about in a coffer by the unhappy but faithful lover for the rest of his life. We learn a great deal about the conditions in which knights lived in the city: "In the region of Saint-Malo there was a renowned city. Two knights lived there in two fortified houses. The qualities of the two barons had made the city famous. One of them had married a wise woman, most courtly and comely. She was widely admired for her observance of customs and good manners. The other was a bachelor well known among his peers for his prowess and great valor. He was fond of the lavishness that brings honor, and he fought in many tourneys and spent a great deal and willingly gave away what he had."

Here the knights have truly laid siege to the city, culturally speaking. A woman is responsible for introducing courtliness, the new code of good manners. A man exhibits the largesse typical of the warrior nobility and takes part in that essential activity of knighthood, the tourney.

*Eliduc* is the strange story of a ménage à trois in which a man, a woman, and the man's lover vie with one another in courtliness and generosity. In the relevant episode, Eliduc, in disgrace with the king of Little Brittany, travels by sea to England. There he takes service with a king who has fallen on evil days. The king, to honor this knight who has come to help him, finds him lodging in a city: "He took lodging (*ostels*) with a very wise and courtly bourgeois. The host gave him a fine room hung with tapestries. To dine with him Eliduc invited poor knights who lived in the town. He forbade all his men to accept remuneration in money or kind for forty days. But on the third day of his stay it was proclaimed in the city that the enemy had come and overrun the country. Soon they would come to the city and assault its very gates. Eliduc heard the uproar of the frenzied crowd. Without further ado he armed himself, and his companions did the same. Fourteen knights with horses were staying in the city." (lines 133–156)

This passage fleshes out our picture of the urban knight. Those knights who are nearly penniless, the poor, live in the bourgeois part of the city, the *bourg,* and engage in economic activity. Eliduc, inviting them to dine with him, makes them promise to refuse all wages, for it was not noble to accept pay for one's work. On the other hand, the bourgeois who receives Eliduc in his home is a courtly man who lives nobly in a house decorated like the residences of the upper class. When enemies threaten the city and the urban populace, deficient in warrior virtues, is gripped with panic ("La gent ki est esturdie," line 152), the knights must come to the defense of the city in which they reside.

*Perceval ou le Conte du Graal,* Chrétien de Troyes's last romance, probably left unfinished because of the poet's death, consists in its surviving versions of two parts. The first recounts Perceval's adventures in the course of an initiation that is also an education. The second tells of the adventures of Gawain, who, when Perceval leaves the court of King Arthur to unravel the mystery of the Grail and the bleeding lance, sets out on his own to deliver a damsel besieged at Montesclaire. According to the homely woman who reproaches Perceval for his silence at the castle of the Grail, this is the highest act of prowess that a knight can perform. The second story is interrupted only by the penitence of Perceval, about which nothing else is said in the tale.

The theme of the city figures only in a general and secondary way in part one, devoted to Perceval's adventures. To be sure, there is a fundamental opposition between the world that Perceval has so much difficulty extracting himself from, the vast forest in which he lives with his mother and where he spent his childhood—a forest to which the "young savage" returns regularly (in line 1295 he is described as *bestiax,* beastlike, crude)—and the court of King Arthur, at which even after his dubbing the Welsh knave never feels at home and which has an urban character in keeping with the monarchical image in courtly poems as well as chansons de geste. Arthur lives in Carlisle (or Carduel, lines 334, 837), Caerleon (lines 3985, 4135, and 4582), and Disnadavon (lines 2730, 2751), but Chrétien does not stress the urban character of these residences. Nevertheless, the contrast between Perceval, the knight born of the wilderness—a character accentuated by the fact that his mother and father are natives of the kingdom of "sea isles," possibly the father's kingdom (lines 417, 423—and Arthur, king of an urbanized court, is a fundamental feature of the story.[18]

In the second part, which details the adventures of Gawain, the city and urban society are present in a very different way, and the knights' image of urban life is much more accurate and realistic. The relation of Arthur's court to its urban setting is stressed, but this is of secondary importance. Three times we are told that the king will hold the great Pentecostal assembly of knights in *la cité d'Orcanie* (lines 8827, 8889, and 8917).

Two episodes tell us something about the urban climate. In the first, Gawain goes to a tournament, but having promised to do battle forty days hence with a knight who has falsely accused him of his father's murder, he does not wish to run the risk of injury and refuses to take part in the combat. The damsels watching the activity make fun of him and express doubt that he is truly a knight. One says: "He is a merchant. Why do you think he came to the tournament? Surely he has brought those horses to sell." Another goes even further: "No, he is a moneychanger. And today is not the day that he is going to distribute the money and plate in his coffers and trunks to the poor knights."

The estate of knight is thus contrasted in scornful, hostile terms with the two estates most typical of the new medieval city: the merchant and the moneychanger. The wealth and avarice of those two rising social groups are stigmatized. They are castigated for lacking the knight's largesse at a time when at least part of the knightly class was sinking into poverty, a victim of the new social and economic order.

Turning a deaf ear to the ridicule, Gawain continues on his way. He meets a young knight who asks him to go see his sister in a nearby city and sue for her love on her brother's recommendation. Gawain comes into view of the city: "The castle was situated on an arm of the sea. He examined it, observed its walls and tower, and judged them strong enough to withstand any attack. He also scrutinized the city, populated with handsome men and beautiful women, and the money-changers' tables, covered with pieces of gold, silver, and small coin. He saw streets and squares filled with good workers employed in the most varied trades. Some made helmets and hauberks, others saddles and shields, still others leather harnesses and spurs. Some furbished swords, others wove and fulled, sheared and combed, and still others smelted gold and silver. Elsewhere people made beautiful and rich plates, cups, tankards, and bowls and precious enamels, rings, belts, and necklaces. It could truly be said that the city was a perpetual fair, for it was so full of riches, wax, pepper, grains, vair and squirrel, and every imaginable kind of merchandise" (lines 5688–5716).

This description is detailed and enthusiastic. It is one of the most positive images of a city in all of courtly literature, an image that is realistic yet embellished—idealized in its realism, one might say. But soon everything changes. The damsel gives Gawain a warm welcome and in accordance with her brother's wishes grants him her love, but a vavasor arrives unexpectedly and accuses the girl of having given herself to her father's assassin. Overcome, the damsel faints. When she comes to, she does not renounce her love for Gawain, but she imagines the "commune of this city" incited against them by the vavasor.[19]

In fact, the vavasor, upon leaving the castle (or tower), "finds, seated side by side, an assembly of neighbors: the mayor, the alderman, and a whole crowd of bourgeois, so big and fat that you can be sure there was no poison in their diet." He describes the situation and urges them to "arouse the whole city." What follows is a classic urban riot: "You should have seen those furious commoners take up axes and gisarmes, while others grabbed shields without straps and still others wielded shovels or parts of doors. The crier sounded the alarm, and all the people assembled. The communal bells were rung so that not a one would miss the call. Not a poor devil among them was without a pitchfork or scythe or club or pick. Never before was there such a ruckus in Lombardy about attacking a slug. Even the pettiest came running, and none arrived empty-handed."

Everything is here: urban rebellion (in which even at this early date bells play a role, as the bourgeois oppose their time to that of the Church and lords), the contrast between the ignoble arms of the populace and the noble arms of the warriors, the astonishment of the knights in the face of popular solidarity, and even the reference to Lombardy, a region that led the way in the creation of the new urban society and that in the middle of the century had repulsed the assault of Frederick Barbarossa, to the stupefaction and scandal of Bishop Otto of Freising, his nephew and chronicler.

To the rebellious populace the damsel shouts: "Hey! Hey! Scum, mad dogs, whoreson rabble,[20] who sent you? What do you want?" Fifty years earlier Guibert of Nogent had exclaimed: "Commune! Execrable word!"

The damsel hurls her chess pieces down upon the mob and threatens to destroy them all before dying, but "the ignoble rioters had made up their minds and declared that they would bring the tower down upon [its occupants] if they did not surrender. The besieged redoubled their efforts and rained down pawns and ivory pieces on the assailants, who, unable to hold, mostly withdrew. Then the people of the commune decided to dig out the ground under the tower with steel picks in order to bring it down."

Meanwhile, the knight who had challenged Gawain chanced to arrive on the scene. "He was astonished to find this mass of commoners shouting and wielding hammers." Anxious that his adversary might be killed by the mob before he could exact his own vengeance, he threatened the attackers but in vain and finally rode off to ask the king for help. "Sire," he said, "your mayor and aldermen are causing you great shame. Since this morning they have been attacking your tower and attempting to knock it down. If they are not made to pay dearly for their audacity, I shall hold you responsible."

The king excused the anger of his people but judged that honor required him to protect his guest: "The king commands the mayor to withdraw his people. They went away. Not one remained after the mayor gave his order."

Thus, the positive image of the city is reversed. The handsome bourgeois and beautiful bourgeoises that Gawain thought he saw when he first arrived have turned into a frightful mob, the laboring classes have been transformed into dangerous classes, and the king himself is able to command obedience only by appealing to the mayor, one of the mob's own, as intermediary, Lords and people are locked in a true class struggle. The devil has sent this mob, and the city is hell.

Before attempting to explain these images of the city and their ambiguity in the warrior milieu, we need to situate them in the broad span of the history of culture and *mentalités,* because the search for permanences and continuities is particularly important in the history of the imagination.[21] Every historical culture is influenced by tradition. Indeed, the degree of traditional influence is an important characteristic of any culture. Most medievalists would agree, I think, that tradition played an especially important role in the culture of the medieval West. That is hardly surprising in view of the fact that tradition is often important in societies governed by a dominant ideology (in this case Roman Catholicism) and that the upheavals of late antiquity and the early Middle Ages for a long time made it necessary for the new society to live more on tradition than on its own creations. Not that medieval society was not creative—in fact I hold that it was enormously so. But for a considerable period its creativity involved mainly choosing among elements inherited from previous cultures, shifting the accent and arranging them in new ways.

Four traditions were important influences in medieval culture: the Judeo-Christian, which first made its influence felt in Europe in the first century and became dominant in the fourth century; the Greco-Roman; the "barbarian," which first affected Rome and then was propagated by the Empire and its successor states; and the indigenous traditions of local cultures dating back to Neolithic times.

Of these four traditions, the last is generally the most difficult to grasp, despite the increasing volume of research on prehistoric and protohistoric times. Fortunately it does not seem to have had much influence on the medieval urban imagination. Perhaps some day archaeologists will have something to say about very old preurban forms, particularly among the Celts; we may then be able to assess their influence on collective culture and *mentalités*.

For similar reasons the barbarian tradition may appear to have been of negligible import. Yet it was probably not without influence, for reasons that I shall explain in a moment.

As for the Greco-Roman tradition, its impact might seem to have been considerable, since the Greek and Roman civilizations were essentially urban. In the twelfth-century works considered here, however, it seems to me to have been quite limited. No doubt this impression is due in part to the limited amount of work that has been done on this subject, most historians of the ancient legacy in the Middle Ages having been interested primarily in "high" culture rather than in collective images and representations.[22] But probably there were also more profound reasons for the relative lack of influence of ancient tradition on the urban imagination prior to the thirteenth century. Many medieval cities could trace their origins back to ancient times; there was physical and geographical continuity. Nevertheless, the medieval city was a new phenomenon. It fulfilled functions different from those of the ancient city, functions associated with a different economy, a different society, and a different symbolism. The ancient contrast between city and country, *urbs* and *rus,* was generally not relevant to the medieval West, where the fundamental dualism was between nature and culture, expressed more in terms of an opposition between what was built, cultivated, and inhabited (city, castle, and village) and what was essentially wild (the sea and the forest, western equivalents of the eastern desert), or again, between men in groups and solitude.

That leaves the Judeo-Christian tradition as the most important influence on the medieval urban imagination, which is hardly surprising. In the Middle Ages the Church had a virtual monopoly on education and the shaping of mental attitudes. The warriors of the dominant strata shared too many common interests with the church not to have been imbued with its teachings.[23] The Bible (and to a lesser extent the Church Fathers) was the supreme authority, reference, and source. An image could become powerful only if supported by or even identified with a biblical reference.

As it happens, the urban theme was fundamental in the Bible. In the Old Testament the city has a rather bad name. Genesis portrays a series of accursed cities. The very first city is founded by Cain (Genesis 4:17). This abominable patronage was remembered in the Middle Ages, and it was even pointed out that when Cain created the first city he also invented weights and measures, precursors of those techniques of counting and reckoning that were so inimical to the freedom, generosity, and abundance that men had idealized ever since creation. Genesis 11:1–9 tells the story of Babel, where man's communal determination to build was vetoed by the Lord, who wanted humans to remain divided so that he might more easily impose his will and punish them. Thus urban solidarity was cursed from the outset. In the story of Sodom and Gomorrah (Genesis 13:13; 18:20; and 19:1–25) the city is a source of lust, the mother of vice. Hence it is not surprising to find that Leviticus advises the Jewish people to live in huts, to remain a people of tabernacles as in the time of the patriarchs.

Little by little, however, a more positive image of the city found its way into the Old Testament. To be sure, in Deuteronomy 9:1 it is the enemies of Israel that live in cities, but these hostile places become the objective of the Hebrew people, and Deuteronomy 20:10–20 inaugurates a series of conquests that culminates in Joshua 2:6 with the conquest of Jericho and the miraculous destruction of its walls.

The Hebrews subsequently become an urban people. The conquered cities are divided among the tribes, and soon there arises a new type of city and new urban themes: the city as refuge and the privileged city (Joshua 13–19, 20–22; Numbers 35:9–34). Other urban episodes are scattered through the Old Testament adding luster to the city's image, such as the story of Samson at the gates of Gaza (Judges 16:1–3).

In the Historical Books the image of the city ceases to be negative. The positive evaluation of the city is obviously associated with the rise of Jerusalem. Jerusalem, first mentioned in Genesis 14:18 along with its priest-king Melchizedek, the first urban ally of the Hebrews, figures prominently in the Second Book of Samuel and the First Book of Kings. Two great kings are responsible for its success: David, who takes the city and transports the ark of the covenant there (2 Samuel 5:6–12 and 6), and Solomon, who builds the Temple and the Palace (I Kings 5–8). Thus the Bible created a physical, institutional, and symbolic image of the quintessential city, beautiful and rich and embellished by monuments, including the seats of the two powers, religious and royal.

The Books of Wisdom and the Poetic and Prophetic Books confirm and enhance the importance of urban images as well as introduce two new themes of far-reaching implication. The Psalms magnify the image of Jerusalem by coupling it with that of Zion, the sacred urban hill (Psalms 48, 69, 122). Isaiah introduces the great contrast between Jerusalem and Babylon, which crystallizes the conflict between the good city and the bad, the city of perdition and the city of salvation, and which ends with the destruction of Babylon (Isaiah 13). The same book also inaugurates an urban eschatology with its prophecy of Jerusalem's resurrection (Isaiah 2). The new Jerusalem will open its bosom and offer eternal salvation not only to Israel but to all nations. Under David Jerusalem became the political and religious capital of Israel and the abode of Yahweh (Psalm 73:2), but at the end of time it will become the meetingplace of all nations (Isaiah 54:11 and 60).

The urban theme also turns up in the New Testament, as if in confirmation of the typological symbolism that medieval commentators saw as a link between the two parts of the Bible. Jerusalem, a city associated with both the life and the death of Jesus, combines the positive, attractive aspects of the city with the negative, repulsive side. Scenes of entry into Jerusalem (Matthew 21:1–17, Mark 11:1–11, Luke 19:28–38, John 2:13 and 12:12–13) express the city's appeal, while a series of apostrophes and maledictions (Matthew 11:20–24 and 23:37, Luke 19:41–44 and 21:5–7) indicate the "Babylonian" side of a city with two faces.

A more ambitious study of the urban theme in the Bible, and especially the New Testament, would have to consider episodes and even isolated expressions that caught the fancy of later commentators, particularly in the Middle Ages. Matthew 5:14 "A city set on a hill cannot be hid"), for example, reinforces the stereotype of the city on the hill.[24]

The epistles of Saint Paul, associated with his preaching in the fundamentally urban zone of Greek cultural influence, gave firm outline to New Testament views of the city. Last but not least, the Book of Revelation focused attention on the urban setting of the end of time and on the great struggle between Babylon, city of evil (chapter 18) and Jerusalem. The heavenly Jerusalem is accorded a special place in the eschatological framework of Revelation (chapter 21), an image that exerted an astonishing influence over the ages.

In Judeo-Christian tradition Paradise was originally a natural place, a garden, to which mankind was promised to return as if returning to its origins, in the Christian Golden Age. Insufficient attention has been paid, I think, to the fact that the garden was gradually replaced by a city (though not without reactions of "ecological" eschatology, which attempted to revive the image of the garden). At the end of time mankind would come to reside for all eternity in a city. The vision of the eternal city, first introduced in Isaiah 54:11, becomes the culmination of the entire Bible (Revelation 21 and following).[25]

Concerning the contribution of the Church Fathers, many of whom were bishops whose work was shaped by its urban setting, I shall mention only the one who had the greatest influence on medieval urban ideology and imagery, namely, Augustine, whose *City of God* gave a definitive urban basis and representation to almost all Christian political theory in the Middle Ages.

Clearly, then, there was ample biblical support for the kinds of urban imagery we found in the twelfth-century works analyzed above. One kind of image was physical yet imbued with values embodying fundamental ideological systems. The urban stereotype was defined by walls, gates, and towers and by materials expressing solidity, wealth, and beauty: stone, marble, silver, and gold. The two dominant powers, religious and civil, were symbolized by Temple and Palace, church and castle.[26] Two basic tendencies predominated. One was to build walls, towers, and monuments that rose up toward heaven. The other was to establish a circulation between internalized culture and external nature via the city gates, an interchange between the rural society of production and the urban society of consumption, fabrication, and trade, between refuge on the one hand and adventure and solitude on the other. The city was an ideal abode in a society in which space was divided, not as in antiquity between right and left, but between high and low, inside and outside.

Yet men also felt ambivalent desire for the city. They saw it as a prey to be captured and conquered. At a still more fundamental level there was the ambiguity of the city itself: Babylon or Jerusalem—or Babylon and Jerusalem, that is, harmony combined with disorder, desire with fear, ruin with salvation.

It is worth noting in passing, moreover, that the third traditional influence mentioned above, the barbarian, seems to have reinforced these biblical images, to judge by the few indications we have. A significant passage in Tacitus's *Germania* (chapter 16) states that, while the barbarians knew nothing of cities, they were attracted by their solidity (the solidity of stone and brick in contrast to the impermanence of wood), wealth, beauty, and function as centers of civilization and power.

I also want to dispel some possible misconceptions about the significance of my conclusions. I do not regard the Bible (and other historical traditions) as the source, in the usual sense of the word, of the cultural and mental images of medieval society, which, like any other society, made a selection from the legacy of the past. Yet these choices were not free. They depended in complex ways on the social structure, the dominant ideology, and the degree to which that ideology emphasized tradition. The originality of a literary work is connected, in my view, with the personality of its author (or authors), which is only partially determined by the conditions of creation. In the West in the twelfth century the influence of Judeo-Christian tradition was very powerful. Urban images were prominent in that tradition, and they were particularly apt for expressing the sentiments of the dominant military strata. The situation of the warrior vis-à-vis contemporary urban realities was captured by biblical images. The success of a theme of the imagination in any society is related to the degree to which the relation between that theme and the rest of the cultural and mental legacy captures the contemporary context.[27]

I come now to the delicate problem of historicism. In following the urban theme in the Bible from Genesis to Revelation (being aware, of course, that the composition followed no neat linear chronology), one has to assume, I think, that a definite relation of some sort exists between the development of that theme in the Old and New Testaments and the historical sedentarization of the Hebrew people. But I do not believe that the history necessarily preceded the ideology or that the images were somehow laid down by the history.

We do not know when and how images of and ideas about very ancient human societies were originally constituted, but what we observe in most cases is that ideology precedes history. History emulates ideology more often than the reverse.[28] This is not to say that ideology is the motor of history, but neither is it the product.

Two related problems of historicity arise in connection with the literary works under study. One has to do with the question of chronology. *Le Charroi de Nîmes* was written "in 1135 at the earliest and in 1165 at the latest" (says Fabienne Gégou on page ix of her translation). *La Prise d'Orange* is said to be a "chanson de geste of the late twelfth century" (according to the subtitle of the translation by Claude Lachet and Jean-Pierre Tusseau). The *Lays* of Marie de France were probably written between 1160 and 1178. Chrétien de Troyes's *Perceval* was most likely written around 1185. Thus the composition of these works may have spanned a certain period of time, with the *Charroi* first, followed by *La Prise* (allowing for the fact that the reworked version that has survived was based on a much older version), followed by the *Lays*, and finally *Perceval*. One might then look for a certain thematic evolution determined in part by the historical context (note the changes in the character of warriors and cities from *Charroi* to *Perceval*) and in part by the internal evolution of literary genres (in particular the shift from epic poetry to courtly poetry). Yet we must be careful not to make too much of such speculation. Not only are the four works nearly contemporary, but it is surely a mistake to think of the history of French literature in the twelfth and thirteenth centuries in terms of a succession of genres. Chansons de geste and courtly romance were produced and consumed at the same time in the same regions. The same themes occur in both, and the same urban images.

Similarly, it would be a mistake to exaggerate the changes in the sociological context of this literature. It is not easy to relate medieval works to particular social groups, and attempts to do so have resulted in diametrically opposed theories (of the fabliaux, for example, and of the *Roman de Renart*). I acknowledge the importance of attempting, as some have done, to determine whether the chansons de geste of the William of Orange cycle express the ideas of the minor nobility rather than the aristocracy and, further, whether in moving from chansons de geste to romance we do not shift our attention from the aristocratic milieu of the barons to the knightly milieu of the middling and minor nobles, who were engaged in battles on two fronts, with the *vilains* (including bourgeois) and with the barons. It is clear, moreover, that the audience for these works often extended beyond the groups that commissioned them and for which they were primarily intended. In the twelfth century, for instance, the chansons de geste were a "popu-lar" success.

Nevertheless, it is undeniable that there was a close connection be-tween the ideology of these works, particularly as regards attitudes to-ward the city, and certain individuals of high or minor nobility, some imbued with the courtly ethic, others not, who defined themselves primarily in terms of military activities and who described themselves as warriors. Violence and courtliness went together, in the twelfth century at any rate, as can be seen in the behavior of the heroes of the works in question, who looked upon cities as women, admiring and desiring them but ultimately taking them with consent if possible, by force if necessary.

How, then, are we to interpret, with the help of these works, the warrior ideology as it pertained to the city and its ever more powerful masters, the bourgeois? Let me distinguish three attitudes, which in practice were often mixed. The first was lust. Far from disdaining cities, warriors were drawn to their beauties and riches. But they wished to exploit these treasures without changing their way of life. Cities were for them places for collecting tribute and taxes as well as places for enjoyment and bases for military activity. They were effec-tive defensive bastions in a military system in which defense was more important than offense. They were also centers where tournaments could be held[29] and bases for military expeditions. Thus the city was a valuable prey.

The second warrior attitude toward the city was one of idealization. Not only was the city beautiful, noble, and rich, it was also a place where the classes, in particular the knights and the bourgeoisie, lived together in harmony under the aegis of the king, an urban utopia. Bib-lical imagery served to express or embellish contemporary realities, but fictitious elements were sometimes added. Take, for instance, the presence of knights in a city's population, a theme given special em-phasis by Marie de France. But twelfth-century warriors generally stayed away from cities, except in Italy, where to Otto of Freising's great surprise nobles mingled with artisans and merchants.[30] Numer-ous passages in our sources suggest a fundamental opposition with re-spect to residence: merchants and bourgeois lived in cities, barons and knights in castles and forests.

This unrealistic portrayal of the city is certainly significant. I am in-clined to view the utopian image of the city and the dream of urban harmony as signs of a desire to exorcise the city of its demons, to ide-alize it by magical means, on the part of warriors who secretly feared the urban environment. They hoped to overcome the relative decline of the military classes, particularly the poor knights mentioned in the *Lays* and *Perceval,* by dreaming of an accord with the bourgeois, of a cultural adaptation whereby the urban classes would accept the knightly values of courtliness and generosity. This, I think, is the deep and no doubt unconscious meaning of the theme of the harmonious city.

Similarly, when William and his companions disguise themselves in the two chansons de geste (especially the *Charroi*), they betray, I think, the uneasiness of warriors vis-à-vis the city and its bourgeois. In this mélange of identification and derision, this travesty, can we not make out the anxious malaise of knights threatened by the social ascendancy of merchants and other citydwellers?

Finally, in *Perceval* we encounter a third image of the city as perceived by warriors, this one in violent contrast to the other two. To be sure, in all the works analyzed the opposition between the warrior's system of values and the bourgeois's system of values is crucial. In anthropological terms this is reflected in contrasts in diet, clothing, weaponry, professional conduct, and especially customary housing. The urban world is the antithesis of the world of castle and forest, jongleur and hunt. But the lure of the city and the dream of urban harmony obliterated this latent antagonism.

In the episode in which Gawain and the damsel are besieged by the commune, the illusion is dispelled. The warriors see the city as it is: an economic, social, political, and cultural organization that is not only different from but profoundly hostile to the system of the warrior nobility, whose ruin the city wants and appears to be capable of bringing about. Apart from wishful thinking, the warriors' only rampart against the conquering bourgeois was the vacillating and already urbanized monarchy.

In the second half of the twelfth century, the inner divisions in warrior attitudes toward the city were expressed by way of the ambiguity implicit in certain biblical images: Babylon or Jerusalem? The Middle Ages were obsessed with urban images of the afterlife. Heavenly or infernal city? The texts capture the uncertainty: "God, this is Paradise!" exclaims William in *La Prise d'Orange* (line 688), while in *Perceval* (line 5958, Hilka edition) the besieged damsel shouts to the men of the commune: "What devil sent you?"

There was no doubt more to the urban imagination in twelfth-century vernacular literature than I have managed to capture here. One theme that would become important later on was that of the marvelous city filled with beautiful places, monuments, and magical wonders.

The theme probably originated in the literature for pilgrim-tourists, of which the *Mirabilia urbis Romae* was the prototype, and found its way into early romances (witness the description of Camille's tomb in *Enéas*, which also incorporates the utopian theme of the harmonious city in which "small and great," "knights and bourgeois, barons and vassals" live side by side). It was a precursor of the urban mythology of the thirteenth and fourteenth centuries, reflecting the desire of new urban communities to create etiological myths and urban *mirabilia* to counter the imaginary genealogies and *mirabilia* of the nobility.[31] In the late twelfth century, however, the urban imagination was essentially divided between the vision of the city of paradise and the city of hell, between Jerusalem and Babylon.

The reader will no doubt find many of my interpretations altogether too categorical. But in pioneering a new field of study, one must resign oneself to the necessity of using rather crude implements. Charles Morazé, who was and remains a pioneer, will, I hope, understand this approach. May these pages, which I dedicate to him, mark a step along the way to a new reading of literary works that will respect their unique nature yet make them available as historical documents in the full sense of the word.

# AN URBAN METAPHOR OF
# WILLIAM OF AUVERGNE

With learning and perspicacity Pierre Michaud-Quantin noticed that
William of Auvergne was a particularly interesting witness to the relation between developments in theology and the growth of cities in the
first half of the thirteenth century.[1]

A passage from the part of the *Summa* that deals with sacraments[2]
adds to our understanding of the contribution made by the bishop of
Paris, who was regent master in theology from 1222 to 1228 and
bishop from 1228 until his death in 1249.[3] In it William compares a
city to the sacramentary septenary.

Considering material things (*materialia*), William of Auvergne emphasizes that they ought not to be prized for themselves but solely
insofar as they may serve to attain perfection. The metaphor is elaborated: "Imagine a city composed of a group of men so perfect (*ima-
ginabimur civitatem aggregatam ex hominibus sic perfectis*) that their lives
consist entirely in rendering honor and service to God, in acquitting
themselves of the duties of nobility of soul (*honestas*), in assisting
others. Clearly, in comparison with this admirable (*praeclara*) city the
rest of mankind is like a wild forest (*quasi silva*) and all other men are as
wood (*quasi ligna silvatica*)." Here, then, is the fundamental opposition
in the medieval system of values, between the city (*civitas*), the real and
symbolic center of culture, and the forest, the geographical and mental
embodiment of wilderness.[4]

In addition to the global opposition between city and forest, William
of Auvergne immediately adds another, which has to do with an essential physical and moral component of the city, the stones of which
parts of it are built. In contrast to crude, unworked quarry stone
(*lapidicina, lapides rudes*) and natural wood, stone that is mortared and
pinned and assembled is, like worked wood (*coementum, et clavi, cae-
teraeque ligaturae inter lapides, et ligna*), a symbol of the mutual love and
spiritual needs that unite human souls.

William uses the same metaphor in other contexts: he compares the

First published as "Ville et théologie au XIIIe siècle: Une métaphore urbaine de Guillaume d'Auvergne," *Razo, Cahiers du Centre d'études médiévales de Nice*, no. 1, "L'image
de la ville dans la littérature et l'histoire médiévales," Université de Nice, June 1979,
reprinted 1984, pp. 22–37.

admirable and splendid city to "societies, groups of men, or cities" (*societates, aggregationes hominum, seu civitates*) as opposed to those false cities that are mere forests or rock quarries (*ad quam caeterae veluti silvae et lapidicinae sunt*).

After stone and wood a third ingredient of the city is mentioned: metal. Once again William contrasts raw ore with metal worked by men to whom God has given strength, technical skill, and artistic sense (*vires, et artem et artificium*) with which to extract and transform the raw material.

Cities are men. And the citizens of cities are truly men in contrast to those other humans who are not really men but animals.[5] Here the city-forest opposition is joined by that other persistent antithesis in the medieval system of values: man versus animal. One is inevitably reminded of the savage, the woodsman, the *homo silvaticus* who obsessed the medieval imagination and who, when encountered in literature and art, was always asked: "Are you man or beast?"[6]

The purposes of this city are religious: peace and happiness under the law of the most perfect monarch, the one true king, God.[7] These important notions remind us of the urban ideology of the first half of the thirteenth century. Peace, an old theme and the slogan of a secular movement since about 1000,[8] now acquired new forms and a new content, which the mendicant orders above all attempted to turn into a political reality.[9] Happiness, a new idea in Christendom, began to take hold in the urban sensibility of the early thirteenth century.[10]

William of Auvergne pursued his comparison still further. How did he view the urban phenomenon? In the first place as an immigration: men *entered* a space defined in terms at once physical, legal, and ethical and, having entered, became different from what they had been before. In a word, they became *citizens*. The first thing that one saw in looking at a city was its gates, by which people gained access to a new status. The city was a civilization.[11]

That civilization, moreover, needed symbolic insignia in order to proclaim its dignity in a visible way. A knight marked his station by strapping on his sword, a minister marked his by possession of keys, and the king his by coronation and installation on the throne. Similarly, those who entered the city had to shed all visible signs of inequality, just as stones, before being used in construction, had to be evened out and trees had to be prepared by removal of their leaves, knots, and gnarls.[12] Members of the new society had to demonstrate their willingness to be associated in a "free" society bound together by mutual aid.[13]

For medieval clerics, the fundamental contrast was between the city, or ordered society, and the forest (desert) wilderness. But those who, like William of Auvergne, were influenced by ancient culture either directly or by way of the Church Fathers (and William in this same passage refers to *civilitas romana*), revived the old antithesis between city and countryside. Those who abandoned the countryside and rural life for the city and became *cives,* citizens and citydwellers, had to give up their rustic ways and country homes and adopt the manners and civility and sociability of the city.[14]

But the spiritual city, whose citizens were "not only servants of God but his sons by his grace and by right of adoption the heirs apparent of the kingdom of heaven" (p. 414), was so much like a material city (*materiali, seu literali civitati in suis visibilibus corporalibus ac temporalibus adeo similis est*) that it needed administrators. Just as kings and governors had ministers and intendants to administer their possessions, the spiritual city needed one or more intendants to administer its riches. Just as ministers reported to their superiors, the administrator of the spiritual city reported to the king of kings and supervised subordinates who reported to him. Thus the spiritual city needed gatekeepers, heralds, dukes, judges, and magistrates (p. 411).

This city was a dream—a clergyman's dream, a bishop's dream—in which all laymen were equal and the ecclesiastical hierarchy, distributor of sacraments, was the only mediator between God and man.

William's metaphor is undeniably urban, and it is reasonable to assume that it was inspired in part by the image of Paris, recently unified within walls constructed by Philip Augustus. Yet it would be a mistake to carry this too far. The bishop of Paris does say that the ideal city that he describes should serve as an example, a book from which the material city may derive inspiration, but to what extent did the inspiration flow in the other direction? To what degree was the Paris of Philip Augustus the model for the city of sacraments?

Pierre Michaud-Quantin has shown the ambiguity of the medieval term *civitas* that William uses: "With the word *civitas* the Middle Ages accepted two ancient traditions, a concept from political philosophy and an administrative term. The first dates back essentially to Cicero, for whom the city was a group of men governed by a single law, *juris societas civium.* But the primary source of inspiration for medieval authors was the work of Saint Augustine. He adopted the formula of the Roman politician but emphasized the moral and emotional factors that unified the members of the city, the *vinculum societatis, vinculum concordiae* that created a *concors hominum multitudo,* a multitude whose hearts beat as one, as the medieval etymologies might have put it."[15]

Clearly William of Auvergne's city was more the city of Saint Augustine than it was the city of Paris. Between the ancient, Augustinian, and episcopal notion of *civitas* (as it was understood in the early Middle Ages), which referred primarily to a group of men sharing a common set of laws and attitudes and which might not resemble a city in form, and the medieval city under the various names by which it was known, there was a difference determined by a change in clerical culture.

This shows how difficult it is to establish any precise relation between the "realities" of the Middle Ages, in this case urban realities, and the mental equipment of clergymen who were the heirs of a different society and culture.

Later, in a series of sermons preached at Augsburg in 1257 or 1263 on the theme of Matthew 5:14 ("A city set on a hill cannot be hid"), Albertus Magnus, expounding a veritable theology of the city, drew upon both a new imagery of the urban phenomenon and a set of biblical and ancient references (not so much Cicero as Plato and Aristotle). Yet ambiguity remained in his "urban" discourse.[16]

# SOCIAL REALITIES AND IDEOLOGICAL CODES IN THE EARLY THIRTEENTH CENTURY: AN *EXEMPLUM* BY JAMES OF VITRY

Medievalists have long been in the habit of comparing what are alleged to be "historical realities" with didactic and imaginative literature of ages past. Formerly the tendency was to look to such documents for information about "real" societies.[1] Within limits such an approach is legitimate. Texts of the kind with which I shall be concerned here, *exempla*, were for a long time exploited as sources of information about the concrete realities of medieval society, and in particular about certain aspects neglected or obscured by most other sources, such as folklore and daily life.[2] These sources give voice to an otherwise silent history. But the method has its dangers. The historian who uses it runs the risk of mistaking imaginary realities for material ones and of distorting the meaning of a text that was not intended to provide evidence of the kind the scholar is after. In recent years a number of eminent medievalists have attempted to redress the balance by treating didactic documents (whether ideological or fictional in nature) on their own terms while examining their complex relation to "objective" social realities of which they are in part a product and in part an instrument of manipulation.[3]

Times of marked social change are ideal for observing the relationship between material and imaginary realities. In the West the birth of a new society between the tenth and fourteenth centuries enables us to examine the changing relations between socioeconomic conditions, ideology, and works of the imagination while avoiding the crude methodology of infrastructure-superstructure and the theory of reflection. A crucial turning point occurred sometime between 1180 and 1240, with variations from country to country and region to region. It involved changes in two of the most powerful ideological instruments wielded by the Church, originator and promulgator of the dominant ideology: namely, preaching and the sacraments.

Originally published in volume 4 of the publications of the Institut für Mittelalterlich Realienkunde Österreichs (1980), pp. 1–7.

The Church adapted its preaching to a new scheme of social classification, more horizontal than vertical and more willing to allow for historical change, for the development of new occupational groups, and for changes in people's everyday lives.[4] Preachers relied not just on the traditional authorities, the Bible and the Church Fathers, but increasingly on arguments provided by the new scholastic methods and on exempla, or edifying anecdotes, taken for the most part from ancient pagan literature and oral tradition and less often from the Bible.[5]

The sacraments were organized into the sacramental septenary, within which the individual sacraments evolved and changed priorities within a hierarchy.[6] To one degree or another marriage was subjected to clerical control; the eucharist took on new importance; and, most important, confession and penitence rose to the top of the hierarchy. The latter development reflected the triumph of the twelfth century's morality of intentions. Private auricular confession replaced public penance, and confessors were instructed to recognize and deal with sins apt to be committed by members of different occupational and social groups. Canon 21, *Omnis utriusque sexus,* of the Fourth Lateran Council (1215), made annual confession compulsory for every Christian, thereby encouraging an already growing tendency toward examination of the conscience. Confessors' manuals composed along casuistic lines replaced the old penitentials, with their schedules of penances.[7]

Preachers and confessors sought to capture the new society of cities, money, and calculation, a society in which princes and their officers, new corporate solidarities, and confraternities played key roles. The family was also important, restructured as it had been by new devotional practices and new ideologies of salvation adapted to changed conditions, attitudes, and sensibilities.

Systems of classification were reformed accordingly.[8] "Objective" classification according to the schema of seven deadly sins persisted,[9] although the hierarchy of sins changed.[10] But a new system of "social" classifications emerged, based on *états du monde,* or social status.[11] A new and deadly serious game was begun: relating the various vices to different social groups. According to one topos the devil had nine daughters, each of whom married a different social group.[12] Another, used by James of Vitry in his early thirteenth-century *Historia Occidentalis,* was to associate characteristic vices with a nationality or language.[13] New classifications were related to old ones in order to justify change through tradition as the Church asserted its ideological dominance.

Here I want to concentrate on an exemplum used by James of Vitry, which is remarkable in that it links all seven deadly sins to a single social group: the knights. James attended the University of Paris in the early years of its existence, at the beginning of the thirteenth century. He was a renowned preacher who, after serving as bishop of Acre in Palestine, became cardinal-bishop of Tusculum, a position in which he remained until his death in 1240. Among those who compiled anthologies of model sermons he was the first to make frequent and systematic use of exempla. The one that I wish to examine here was previously studied by Crane,[14] but isolated from its context.[15]

The exemplum in question occurs in sermon 52, the second of three sermons that James addressed to powerful lords and knights (*ad potentes et milites*), the first of the lay status groups included in his anthology of *sermones ad status*. James dealt first with priests and monks, next with a group whose members had voluntarily or involuntarily endured trials that gave them a status intermediate between the clergy and the laity: lepers, victims of other diseases, paupers, people in mourning for relatives or friends, crusaders, and pilgrims. Finally, he considered the *potentes,* the powerful, a term used in the early Middle Ages to refer to nobles, aristocrats, as opposed to *pauperes,* paupers.[16]

The three sermons abound with exempla in which men are compared with animals. This proved to be not only an effective rhetorical device but a powerful ideological weapon. The unicorn, wolf, lamb, and crane figure in the first sermon; the ape, bear, eagle, fox, lion, and rat in the second; and the rose and the serpent in the third.

The theme of the second sermon is Luke 3 : 14: "And the soldiers likewise demanded of him, saying, And what shall we do? And he said unto them, Do violence to no man, neither accuse any falsely; and be content with your wages." The sermon begins with a traditional exhortation to convert and to respect the word of God. Two exempla depict a knight who willingly listens to the sermons but does the opposite of what they preach and another who refuses to hear mass. Next comes a passage on tournaments, a justification of the *ordo militaris* as part of God's will for the defense of the oppressed and of churches and for the promotion of peace, justice, and security. There is a disquisition on the various orders that make up the Church based on an organic metaphor for society, with Christ as the head, priests and prelates as the eyes, princes and knights as the hands,[17] and so on. There is also an attack on corrupt knights who oppress churches and the poor rather than protect them and an excursus on the ephemeral nature of secular power. Then come the comparisons with animals:

the eagle is like those who accept mortmain and oppress widows, orphans, and paupers, and similarly for the other animals. Along the way there are condemnations of "wicked customs" such as tallages and other unjust exactions and of wicked provosts and seigneurial officers. The great (*majores*) are exhorted not to drive the small (*minores*) to despair.

Although the text is not presented as an exemplum, it is one nonetheless. It is introduced by the word *memini,* which, like the more common *audivi,* indicates a personal exemplum, and it culminates with the conversion and salvation of the hero of the exemplum, a knight (*quidam miles*) whom James persuades to abandon tournaments and who eventually comes to hate them.

James demonstrates that the seven deadly sins are the inevitable accompaniment of every tournament. The first sin is pride, *superbia,* because impious (the word is from the Old Testament) and vain knights compete for the praise of other men and vain glory. Competition leads to envy (*invidia*) for supremacy in strength and glory. Wrath (*ira*) and even hatred (*odium*) are also involved, for the aim is to strike other men, to hurt them, indeed to wound them mortally. Dispiritedness (*acedia vel tristitia*) is too often the result, for knights under the dominion of vanity find spiritual goods insipid, and if defeated they slink away in shame, another reason for sadness. They also succumb to greed (*avaritia vel rapina*), for when they defeat an enemy they take him prisoner, demand an excessive ransom, and strip him of mount and arms. To pay the cost of combat and to finance their journeys they impose intolerable burdens on their men in the form of heavy exactions; they rob them mercilessly, trample crops in the field, and inflict material and physical damage on poor peasants. They are also guilty of gluttony (*castrimargia*), for they invite one another to banquets and spend what rightfully belongs to the poor on culinary debauch. And they also indulge their lust (*luxuria*), seeking to prevail in combat in order to please immodest women, whose coats of arms (*insignia*) they have taken the habit of wearing as banners (*pro vexillo*). Because of these evils and cruelties the Church has rightly decided to refuse Christian burial to those who perish in tournaments. The wicked are destined, the Bible says, for the "depths of the sea," for the "depths of bitterness and pain," that is, for Hell.

In this passage James of Vitry is accusing knights who engage in tournaments of all the sins of all the "estates" of society. Foremost among them of course are the specific sins of the warrior: pride (or vainglory), wrath, and avarice in the form peculiar to knights, namely, rapine. But they are guilty as well of the sin common to men of every class: lust. More than that, they exhibit the vices characteristic of every class: envy, the sin of peasants and paupers; avarice, the sin of bourgeois merchants; and gluttony, the sin of the clergy. James is clear that the seven deadly sins form a series: he numbers them, "first," "fourth," "fifth," and so on. Thus, the system of seven sins, which had been fractured by the new emphasis on status and the new assumption that certain sins are characteristic of particular status groups, could under certain circumstances be reconstituted and applied to a single group. What circumstances? Occasions particularly propitious to the commission of sins, such as tournaments.[18]

The antitournament theme was a common one in thirteenth-century literature, especially in the first half of the century. This was a clerical literature, a literature dominated by the clergy, yet one in which the passion of warriors for a sport that conformed to their system of values is frequently evident.

The *Histoire de Guillaume le Maréchal* (History of William the Marshall, circa 1226) provides the best available portrait of knights who pay huge ransoms and pursue glory (or vainglory, as the priests called it) and prizes and leave in their wake trails of red blood.[19]

A tournament also figures importantly in Jean Renart's *Roman de la Rose,*[20] which depicts the "fantasy of glory of the tourneying knights."[21] Their one idea is "to distinguish themselves weapons in hand." We are shown a joust, really nothing more than an interminable exchange of blows that shake both combatants and spectators, rending shields and helmets, breaking lances, slashing doublets, unseating knights. Yet no one is killed or apparently even injured. The jousters are seeking profit as well as glory: "Ah! If only you had seen the prisoners on every side being led away to each nation's camp! What profits for some, what losses for others!" Although William is a victor, he shows his largesse: "William, wearing a meager doublet, came away with nothing but his glory. Disarming straightaway, he gave everything to his heralds, both arms and horses." He had fought eight jousts in a row, vanquished all his adversaries, and won seven warhorses, but from his last victim he took nothing, in honor of his courage. He had also won love, more for his beauty than for his valor: "to him alone an open face had brought the love of many a lady." Joyfully he celebrated his victory: "They found tables covered with cloth, good wines, and dishes prepared to each person's taste." This banquet is the positive counterpart of the one that James of Vitry describes as an example of sinful gluttony. Yet sadness is one sin that does not afflict William of Dole and his companions: "Our hero did not look sad. . . . William sat among companions who radiated gaiety."

In the chantefable *Aucassin et Nicolette,* Aucassin readily prefers the Hell promised to tourneying knights by clerics such as James of Vitry to the Heaven of "lame, one-armed old priests . . . who die of hunger, thirst, cold, and misery." Indeed he says: "I want to go to Hell, for it is to Hell that handsome clerics go, and handsome knights who die in tourneys or in illustrious battle, valiant men of arms and nobles." [22] By contrast, Rutebeuf, in his *Nouvelle complainte d'outremer,* passes the various estates in review in order to heap opprobrium on them all. After considering barons and before turning to "young squires with downy skin," he devotes considerable attention to tourneying knights: "Habitués of the tournaments, you who freeze in winter while searching for opportunities to joust, you can commit no greater folly! You spend, you waste your time and your lives and the lives of others, indiscriminately. You eat the shell instead of the meat, you choose vainglory over Paradise." [23]

How did real tournaments differ from literary ones? The fact is that our most detailed sources are literary ones, and much of what we know of the reality of tournaments is based on them. Georges Duby, who has given the best description and explanation of the tournament "system," relied primarily on Lambert of Ardres's *Histoires des comtes de Guines* and on the previously mentioned *Histoire de Guillaume le Maréchal,* but he interprets these sources in the light of other knowledge of the world in which the knights lived and fought. [24]

The contestants in the tournaments were young unmarried knights. Although James of Vitry does not allude to this fact, it seems likely that it contributed to his assessment of their sinful ways. In a world in which the layman's duty was to marry and procreate, and celibacy (at least since the Gregorian Reform) was the province of the clergy, the young knight was already at odds with his estate. What is more, celibacy was supposed to be coupled with virginity, but the young knight sought relations with women. In Duby's words: "Tournaments became schools of courtesy. . . . Everyone knew that among the prizes to be won was the love of the ladies." Tournaments—"marriage markets," as they have been called—also afforded opportunities for finding a wife, but in conditions that the Church considered suspect. Signs of this link between tournaments and marriage can be found in a fabliau that can hardly be considered religious in spirit, the *Dit des cons.* [25]

For these young warriors tournaments provided a needed outlet, a safety valve, a decompression chamber. In the early thirteenth century, however, the Church indicated an approved and blessed arena in which idle knights could hone their military skills: the Crusade. James of Vitry, who was bishop of Acre and who placed crusaders high on his list of social estates, was even more imbued with the crusading spirit than most of his colleagues. Even before the advent of the tournament, Saint Bernard, who in his *De laude novae militiae* propagandized in favor of holy knighthood, was also among those who deplored knightly vainglory. He was frightened by bands of violence-prone young warriors such as he saw passing through Clairvaux. Tournaments were in effect a team sport. The Church, which encouraged pious confraternities but discouraged associations based on nonreligious affinities, opposed these devil-inspired groups. Young knights fought not only for the sake of love and violence but also for money. No one has shown better than Georges Duby the economic significance of tournaments, the Latin word for which, *nundinae,* also meant fairs. The purpose of jousting was to capture men, horses, and arms. Fortunes were made and lost in the lists. The transfer of wealth was comparable to that which took place among merchants in the fairs.

The circulation of money was considerable. Or, more precisely, since currency was still rare, the exchange involved a complex traffic in loans, pledges, contracts, debts, and promises—just as "at the end of the fairs," to quote Duby again. The tournament became a financial rival of the Church: "The role of tournaments in the twelfth-century economy was equivalent to the erstwhile role of pious donation in a population that the priests kept on a tight leash. Here was yet another reason for the Church to condemn this sport, for it competed with alms and opened a chink through which the spirit of gain could infiltrate the aristocratic mentality."

It is not hard to see why the Church was so harshly critical of an activity that harmed both its spiritual and material interests. As early as 1130 the Councils of Reims and Clermont, which were attended by Pope Innocent II, condemned "those deplorable meetings or fairs" which in 1179 the Third Lateran Council called by name: tournaments. Yet the *oratores* did not entirely condemn those *bellatores* who died in the lists. The Church refused them Christian burial, as James of Vitry observed. But it allowed them "penitence and viaticum."

James of Vitry's *exemplum* is an interesting piece of evidence for understanding the war between the oratores and the bellatores. The rivalry between the first two orders of medieval society had a long history. The Church condemned the tourneying knights not only for the sins inherent in their estate but also for sins that broke with that estate:

the pursuit of profit and ostentatious licentiousness. But the criticism of the tournament was not only part of this long history; it also reflected the concerns of a particular historical moment. At the turn of the thirteenth century the tournament was replacing the Crusade, interest in profit was emanating from the fairgrounds, and pious donations were being diverted into frivolous expenditure on sport.

A system of classification could express this clash of orders and serve the Church's didactic aims more effectively if it combined traditional beliefs with changes reflecting current circumstances. By combining the seven deadly sins with the system of estates, early thirteenth-century oratores were able to mount, at the theoretical level, an effective attack on the new sport of the bellatores: the tournament.

# Appendix

Excerpt from sermon 52 *Ad potentes et milites* by James of Vitry, based on Luke 3:14, Interrogabant milities Johannem dicentes, etc.

Transcription: Marie-Claire Gasnault, based on BN Latin 17509 and 3284 and Cambrai BM 534.

See also T. F. Crane, *The Exempla or Illustrative Stories from the Sermones Vulgares of Jacques de Vitry* (London, 1890), reprinted by Kraus Reprint (Nehdeln, 1967), no. 161, pp. 62–64 and 193.

*Contra torneamenta et de malis que de torneamentis proveniant.* Memini quod quadam die loquebar cum quodam milite qui valde libenter torneamenta frequentabat et alios invitabat, precones mittens et hystriones qui torneamenta proclamarent, nec credebat, ut asserebat, hujusmodi ludum vel exercicium esse peccatum. Alias autem satis devotus erat. Ego autem cepi illi ostendere quod VII criminalia peccata coritantur torneamenta. Non enim carent superbia, cum propter laudem hominum et gloriam inanem in circuitu illo impii ambulant et vani. Non carent invidia, cum unus alii invideat, eo quod magis strenuus in armis reputetur et majorem laudem assequatur. Non carent odio et ira, cum unus alium percutit et male tractat et plerumque letaliter vulnerat et occidit. Sed et inde quartum mortale peccatum incurrunt, quod est accidia vel tristicia: adeo enim vanitate occupantur quod omnia bona spiritualia eis insipida redduntur; et quia non prevalent contra partem aliam, sed cum vituperio sepe fugiunt, valde constristantur. Non carent quinto criminali peccato, idest avaricia vel rapina, dum unus alium capit et redimit,[26] et equum quem cupiebat cum armis aufert illi contra quem pugnando prevaluit. Sed occasione torneamentorum graves et intolerabiles exactiones faciunt et hominum suorum bona sine misericordia rapiunt, nec segetes in agris conculcare et dissipare nonformidant et pauperes agricolas valde dampnificant et molestant. Non carent torneamenta sexto mortali peccato, quod est castrimargia, dum mutuo propter mundi pompam invitant ad prandia et invitantur: non solum bona sua, sed et bona pauperum in superfluis commesationibus expendunt et de alieno corio largas faciunt corrigias. "Quicquid delirant reges, plectuntur Achivi."[27] Non carent septimo mortali peccato, quod dicitur luxuria, cum placere volunt mulieribus impudicis, si probi habeantur in armis, et etiam quedam earum insignia quasi pro vexillo portare consueverunt. Unde propter mala et crudeliatesque ibi fiunt, atque homicidia et sanguinis effusiones, instituit ecclesia, ut, qui in torneamentis occiduntur, sepultura christiana eis denegetur. "In circuitu quidem impii ambulant" [Cf. Psalms 12:8] "Unde cum mola asinaria," ide est cum in circuitu vite laboriose, "demerguntur in profundum maris," id est in profunditatem amaritudinis et laboris. [Cf. Matthew 18:6] Cum autem dictus miles hec verba audiret et aperte veritatem, quam nunquam audierat, agnosceret, sicut prius torneamenta dilexit, ita postea semper odio qui habere cepit. Multi quidem propter ignorantiam peccant, qui, si audirent veritatem et diligenter inquirerent, non peccarent, sicut memorati milites diligenter interrogabant Johannem Baptistam: "Quid faciemus et nos," quibus ipse respondit ut neminem concuterent violentiam faciendo nec calumpniam facerent falso aut fraudulenter accusando, sed contenti essent stipendiis, que ideo, teste Augustino, constituta sunt militantibus, ne dum sumptum queritur, predo grassetur.

## Against Tournaments and the Evils That Result from Them

I remember that one day I was speaking with a knight who often went to tournaments and who invited other knights by sending heralds and histrions to announce that a tournament was being held, and he did not believe, or so he assured me, that this sort of game or exercise was a sin. What is more, he was in fact rather devout. I undertook to prove to him that the seven deadly sins went along with tournaments. Knights do not lack for pride, since for the praise of men and vainglory the impious and vain make the rounds. They do not lack for envy, for each man envies the other for being judged a stronger contestant and for drawing greater praise. They do not lack for hatred and wrath, for each man strikes the other, hurts him, and often mortally wounds and kills him. Hence men incur the fourth mortal sin, which is dispiritedness or sadness. They are in fact so obsessed by vanity that all spiritual goods seem insipid. And when they do not defeat their adversary but flee in reproach, they are deeply saddened. They do not lack for the fifth mortal sin, which is avarice or theft, for each one who makes his enemy prisoner ransoms him and takes the horse, which he coveted, and the arms from him whom he has defeated in battle. Because of tournaments, knights make heavy and unbearable exactions. They mercilessly rob the property of their men. They do not fear to trample underfoot and scatter the crops in the fields, and they greatly harm and molest the poor peasants. These tournaments are not lacking in the sixth mortal sin, gluttony, for the knights hold banquets and seek invitations to others in sacrifice to worldly pomp. They spend on superfluous eating not only their own wealth but that of the poor, and of other men's skins they make broad belts: "When the kings are mad, the Greeks are beaten." (Cf. Horace, *Epistles*, 1.2.14) They are not lacking in the seventh deadly sin, which is called lust, for they want to please immodest women by distinguishing themselves in combat and even by wearing certain female items as banners. Hence, because of the crimes and cruelties committed in tournaments, because of the homicides and bloodlettings, the Church has refused Christian burial to those who die on the tournament field. "The wicked walk on every side." (Cf. Psalms 12:8) "With a millstone for a soul," that is, in the circuit of a toilsome life, "they are drowned in the depths of the sea," that is, in bitterness and toil. (Cf. Matthew 18:6) When the knight had heard these words and openly recognized the truth, which until then he had ignored, just as he had previously loved tournaments, from then on he always hated them. Many indeed sin out of ignorance, who, if they listened for and diligently searched out the truth, would sin no more, like those soldiers who dutifully asked John the Baptist: "And what should we do?" He answered them that they ought to strike no one out of violence and slander no one with false or dishonest accusation, and that they should be content with their wages, which according to Augustine were instituted in order to prevent soldiers seeking their livelihood from acquiring booty through violence.

# PART FIVE

# DREAMS

# CHRISTIANITY AND DREAMS
# (SECOND TO SEVENTH CENTURY)

Beginning in the fourth century, when Christianity became the dominant religion and ideology in the West, and continuing during the subsequent transitional period known as late antiquity or the early Middle Ages, dreams and their interpretation, important matters in many societies, became cultural phenomena with which Christians had to deal.[1]

Like any new cultural system, Christianity began with a legacy from the past. Among the important influences on its development was Greco-Roman culture, called "pagan" culture by the Christians. Cultivated fourth-century Christians felt anxiety about this legacy, perhaps best expressed in an account of a dream of Saint Jerome's.[2]

Dreams and their interpretation were a matter of particular perplexity and anxiety for Christians. In the hope of clarifying the views of the faithful in the Middle Ages, I shall briefly discuss biblical, Greek, and Roman traditions of dream interpretation. (For lack of competence I will not discuss the influence of "barbarian," i.e., Celtic, Germanic, and Slavic, traditions, which did not become apparent before the seventh century.)

With that discussion as background, I shall then turn to the uncertainties and contradictions in Christian dream theories and beliefs in the second, third, and fourth centuries. Finally, I shall discuss the development of misgivings about dream interpretation and the elaboration of a new Christian typology and theory of dreams that occurred between the fourth and seventh centuries.

## I. The Biblical Heritage

### A. Frequency of Dreams in the Old Testament, Rarity in the New

E. L. Ehrlich counted some thirty-five dreams in the Old Testament,[3] whereas Martine Dulaey found forty-five.[4] In an appendix I have listed some forty-three dreams drawn from the work of both of these scholars.[5]

First published in the proceedings of the colloquium "I sogni nel Medioevo," Lessico Intelletuale Europeo, Rome, 1983 (Rome, 1985).

In the New Testament, however, we find only nine dreams (including apparitions and visions).[6] Five are in Matthew, four of which concern the birth of Jesus (Matthew 1:20, 2:12, 2:13–19, 2:22), the other being the dream of Pilate's wife. The other four are in the Acts of the Apostles (16:9, 18:9, 23:11, and 27:23), and all concern Saint Paul, whose apostolate took place in a part of the world influenced by Greek culture with its long tradition of oneiromancy and in which those who received divinely inspired nocturnal visions enjoyed great prestige.

### B. The Biblical Legacy with Respect to Dreams

*a.* Dreams inspired by Yahweh are a case apart, for this was a god who transmitted warnings and orders both to his chosen people (the Jews in the Old Testament) and to high-ranking pagans (Pharaoh, Nebuchadnezzer). Royal dreams have been considered special since earliest recorded times.[7]

*b.* The Bible distinguishes between clear visions and dreams requiring interpretation, a distinction usually but not always expressed in the Vulgate by the opposition between *visio* and *somnium*. In any case, *waking dreams,* daydreams, were traditionally excluded from the Christian category of dreams. Dreams are a phenomenon of sleep, a vast territory for religious anthropology to explore. The frontier between sleep and wakefulness is not always apparent, however. In Numbers 12:6–8 Yahweh seems to place *visio* and *somnium* in one class, face-to-face apparitions in another: "Audite sermones meos: Si quis fuerit inter vos propheta Domini in visione apparebo ei, vel per somnium loquar ad illum. At non talis servus meus Moysses, qui in omni domo mea fidelissimus est: ore enim ad os loquor ei, et palam, et non per aenigmata et figuras Dominum videt." [And he said, Hear now my words: If there be a prophet among you, I the Lord will make myself known unto him in a vision, and will speak unto him in a dream. My servant Moses is not so, who is faithful in all mine house. With him will I speak mouth to mouth, even apparently, and not in dark speeches; and the similitude of the Lord shall he behold.] This text proposes a hierarchy of dreamers based on the relative clarity of the dream message, determined by the dreamer's familiarity with God. In the Old Testament one might accordingly single out Moses and more generally the patriarchs who experience visions in which Yahweh speaks clearly, as opposed to the kings and prophets who experience more enigmatic dreams and visions and, finally, the pagan kings, recipients of obscure dream messages.[8]

*c.* Dreams and fear: frightening dreams, accompanied by psychic and physical signs, anxiety, and trembling, constitute an important topic in the historical anthropology of dreams. In the Old Testament the best examples are the nightmares of Job (4:12−16; 7:13−14).[9]

*d.* Dreams act through a combination of vision and words, sight and hearing. Apparitions speak, and their words, whether clear or obscure, are obviously part of the message. Silent visions are rare. In the dream in which Jacob sees a ladder reaching from earth to heaven, for example, he also hears Yahweh speak to him.[10] It has been suggested that there are more words in Old Testament dreams and more silent visions in New Testament ones, because the Jews emphasized the sense of hearing and the Greeks that of sight. This kind of explanation should be treated with extreme caution, however.

*e.* There are no apparitions of the dead or of demons in biblical dreams. Ghosts are in general closely related to dreams, and it is therefore remarkable that the dead do not appear in biblical dream visions. Similarly, while numerous angels appear in biblical dreams, demons are absent. The dream was not a means of access to the dead or to demons.

*f.* The rejection of dreaming. Yahweh sometimes acts through dreams, but more often dreams are dangerous illusions. From God emanate true dreams, but there are also deceitful "dream-senders" who propagate dreams through false prophets. Yahweh revealed to Jeremiah that false prophets were sending false visions in his name: "Then the Lord said unto me, The prophets prophesy lies in my name: I sent them not, neither have I commanded them, neither spake unto them: they prophesy unto you a false vision and divination, and a thing of nought, and the deceit of their heart" (Jeremiah 14:14).

Dreams are illusions, often nocturnal illusions that can lead to heresy. They may be temptations or trials. "If there arise among you a prophet, or a dreamer of dreams, and giveth thee a sign or a wonder, and the sign or the wonder come to pass, whereof he spake unto thee, saying, Let us go after other gods, which thou hast not known, and let us serve them; thou shalt not hearken unto the words of that prophet, or that dreamer of dreams: for the Lord your God proveth you, to know whether ye love the Lord your God with all your heart and with all your soul" (Deuteronomy, 13:1−3).

The condemnation of dreams is especially harsh in Ecclesiastes and Ecclesiasticus. "For a dream cometh through the multitude of business" (Ecclesiastes 5:3), and "in the multitude of dreams and many words there are also divers vanities" (Ecclesiastes 5:7). In Ecclesiasticus, one aspect of man's misery is his inability to find repose in sleep owing to dreams that bring back the day's troubles and pursue the dreamer "as if he were escaped out of battle" (Ecclesiasticus 40:5–6).

Jewish rabbis dissuaded their followers from divination by means of dreams, this being a pagan or Chaldean custom whose influence, exerted through magi, had almost corrupted the Jews during their captivity in Babylon. God ordered Moses to tell his people not to seek to interpret dreams: "Neither shall ye use enchantment, nor observe times" (Leviticus 19:26). For there was no point examining dreams: Yahweh had spoken, and there was nothing that a dream could add to the word of God.

Significant dreams in the Bible tend to establish a link between heaven and earth rather than between the present and the future as in pagan oneiromancy. Time belongs to God alone. The dream, rather than reveal the future, puts the dreamer in contact with God.

## II. Pagan Dreams

A. Main Characteristics of Dreams in the Greco-Roman Culture to the Second Century A.D. [11]

*a.* There is a fundamental distinction between true dreams and false dreams. This concept is discussed in two well-known texts: book 19 of the *Odyssey* (lines 560 ff., Penelope's dream) and book 6 of the *Aeneid* (the description of the underworld). Since Virgil took his inspiration from Homer, both poets used the same image to express this idea. Penelope sees a dream world, very much like Hades, with two gates, one ivory, from which false dreams (those which ἐλεφαίρονται [deceive]) emanate, the other of horn, through which true dreams (those which κραίνουσιν [are fulfilled, come true]) escape into the world. Similarly, Aeneas in Hades sees true dreams passing through the *porta cornea* while false dreams emanate from the *porta eburnea* (*Aeneid* 6.893–898).

*b.* Dreams, the dead, and the other world. Pagan dreams were much more objectified than were dreams in Jewish or Christian thought. They were shadows, phantoms, vaporous forms with a place of their own in the underworld. The world of the dead was also the land of dreams. Dreams, death, and the afterlife were closely connected. Dreams were ghosts.[12]

*c.* True dreams predominated. Both ordinary people and intellectuals considered the vast majority of dreams to be true and reliable.

Nevertheless, in Greek and Roman philosophy there was a persistent current of hostility to dreams, which were said to be illusory and antithetical to truth and reason. Hesiod, in his myth of the origins of dreams ( Ὄνειρος) described the dream as a son of "shadowy Night," a brother of "black Earth," of Sleep (Ὕπνος), and odious Death (θάνατος).[13] Many nocturnal phenomena, including dreams, were surrounded by darkness and fear. In philosophy, unlike Pythagoras, Democritus, and Plato, who believed in the truth of dreams, Diogenes was the first to profess total incredulity, and Aristotle offered a rationalist critique in which he proposed psychological and physiological explanations for most types of dreams, resulting, it has been said, in "a radical devaluation of dreams."[14] As for historians, Thucydides and Polybius excluded dreams from their works.

A critical, rationalist attitude toward dreams developed simultaneously in medicine. A treatise from the Hippocratic corpus entitled περὶ ἐνυπνίων (*On Dreams*, ca. 400 B.C.), which constitutes book 4 of περὶ διαίτης (*On Diet*), gave an empirical basis to dream science and related dreams to physical state and disease.[15] In the second century A.D., Galen's treatise *On Diagnosis through Dreams* (περὶ τῆς ἐξ ἐνυπνίων διαγνώσεως) was in the Hippocratic tradition, and Oribasius also helped to move the medical science of dreams away from oneiromancy.[16]

*d.* Two dream typologies: predominance of an internal criterion of classification. Two dream typologies were developed in antiquity. One was based on the origin of the dream, but as Behr aptly put it, the ancients were more interested in the result of the dream than in its origin. In general they believed that the origin of dreams was in some vague way divine. But they did believe in the existence of "dream senders," Hermes foremost among them. Dreams could also originate with the dead. The Stoics apparently outlined a dream typology in which there were three possible origins.[17] This was perfected in the first century B.C. by Posidonius, who bequeathed it to his pupil Cicero. The latter formulated it in his *De divinatione* (1.64), our best available source. According to Cicero, dreams could originate with man (or, more precisely, with his spirit, which produced dreams of its own accord), with immortal spirits, which filled the air, or with gods, who addressed themselves directly to sleeping individuals.[18] Christianity would adopt this typology with some changes.

The second dream typology was essentially utilitarian. The point was to distinguish those dreams that foretold the future from those upon which one could not rely. Derived from the Homeric myth of the gates of ivory and horn, which was adapted by Plato, this classification may have been linked with the classification by origin in a "popular" typology.[19] Conflation of true and false dreams with premonitory and nonpremonitory ones led to a system of three classes of dreams: nonpremonitory, divinely-inspired premonitory, and demon-inspired premonitory (demons being inhabitants of the air, not necessarily either good or bad). But Posidonius, who provided Cicero with his typology, included a fourth category, dividing premonitory dreams into two groups, clear or enigmatic, thus perpetuating the dominant typology based on the nature of the dream. Under the influence of medical theories (which traced dreams to indigestion, intoxication, illness, and so on), a fifth category, composed of illusory dreams, was added to the system in the first few centuries of the Christian era, yielding a system of five categories. Premonitory dreams could belong to one of three categories: *oneiros* (*somnium*) or enigmatic, *horama* (*visio*) or clear vision, and *chrematismos* (*oraculum*) or divinely inspired but often enigmatic. Nonpremonitory dreams were of two types: the *enupnion* (*insomnium*), meaning a dream, symbolic or not, that referred only to the past or to ordinary events, and the *phantasma* (*visum*), or pure illusion.[20]

Note that this typology is quite similar to the one implicit in the Old Testament, with its division between clear and enigmatic and its incipient distinction between "dream" and "vision," which would be greatly elaborated, albeit not without ambiguity, in the Middle Ages.

*e.* A mystical conception of the dream: the dream of the soul liberated from the body. According to a philosophical tradition that dates back to Pythagoras, dreams and souls are closely associated. Dreams occur at night when the soul is liberated from the body, and their value depends on the purity of the soul. Plato added depth to this theory (*Republic* 9.1). The Stoics developed this mystical tendency in dream criticism, and in the third century B.C. the Stoic theoretician Chrysippus, influenced by this tradition, wrote a treatise on oneiromancy, now lost, which seems to have been quite influential. Others influenced by the mystical tradition include Cicero and the first Christian author of a dream theory, Tertullian.

*f.* One of the most remarkable aspects of the ancients' attitude toward dreams was their reliance on specialists for dream interpretation. Three types of oneiromancers can be distinguished: the "popular" soothsayers plied their trade in public places; learned dream specialists consulted specialized works and gave consultations in their homes or in temples as well as at markets and banquets; and an elite group wrote treatises on the meaning of dreams, usually supported by case studies drawn from their own experience and that of other specialists, transmitted orally or in writing. The oneiromantic literature seems to have been abundant, but only a small portion of it has survived.[21]

Although divination by means of dreams was popular among the ancients, it was considered less important and less dignified than divination by means of sacrificial entrails and birds. Augurs and haruspices were priests and as such more highly esteemed than oneiromancers.[22]

Oneiromancy was disturbing to nonspecialists because it yielded multiple interpretations dependent on individual and collective factors. Artemidorus made extensive use of what has been called the "law of antithesis," a tradition "according to which dreams could announce precisely the opposite of their content."[23]

## B. Changing Attitudes toward Dreams between the Second and Fourth Centuries

As E. R. Dodds has pointed out, pagans and Christians in this period coexisted in an anxious climate, which affected their dreams.[24] A flourishing interest in dreams and dream theory is evident in the East, as can be seen from the works cited below. Dreams played a substantial role in the philosophical revival that took place in the third century, particularly among neo-Platonists in those crossroads cities of religion, philosophy, and culture, Alexandria and Rome. Plotinus and his disciples Porphyry and Iamblichus brought dreams into their philosophy, which sought to put the individual into direct contact with God through ecstasy and contemplation.[25]

In addition to Artemidorus of Daldis's *Oneirocriticon* (second century A.D.),[26] there is evidence that the dream theories of the learned and the traditionally distinct oneiromancy of the populace tended to converge. Artemidorus indicates that in writing his treatise and compiling lists of dreams to be included he consulted not merely his own well-stocked library on the subject but also "the soothsayers of the marketplace."[27]

Much use was made of the practice of stimulating dreams by incubation, associated with the temples of certain healing gods such as Serapis and especially Asclepios. Aelius Aristides, an adept of this practice, has left an extraordinary account in his *Sacred Tales,* in which he tells of cures in the temples of Serapis and Asclepios.[28] Although he received therapeutic formulas directly from the god, he seems to have been even more interested in the personal contact with the deity, whose apparitions, perceived as "real," left him ecstatic. The god also commanded him to engage in extremely intense activity such as running and swimming in cold water. The work thus reveals the power of a personal religion in which dreams were a means of contact with divinity.[29] The afflicted joined therapists and others interested in dreams in endless discussions of the dreams stimulated by incubation and their meaning. Here we encounter the notion of a link between dreams and health that can also be found in the Middle Ages, for example in Hildegarde of Bingen's *Causae et curae* (twelfth century). Aelius Aristides marks the appearance of a literary genre that Georg Misch has aptly named "oneiric autobiography," autobiography in which the salient events are healing or premonitory dreams or perhaps simply dreams illuminated by the presence of a god.[30] In some respects Augustine's *Confessions* are an oneiric autobiography, and Guibert of Nogent's twelfth-century *De vita sua* is even more so. The autobiographical tales collected by Julio Caro Baroja in his astonishing sixteenth-century work, *Vidas mágicas,* are yet another manifestation of a genre of which examples can also be found in Romantic and Surrealist writing.[31]

If Artemidorus with his vast experience and broad knowledge of the sources is to be believed, the social and political structure and intellectual climate of the Greek city had a profound influence on dream interpretation. The meaning of a dream depended not only on the character of the dreamer but even more on his occupation, legal status, and social position. The *Interpretation of Dreams* contains a typology based on occupation and civic function. The meaning of a dream depended on whether the dreamer was a citizen, a slave, or a metic. There were profound differences between the dreams of men and women. Relations between parents and children are a recurrent topic of the treatise. But the advent of Christianity changed the nature of the city profoundly, and this proved to be a handicap to an oneiromancy so deeply enmeshed in the ancient urban structure. In pagan (especially Greek) cities in late antiquity there was also widespread hostility to divination, which affected oneiromancy and diminished its capacity to resist the onslaught of Christianity.

In this and other areas, such as sexuality and the quest for God, Peter Brown, Paul Veyne, Michel Foucault, and Aline Rousselle have shown that the great change in sensibilities and behaviors that would triumph with Christianity actually began in the pagan world of late antiquity.

In the late fourth century at least one very important treatise reveals a tendency toward "democratization" of dreams. At the same time, and as if in counterpoint, dreamers themselves were categorized according to a traditional hierarchy.

The democratization of dreams is evident in the work of the Greek neo-Platonist Synesius of Cyrene (ca. 370–414). A member of an important family that claimed to descend from the kings of Sparta, Synesius, who once delivered a speech "On Royalty" to the Emperor Arcadius, later converted to Christianity and became bishop of Ptolemais. A number of treatises from his Christian period have survived. He was still a pagan when he wrote the astonishing work *On Dreams* (περὶ ἐνυπνίων), in which he counseled that there was no need to resort to oneiromancers because every man and woman was capable of interpreting his or her own dreams. He saw this, moreover, as one of man's fundamental rights. To each his own dreams and their interpretation. No authoritarian state or tyrant could deprive anyone of this right. Sleep and dreams were the prime domain of individual liberty.[32]

The most comprehensive ancient treatise on dreams is Macrobius' *Commentarius in Somnium Scipionis,* which dates from the end of the fourth century.[33] Macrobius (born circa 360; died after 422) was a member of a small but important group of writers and encyclopedists who began as pagans but died Christians and who attempted to condense and popularize the classical liberal arts and the philosophy and science of antiquity. The last and most illustrious representative of this group was Isidore of Seville. The dream theory set forth by Macrobius in his *Commentary on the Dream of Scipio* became the key to a renaissance in the study of dreams in the twelfth century, exemplified by the pseudo-Augustine's *De spiritu et anima* and by John of Salisbury's *Policraticus.* In particular, Macrobius stressed the traditional idea that there is a hierarchy of dreamers, and that only the dreams of persons invested with supreme authority could be regarded as authentic and irrefutable premonitory dreams. In a closely reasoned argument he questions the validity of basing a dream theory on Scipio's dream, since at the time of the dream Scipio was neither the leader of a city nor a supreme magistrate. Nevertheless, the distinction of both his natural father (Aemilius Paulus) and his adoptive father (Scipio Africanus), as well as his cultivation and innate gifts, entitled him to dream an authentic dream about the destruction of Carthage for which he would be responsible. Macrobius thus reaffirmed the notion of a hierarchy of dreamers (including the special case of the royal dream), a legacy of earliest antiquity that would later be revived in medieval Christian dream theories.

But the dominant dream typology in the ancient world involved classification according to the nature of the dream, and two pagan intellectuals in the fourth century gave its definitive formulation. The neo-Platonic philosopher Chalcidius included a brief treatise on dreams in chapters 250–256 of a Latin commentary on Plato's *Timaeus*, in which he distinguished three types of dreams according to their origin. The first and third types were further subdivided into two categories, yielding five types of dreams in all:

I. Dreams that originate in the soul. These are divided into two subcategories:

    A. Dreams stimulated by external impression and without significance for the future. These dreams were described by the word *somnium*, the Latin equivalent of the Greek ἐνύπνιον and φάντασμα.

    B. Dreams produced by the superior part of the soul but generally obscure. The word for such dreams was *visum* or ὄνειρος.

II. Dreams containing information transmitted by angels or demons sent by God. In this case the word was *admonito* (χρηματισμός).

III. Dreams that came directly from God, which were therefore clear. These corresponded to the Greek category ὅραμα.[34]

But the most complete statement of the five-part typology was given by Macrobius in his *Commentary on the Dream of Scipio*. Two categories of dream were without "utility or significance." These corresponded to Virgil's "false dreams." The first was the *insomnium* (ἐνύπνιον), which could have three sources: soul, body, or fortune. The second was the *visum* (φάντασμα), which attacked the sleeper in the early stages of sleep with fleeting and illusory forms. Macrobius added a further category, the ἐπιάλτης, corresponding to our nightmare. In common parlance ( *publica persuasio*, interpreted by some historians of religion to mean popular culture) this word referred to oppressive sensations during sleep. Freud's biographer and disciple Ernest Jones, who ascribes the invention of the nightmare to the Middle Ages, has persuaded me that the ἐπιάλτης, which Macrobius does not translate into Latin, should be eliminated from the five-part dream typology.[35] The three remaining categories of true or premonitory dreams were thus the *oraculum* (χρηματισμός), in which a relative, "holy" person (especially a priest), or divinity revealed a future event;

the *visio* (ὅραμα), which revealed an image of the future as it would come to pass; and the *somnium* (ὄνειφος), which foretold the future, but darkly. Thus, pagan antiquity's last word on dreams reaffirmed a typology based on the nature of the dream.

Finally, just as certain cities began to proscribe divination, on a broader level the "state" tended to view all forms of divination, including oneiromancy, as magic, which was repressed and condemned "for reasons of state."[36] Although traditional forms of oneiromancy were still flourishing at the time of Christianity's triumph, repression was increasingly the order of the day.

## III. Christian Doubts

Prior to the fourth century and the recognition of Christianity as an authorized and then official religion, Christians showed first an interest in dreams, then anxiety about them, and finally, uncertainty.

### A. Increased Interest in Dreams

It is striking that at least until the middle of the third century, Christians exhibited such a lively interest in dreams that in many texts they were closely associated with important aspects of contemporary Christian life: conversion, contact with God, and martyrdom.

*a. Dreams and conversion.* Conversion to Christianity was often associated with dreaming. Thus Origen (185–254) wrote in *Contra Celsum* (1.46): "Many came to Christianity in spite of themselves, a certain spirit having turned their hearts from hatred of the doctrine to resolution to die for it by presenting them with a *vision or dream* (ὕπαρ ἢ ὄναρ). I have seen many examples of this. If I were to put them down in writing, eyewitness though I was, I would offer a broad target for the derision of unbelievers, who would think that I too, like others whom they suspect of having forged such fictions, am telling them stories. But God is witness of my conscience and of his desire to confirm, not by fraudulent stories, but by clear and multifaceted truths, the divine teaching of Jesus."[37] Note the distinction between vision and dream, which would assume such importance in the Middle Ages.

*b. Dreams and contact with God.* Dreams and visions were also a means of access to God, an opportunity for direct contact with the deity. No one expressed this better than Tertullian (160–240), the first great Christian theorist of dreams: "Most men owe their knowledge of God to visions" (*De anima* 47.2).[38]

According to Saint Cyprian, God is permanently present in every Christian by way of dreams and visions, and above all that supreme form of dream known to a few Christians, namely, ecstasy. "That is why the divine governance is constantly correcting us night and day. In addition to nocturnal visions, by day the Holy Spirit fills us in ecstasy with the innocence of children and makes us see with our eyes, hear, and speak the admonitions and instruction that God makes us worthy to receive."[39]

Adapting the ancient hierarchy of dreamers to a Christian context, Cyprian claims for bishops, himself among them, the privilege of being especially favored by God to receive visions and to be questioned by God, as were Old Testament patriarchs and prophets. In letter 11 he makes this point twice: "Indeed, and this is the main reason that has impelled me to write you, and you will know that, because the Lord has deigned to reveal himself in us (*sicut Dominus ostendere et reuelare dignatur*), it was said to us in a vision . . . (*dictum esse in visione*)." Later he adds: "For not long ago this reproach was also made to us, my dear brothers, in a vision (*per visionem*), that we are somnolent in our prayers and do not speak to God like people who are awake."

Here, however, Cyprian is distorting the traditional link between visions and dreams among both Christians and pagans. Without specifying the state he was in when he had the visions that he reports, he exhorts Christians to avoid sleep and maintain a constant vigil, thus depriving them of the principal opportunity for dreaming: "Shake off and break the bonds of sleep, and pray urgently and attentively in accordance with the precept of the apostle Paul: 'Persevere in prayer and stay awake while praying.' Indeed, the apostles never ceased to pray, day or night." We detect an opposition between prayer and sleep, hence also between prayer and dreams.

*c. Dreams and martyrdom.* In the new Christian hierarchy of dreamers, it is hardly surprising to find the martyr, the Christian hero par excellence, ranked above the bishop. By dint of virtue and sacrifice, martyrs were worthy of the noblest visions, those that revealed the afterlife and the future. Consider one notable example, the visions of the martyrs Perpetua and Saturus in the celebrated *Passio S. Perpetuae et Felicitatis,* based on notes dictated by Perpetua in prison, which recounts the martyrdom in 203 of a small group of Christians in Carthage. This group was so plainly associated with Tertullian that some scholars have argued that he must have been the author of this Passion.

The text recounts five visions experienced in prison by Perpetua and one of her companions, Saturus. Four were Perpetua's, two concerning herself and her companions and revealing the future and two concerning a younger brother and offering a glimpse of the other world. Saturus's vision added further details to what Perpetua's visions had revealed about the future of the group of martyrs.

Two features of these accounts of dream-visions are worth noting. First, the martyrs are *worthy* of receiving them, particularly Perpetua. Indeed, her merits are such that she even has the right to *demand* a vision and to converse with God.

The first time it is her brother who urges her to ask God to reveal the future in a vision: "Then my brother said to me, 'Honored sister, you already possess such great merit that you are worthy of asking for a vision, and you will be shown whether it is martyrdom or release that awaits us" (Domina soror, iam in magna dignatione es, tanta ut postules visionem et ostendatur tibi). Perpetua, knowing that she can converse with God (Et ego quae me sciebam fabulari cum Domino) did ask, and in response she was shown a vision (Et postulavi et ostensum est mihi hoc). She saw a ladder bristling with arms rising up to heaven, with a dragon at its foot. Saturus helps her to mount this dragon, which carries her to a large garden where she is welcomed by a shepherd dressed all in white, who gives her a piece of cheese to eat. From this she understands that martyrdom lies in store.

Her next two dreams offer a first glimpse of what would later become Purgatory.[40] Without doing anything to bring it about, Perpetua is shown a vision of a young brother who had died some time earlier and who is suffering in an unfriendly garden in the other world. This time she prays that her young brother be given to her (ut mihi donaretur), in other words, that he be delivered from his trial. In another vision on the eve of her martyrdom she sees a strange vision of the combat in which she will engage the next day, not with the beasts but with the devil.[41] Saturus is also blessed with a premonitory vision (Et Saturus benedictus hanc visionem suam edidit) in which he sees himself and his companions welcomed into Paradise. "Such are the noteworthy visions of the most blessed martyrs Saturus and Perpetua, dictated by themselves."[42]

## B. From Dreams to Heresy

Within a short time, however, Christian leaders discovered a connection between dreams and heresy. After Judas, Christianity's first great sinner was Simon Magus, the first heretic in Samaria according to the

Acts of the Apostles (8:9–25). His controversies with Peter and Philip, who brought back into the Church the many disciples he had seduced, became legendary. Saint Irenaeus in his *Treatise against Heretics* (late second century) described Simon Magus and his followers as "sowers of dreams": they relied "on demons known as *paradromes* and *oniropompes.*" Similarly, in the apocryphal Gospel of Nicodemus, or Acts of Pontius Pilate, Pilate's wife dreams a dream instigated by a magician.

Saint Hippolytus (third century) speaks in his *Commentary on Daniel* (4.19) of a religious leader who uses visions and dreams to deceive many disciples, to whom he falsely heralds the end of the world: "He was head of a church in Pontus, a pious and modest man who, lacking solid knowledge of Scripture, placed greater credence in his own visions (τοῖς ὁράμασιν οἷς ἀυτὸς ἑώρα). After a first, a second, and a third dream (ἐφ ἑνὶ καὶ δευτέρω καὶ τρίτῳ ἐνυπνίῳ), he began to forecast the future to his brothers as though he were a prophet: 'This is what I have seen, this is what awaits ignorant and thoughtless men who with all their zeal place their faith in human traditions and in their own errors and dreams (τοῖς ἑαυτῶν ἐνυπνίοις), in myths and old wives' tales.'"

Attempts to establish direct contact with God and to reveal the future through visions and dreams played an important role in many sects declared heretical by the Church and especially among those important rivals of the Christians, the Gnostics. Dreams and visions were a major interest of the Ebionites or Nazarenes, a Judeo-Christian sect that was probably at the root of gnostic beliefs. Its core group consisted of descendants of the first Christian community in Jerusalem who emigrated during the war between the Jews and the Romans in A.D. 66–70, crossing the Jordan to Pella; it was responsible for the so-called *Clementine (or pseudo-Clementine) Homilies,* which were continually revised down to the fourth century.

Another influential sect was composed of disciples of Valentine, an Egyptian who preached in Rome in the middle of the second century; their beliefs are known from the *Gospel of Truth* found at Nag Hamadi in Egypt. In Valentinian gnosticism, man is made of three elements: the pneumatic or spiritual, which returns to the father; the psychic, which remains at the gates of Pleroma (symbolizing the plenitude, totality, and inexpressible richness of God's being), and the *hylic* or material, which is destroyed. In particular, the pneumatic element includes dreams and visions in which the ascent out of the material and toward the Father can be seen and which contribute to that ascent.

The gnostic sect of Capocrates, centered in Rome in the mid-second century, was accused by Christians of amoral behavior and debauchery. The fact that members of this sect attached great importance to dreams and visions helped to discredit dream interpretation among orthodox Christians.

Ecstatic visions and dreams were further discredited by their importance to the followers of Montanus, a Phrygian who between 160 and 170 fell into ecstatic trances during which he issued prophetic warnings. Tertullian joined the Montanists sometime around 205, and ecstasy occupied an important place in his dream typology. Many members of this ascetic, prophetic, and millenarian sect went to Pepuza in Phrygia to await the descent to earth of the heavenly Jerusalem. The connection they saw between ecstasy, dreams, and prophecy further compromised the interpretation of dreams in the eyes of the orthodox Church.[43] In spite of this, an orthodox bishop like Saint Cyprian did not hesitate in the middle of the third century to see ecstasy as a peculiarly Christian state.

## C. Tertullian and the First Christian Theology of Dreams

Between 210 and 213 Tertullian, at that time a Montanist, composed a treatise on dreams that has been preserved as chapters 45–49 of his *De anima*. Thus it was a semi-heretic who elaborated the first coherent Christian theory of dreams, from which we can gain a good idea of Christianity's uncertainty with respect to oneiric phenomena.[44]

*a. The dream, between sleep and death.* The place that Tertullian's theory of dreams occupies in *De anima* is worth noting. It comes between sections on sleep and death. Tertullian refers to dreams (*somnia*) as the business of sleep (*negotia somni*). Thus dreaming, though it occurs in sleep, is considered a part of the active life. Yet a dream is nothing but an accident of sleep, and its activity depends on the movements of the soul, which is always mobile. The soul, liberated from external influences during sleep, emits productions of its own, dreams among them.[45]

After what is apparently a digression on dreams, Tertullian returns to the main theme of his argument: death. Although he seems to be influenced by the ancient tradition of a link between dreams and death, he denies that death is a repository of dreams. After death, he believes, the soul either goes to Hell or awaits resurrection in the flesh, except for the souls of martyrs, which go directly to Paradise. No soul can return from Hell, and if in our visions we think we see returned souls, they are *phantasms* sent to us by demons.[46]

b. *There are true dreams.* Although Tertullian was suspicious of dreams, he believes that "true" dreams exist and almost goes as far as to say that dreaming is a part of human nature. "Who could be so alien to the human condition," he writes, "that he never once perceived a faithful vision" (Quis autem tam extraneus humanitatis ut non aliquam aliquando visionem fidelem senserit? *De anima* 46.3).

Drawing upon his vast knowledge of "pagan" culture, Tertullian listed a whole series of prophetic dreams of the Greeks and Latins that predicted the future acquisition of some sort of power or a danger that lay in store for the dreamer or an impending confrontation with death.

c. *A tripartite dream typology based on origins.* Tertullian begins by asserting the need for a Christian doctrine on dreams. He is familiar with most of the pagan theories on the subject. He knows that Epicurus was hostile to dreams, that Aristotle believed that dreams are generally pointless but occasionally "true," and that the inhabitants of Telmessa in Lycia of whom Cicero spoke impugned not the dream but the interpreter if a prediction turned out to be wrong. He himself made extensive use of the now lost treatise on dreams by Hermippus of Berytus, a contemporary of Hadrian who was probably also an important source for Artemidorus.

Sifting through these divergent opinions, Tertullian settled on a typology according to origins. He adapted the classifications found in his sources to the needs of Christianity. Accordingly he held that most dreams are sent by demons. At the beginning of chapter 47 he says: Definimus enim a daemoniis plurimum incubi somnia. Occasionally good demons send true and profitable (vera et gratiosa) dreams, but more often they are "vain, deceptive, disturbing, and lubricious" (vana et frustatoria et turbida et ludibriosa).

God, however, also sends prophetic dreams. Tertullian argues (47.2) that most men come to know God through visions. Even pagans may be so blessed. Yet evil demons are constantly seeking to tempt even saints with dreams by day and by night.

A third category consists of those dreams instigated by the soul itself in response to circumstances (tertia species erunt somnia quae sibimet ipsa anima videtur inducere ex intentione circumstantiarum).

Like many other Christians of his time and even more like heretics such as the Montanists, Tertullian identifies a fourth "form" (rather than origin) of dreams, namely, those associated with ecstasy (ea autem, quae neque a deo neque a daemonio neque ab anima videbuntur accidere . . . ipsi proprie ecstasi et rationi eius separabuntur).

Contrary to the assertions of the comic poet Epicharmus, however, the soul and ecstasy do not produce dreams by chance (non est ex arbitrio somniare . . . quomodo ipsa erit sibi causa alicujus visionis).

In chapter 48 Tertullian discusses the conditions under which man produces dreams, whether through his soul or through his body. Dreams occur primarily at the end of night and the period of sleep, at different times depending on the season. They also depend on the position of the sleeper's body, his diet, and his degree of sobriety. Sobriety and fasting are favorable to dreams. Far from preventing ecstasy, as some argue, they encourage it to flourish in God (ita non ad ecstasin summovendam sobrietas proficiet, sed ad ipsam ecstasin commendandam, ut in deo fiat).

*d. Dreaming is possible anywhere: against incubation.*    Tertullian condemns any attempt to confine dream interpretation to a particular place, such as the *sacrarium* of an oracle (46.13) or a temple in which incubation was practiced (48.3). Incubation is nothing but a superstition. "The force [of the soul or ecstasy] is not circumscribed by the boundaries of sacred places. It wanders, flying here and there, and remains free. No one can doubt that houses are open to demons and that men are encircled by 'images' not only in sacred places but even in their rooms" (46.13).[47] Furthermore, "it is a superstition to prescribe fasting for those who practice incubation near oracles in order to obtain cures [for their ills]."[48]

Incubation nevertheless survived under Christianity. The hagiographic compilations of Gregory of Tours mention numerous instances of incubation near the tombs of saints in the hope of receiving a healing formula in a dream, and instances of incubation were still being recounted in the late Middle Ages.[49]

*e. Everyone dreams.*    Caught between belief in dreams and suspicion of them, Tertullian nevertheless insists that dreaming is a universal human phenomenon. In his final chapter on dreams, chapter 49, he extends the dream experience to all mankind. Small children dream, opinions to the contrary notwithstanding, and the Atlantes of Libya, said to sleep a blind sleep, may also dream. To be sure, the dreams of barbarians and of tyrants like Nero are inspired by demons, but dreams also emanate from God (sed et a deo deducimus somnia). Can he not send dreams to the Atlantes or any other people on earth? It is wrong to assume that any soul is immune from dreams (dum ne animae aliqua natura credatur immunis somniorum).

Thus, despite his uncertainties, Tertullian lent his authority to the new universality in dream theories, which a little less than two centuries later would result in the democratization of dream interpretation as taught by Synesius.

## IV. Genesis of a Christian Oneirology

Between the fourth and the seventh centuries a Christian oneirology took shape in theory and practice. In the works of the Church Fathers, however, we find no statement of doctrine concerning dreams, and not until Gregory the Great and Isidore of Seville do we come upon a succinct and comprehensive statement of the Christian view. For the most part we must infer early Christian attitudes from brief or inadvertent remarks. About practice we know very little. Many dreams were not recorded, either because they were deemed unworthy of being written down or because suspicious ecclesiastical authorities wanted them left out of the tradition. Other dreams were recorded, but they often give the appearance of having been dressed up for literary purposes, watered down or altered by self-censorship or ecclesiastical control. Some are little more than cultural commonplaces. Nevertheless, it is possible to say something about Christian attitudes toward dreams and to describe the broad outlines of Christian oneirology.

### A. Major Changes and Suspicion

Attitudes and doctrine concerning dreams had begun to change in pagan antiquity, but Christianity introduced profound changes and the Church attempted to persuade its followers not to engage in the interpretation of dreams.

*a. Expanding the range of significant dreams.*   Nevertheless, Christianity seems to have brought about profound cultural changes that resulted in much broader criteria for judging whether or not a dream was meaningful. Ancient oneirocriticism from Homer to Artemidorus and Macrobius was concerned only with prophetic dreams. True dreams, those which passed through the gate of horn, were useful and significant because they could be used to predict the future. False dreams, which passed through the gate of ivory, were meaningless because they had nothing to say about the future.

By contrast, Christian oneirocriticism was potentially applicable to all dreams, and all dreams were potentially meaningful. This was in part a result of the "democratization" of dreaming alluded to earlier and in part a consequence of the omnipresence of the divine will (whether directly effective or apparently thwarted by the deceptions of demons or the sins of man). God's will affected all human activities, especially those involving close contact with the supernatural.[50]

But the apparent triumph of the dream cut two ways. Every dream was now meaningful, but some were true and others false, for the distinction between true and false dreams was maintained. What new criteria determined a dream's truth?

*b. Suppression of dream interpretation and condemnation of divination by dreams.* Christianity did away with all those whose special skill was the interpretation of dreams. Divination by dreams was prohibited at an early date. Canon 23 of the First Council of Ankara (314) decreed: "All who observe auguries or auspices or dreams or divinations of any kind according to the custom of the pagans or who invite men into their homes for the purpose of conducting inquiries by the art of magic . . . shall confess and do penance for five years."[51] Since no one took the place of the traditional oneiromancers, the Christians were left to their own devices when it came to the interpretation of dreams, whereas their ancestors had relied on specialists when it was a matter of any importance. For centuries this created a type of society that deserves more study than it has yet received, a society in which dreaming was impeded, which suffered from disorientation in the oneiric realm.

Early medieval dreamers did of course manage to muddle through. The prohibition against incubation was not universally respected, as we have seen. In practice men and women probably continued to turn to "sorcerers" and "witches" for the interpretation of their dreams, and some no doubt turned to the new men of learning, monks and priests. But they did so in a semiclandestine manner; the tolerance of the Church was provisional and might be revoked at any time.

*c. Triumph of classification by origin.* Until the twelfth century there was only one Christian dream typology based on three possible sources of dreams: God, demons, and man through either the body (as a consequence of diet, physical constitution, illness, etc.) or the soul (memory, purity/impurity, and—the ultimate—ecstasy). Whether by inadvertence or by design, however, official Christianity never adopted clear criteria for determining the origin of a dream. Given the difficulty of distinguishing between good (God-inspired dreams), evil (demon-inspired ones), or mixed good and evil (human-inspired), the Christian attitude toward dreams was fundamentally one of suspicion.

## B. The Reasons for Mistrust

From the fourth century onward a variety of factors combined to make dreams and their interpretation objects of growing mistrust. Associated with the body, dreams, along with gesticulation, laughter, and sexuality, were viewed as demonic, hence suspect. (Ironically, since the sixteenth century, and especially in the nineteenth and twentieth centuries, these behaviors have been regarded as specifically human.)

*a. The diabolization of dreams.*   In the fourth century Christians made a fundamental change in the way they viewed the supernatural world, what I call the reduction to Unity (*la réduction à l'Un*). Even in the pagan religions of late antiquity there had been a strong tendency for polytheistic beliefs to condense into some form of monotheism. Now the diversity of aerial divinities was similarly reduced. Pagan demons were both good and bad, but in late antiquity they were divided into two more or less distinct groups, good on one side, bad on the other. Christianity consecrated this distinction by calling the good demons angels and limiting the use of the term *demon* to evil spirits. The angels became God's militia and served as divine messengers, delivering among other things "true" dreams, whereas the demons were unified under the command of a general—Satan—who was admittedly inferior to God yet capable with God's permission of deceiving sinful mankind.

This resulted in what I consider to be a fundamental change in the tripartite typology of dreams. Whereas Tertullian still saw false dreams as inspired by *demons* (in the plural), now they were said to be inspired by *the* Devil, by Satan himself (in the singular). The entry on the scene of the Enemy of man led to an association between dreams and the domain of Satan.

*b. Dreams and heresy.*   The Church's mistrust of dreams was exacerbated by the extreme importance attached to visions and dreams in certain heresies, particularly those of Gnostic stripe. Eusebius, in his early fourth-century *Ecclesiastical History* (5.28.7–12) recounts, in a manner that reveals persistent uncertainty as to the value of visions, the story of a disciple of the heretic Artemon Natalias, who had been favored with a number of visions in which Jesus called upon him to abandon his errors (δι' ὁραμάτων πολλάκις ἐνουθετεῖτο ὑπὸ τοῦ κυρίου), but who paid little attention to these visions (ἐπεὶ δὲ ῥαθυμότερον τοῖς ὁράμασιν προσεῖχεν). Eusebius was still influenced by the early Christian notion of contact with God through dreams, especially in the case of a "confessor" (ὁμολογητής).

After Christianity gained first toleration and then recognition as the official religion, the church hierarchy sought to exert tighter control over the religious life of the faithful. In particular, it sought to prevent direct contact between God and the faithful, that is, contact without the benefit of the Church as intermediary. Dreams were viewed with suspicion because they were seen as a way of circumventing the Church's role as mediator.

*c. The future belongs to God alone.* For pagans the great attraction of dreams was that certain ones were thought to reveal the future. But in the Christian religion the future was the province of God alone. God voluntarily relinquished parts of his province to man, including dominion over time and knowledge. In the twelfth and thirteenth centuries grave theological difficulties arose when men sought to sell what belonged to God alone, namely, time (by means of usury) and knowledge (by means of payments by students to their teachers). As for knowledge of the future, no human technique could wrest this privilege from God, and God only rarely shared his secret with selected humans. Certain saints were warned by visions of their impending deaths, and certain sinners were chosen by God to journey in a dream to the other world, with the idea that the sight of the punishment of souls in Hell and Purgatory and the beatitude of souls in Heaven's outer precincts would incite them to repent and prepare for salvation. But for these extremely rare exceptions, dreams ceased to foretell the future.

*d. Dreams and sex.* Dreams were also compromised by their association with sexuality. The devil inspired dreams that stirred the flesh, particularly the sex organs, as part of his temptation, and man's lustful body and concupiscent soul produced images in his dreams that were repressed by his conscious mind. When man slept he was prey to indecent dreams. The temptations of the night assailed him. Dreams were the cause of "nocturnal pollutions." As time went by the temptations of Saint Anthony were increasingly represented in sexual terms. No one did more to cast dreams in this light than Augustine.

## C. Augustine and Dreams

It would be surprising if Augustine, who had such a profound influence on the entire period from late antiquity to the Industrial Revolution, had not played an important role in this as in other respects. Here I can touch only briefly on his contribution. Interested readers may wish to consult the work of Pierre Courcelle and Martine Dulaey.[52]

*a. Africa and dreams: oneiric autobiography.* With learning and perspicacity Pierre Courcelle has helped us to understand Augustine's attitudes toward dreams in relation to his African milieu. I had best let him speak for himself:

> Another autobiographical tradition that enjoyed considerable influence in Africa in the third and fourth centuries was of Hellenistic origin and involved accounts of visions, which, as Festugière points out, permitted the author "to put himself forward and as it were offer us his confession."[53]
>
> In the African churches of Tertullian's day visions that occurred during services were carefully recorded in the form of first-person accounts. Such visions were common not only among Montanists but also in the bosom of the Great Church, where they were especially numerous in times of persecution. Both daytime and nighttime visions were involved, the latter being dreams. Christians imprisoned and awaiting interrogation and martyrdom experienced numerous visions, which they took care to communicate to their companions either orally or in writing. These became the bases of hagiographies. We find such first-person accounts inserted unaltered in the gravest of documents. . . . These visions were characterized by suddenness, often signaled by the word *ecce,* and apparent reality, signaled by the word *quasi.* The visionary generally both saw and heard a heavenly creature, either Christ or an angel or a martyr or another deceased individual. . . . Augustine, like his African contemporaries, read and appreciated these autobiographical accounts of visions. He mentions several times the *Passio Perpetuae,* a text that was on occasion read out as part of the service prior to his sermons. . . . He also recorded visions experienced by friends and acquaintances.[54]

This passage confirms several points made earlier. Certain Hellenistic traditions survived in Christian attitudes. The dreams of martyrs enjoyed a special status. Visions were popular among heretics such as the Montanists. Both pagans and Christians in the fourth century, and especially Africans, had a lively interest in dreams and their interpretation. Finally, many dreams involved more than one of the senses, especially sight and hearing.

Yet the combination of words indicating the apparent reality of these visions with expressions of incredulity on the part of Augustine discloses the existence of certain doubts. As Courcelle observes, the *ecce* suggests truth but the *quasi* betrays doubt. In the *Confessions* Augustine presents himself as the hero of an oneiric autobiography of the sort that his contemporaries in Africa found so interesting. In his conversion, the great event of his life, dreams play a major role. His mother has a dream that predicts that he will convert. (The climate is both pagan and Christian, so prophetic dreams are in order, and Augustine can without undue pride portray his life as one of privileged contact with God.) In the twelfth century Guibert of Nogent would tell the story of his life by intertwining his own dreams with those of his mother. Similarly, Augustine and Monica form a couple, a fact of fundamental importance in both Augustine's earthly life and his religious vocation. By attributing the first dream of his conversion to his mother he was emphasizing the importance of dreams in his life.

While Augustine lies gravely ill, Monica in a dream sees a young man who assures her not only that he will recover physically but that he will in the future be healed spiritually as well. On the "wooden rule" on which she is standing she sees a "shining youth" and then Augustine himself, and she hears God say: "That where she was, there was I also." (*Confessions,* 3.11.19, Pusey translation).

A convert by the time he wrote the *Confessions,* Augustine was in no doubt as to the meaning of the dream. The young man who consoled his mother and predicted his conversion was none other than God himself or an angel sent by him (common in African visions, as Courcelle noted).

Augustine's conversion, which took place in August of 386, nine years after his mother's dream, is described in the famous garden scene at Milan (*Confessions* 8.12.28–29, cited below after the translation by E. B. Pusey). After a conversation with his friend Alypius, Augustine succumbs to a fit of crying, during which he asks God "How long? How long, Lord, wilt thou be angry, for ever? . . . How long? how long, tomorrow and tomorrow?" (Et tu, domine, usquequo? usquequo, domine, irasceris in finem? . . . Quamdiu, quamdiu cras et cras?) Then he lies down in his garden at Milan, underneath a fig tree. He hears a voice coming "from a neighboring house, as of a boy or girl . . . chanting and oft repeating 'Take up and read; Take up and read'"

(Tolle, lege). Then he opens the Gospels and his eyes fall on a passage from Paul's Epistle to the Romans 13:13: "Not in rioting and drunkenness, not in chambering and wantonness, not in strife and envying: but put ye on the Lord Jesus Christ, and make not provision for the flesh in concupiscence."

The interpretation of this scene has been the subject of much discussion. I agree with Courcelle that Augustine heard what he took to be a supernatural voice bearing the word of God (quasi *pueri an puellae*, like the voice of a small boy or girl). He thus experienced what might be called (with apologies for the mixed metaphor) an auditory vision. His conversion then falls within the ancient Christian tradition of conversion through a dream (in this case brought on by Augustine's words to God). Even though the *Confessions* go far beyond the traditional oneiric autobiography, the heart of the work belongs to that tradition.

*b. Augustine's growing distrust of dreams.* As Martine Dulaey points out, Augustine, while still a pagan, seems to have based his theory on Cicero's doctrine, which can be summed up by the following formula: "Dreams are generally misleading, but. . . ." He asked his mother how she distinguished between true and false dreams, but she was able to supply no more than a vague criterion: "a special taste, impossible to explain in words" (Courcelle, p. 103).

Shortly after his conversion, late in 387, Augustine was apparently still taking his inspiration from Cicero (*De divinatione* 2.128 and 2.139), from whom he borrowed the following definition (*De quantitate animae* 33.71): "At regular intervals the soul withdraws from the exercise of the senses. It repairs their activity by taking a vacation, as it were. It combines innumerable manifold images with which it has been supplied by their agency. That is what makes sleep and dreams."

He was interested in what went on inside man (especially in the soul) and what could appear in dreams. Taking an approach reminiscent of Tertullian's, he borrowed from the neo-Platonist Porphyry the idea that the soul is carried by the *pneuma* and therefore possesses powers of imagination. Dreams are among the images produced by the soul.[55] Yet his correspondence with Nebridius shows that he also believed that demons (good as well as evil) played a part in the production of dreams.[56] In any case he was interested not so much in elaborating a theory of dreams as in recording a few remarks based on observation of concrete psychological facts.

His *De genesi ad litteram* 12.18 (circa 414) contains a rough classification of dreams. Broadly speaking he divides them into two groups, true and false. True dreams are further divided into two subgroups, clear and symbolic. This is nothing but the bare skeleton of the pagan theory that gave rise to the five-part typology. But Augustine is interested in finding a criterion for distinguishing between true and false dreams. With his mother's experience in mind, perhaps, he speculates that in false dreams the soul is perturbed (*perturbata*), whereas in true dreams it is calm (*tranquilla*).[57] He also discusses the notions of *phantasia* and *phantasma*.[58]

Ultimately he combines internal and external factors to arrive at a theory not unlike the prevailing Christian typology based on origin. He begins with man, body and soul. The soul is at the root of the process, however, and plays the leading role. Yet external stimulus also has a part to play. Dreams are inspired by spirits: angels or demons.[59] Diabolical dreams exist. (Augustine had read the confession of Saint Cyprian, written some time between 360 and 370, in which it is said that Cyprian saw "the devil and his court.") Nevertheless, Augustine does not place much emphasis on the devil or demons as originators of dreams. Angels for their part produce numerous visions, upon which they direct "the intentional force of the soul," but it is the soul that plays the key role. "Everything takes place within man's spirit, even if angels come from outside."[60] Dreams that come directly from God are quite rare, as the experience of his mother Monica proved.

As Augustine grew older his misgivings about dreams apparently increased. While still a pagan in Milan he had gathered a considerable body of information about dreams. As a specialist in the interpretation of dreams he collected accounts of dreams, one of which he recounted at a much later date: "When I was in Milan I heard the following report. A man was hounded for a debt incurred by his father during his lifetime, and he was shown the note his father had signed. The man was saddened and surprised to think that his father had not mentioned this debt on his deathbed, when he made his testament. In his anguish, his father appeared to him in a dream and told him where to find the receipt that canceled the note. He found the document, produced it, rejected the accusation, and even recovered the note that his father had signed, which his father had not reclaimed when he paid off the debt."

As Courcelle notes, "Augustine at first shared the common opinion that the soul of the father, concerned about his son, came to him in sleep in order to deliver him from his worries by providing him with the information he lacked." Later, however, after establishing the "falsity" of a vision that one of his disciples had of him, he ceased altogether to believe in this dream. Subsequently, when he came to consider beliefs about ghosts in *De cura pro mortuis gerenda* (421), he gave vent to his misgivings about dreams in which the dead appeared, for in his view these were associated with the cult of the dead.[61]

His experience as a pastor in the conflict with the Donatists, also much taken by dream visions, made him aware of the links between dreams and heresy. His aversion to the flesh and to concupiscence (particularly in its sexual forms) as a result of his experiences and the nature of his conversion made him acutely aware of the danger of a particularly obtrusive type of dream, the erotic. Earlier, in *De genesi ad litteram* 12.15, he had asked how we know whether men are responsible for sexual dreams and where they come from.[62]

In sum, Augustine reduced dreams to an essentially psychological phenomenon. The soul active in the dream was not yet purified, however, and oneiric images were different from other images. At bottom dreams made Augustine uneasy. As Martine Dulaey observes, he did not regard dreams as a privileged means of access to the truth.

Dream interpretation was not the area in which Augustine had the greatest influence on medieval beliefs and practices. He was imbued with ancient pagan and Christian uncertainties about dreams, and his writings lack a true theory of dreams. Despite the shrewdness of his psychological analyses, therefore, he was not a "doctor of oneirology." His very reserve contributed to early medieval misgivings on the subject.

Nevertheless, with the revival of ancient dream theories in the twelfth century, Augustine's views, unlike the tripartite Christian typology of origins, were not discredited. Because of his interest in the role of the soul or *pneuma* in dreaming, he actually became the father of the new Christian oneirology, and authorship of the treatise that marked the birth of this new discipline, entitled *De spiritu et anima,* was ascribed to him.

## D. Dreams under Surveillance

Because the Church felt such qualms and misgivings about dreams it sought to exert fairly strict control over them. A new elite of dreamers was singled out and authorized to seek the meaning of their dreams. At the same time, dreams helped to impose a new ideology, a new system of values, a new relation with the divine, and a new hierarchy of symbolic power derived in part from dreams.

*a. The new elite.*    The Church agreed to the perpetuation or revival of one traditional elite with respect to dreams, namely, kings. Emperors who converted to Christianity enhanced their prestige through dreams. The two founders of the Christian Empire, Constantine and Theodosius the Great, had previsions of decisive victories over pagan or heretical enemies through dreams, and by stiffening their resolve and bolstering their confidence these visions may have contributed to their success.

Constantine's dream is well known. In 312, on the eve of a decisive battle with Maxentius at the Milvian Bridge, Constantine in broad daylight saw a cross in the sky bearing the words *In hoc signo vinces* (By this sign thou shalt conquer). That night in a dream he saw Christ urging him to place the sign of the cross on a banner. Constantine defeated Maxentius. In the following year he issued the edict of Milan recognizing Christianity and restoring the rights of Christians.[63]

In 394 Theodosius engaged in another decisive battle at Frigidus in Illyria against the pagan usurper Eugenius, a creature of the Frank Arbogast, who, after murdering the legitimate emperor, Valentinian II, Theodosius's brother-in-law, led an army of barbarians, mainly Goths, in an attempt to wrest the Western Empire from the grip of Christianity. Theodosius, on the other hand, sought to reunify the Empire and establish Christianity once and for all. He therefore cast his mission as a holy war, for which he prepared by making pilgrimages and consulting the hermit John in Thebaid.

According to Theodoretus, the first day of battle went very badly for Theodosius and his army, and in the early hours of the following morning the emperor, so exhausted that he could not prevent himself from falling asleep, had a dream: "Shortly before the crowing of the cock, sleep overcame his resolve [to remain awake]. Lying on the ground, he seemed to see two men dressed in white and riding white horses, who commanded him to be bold, to dispel all fear, and to order the soldiers to take up arms and range themselves in order of battle at first light. They said that their mission was to help the soldiers and to fight at their head. And one of them said that he was John the Baptist and the other, the apostle Philip."

A soldier had the same vision and was brought before Theodosius, who commented thus: "'It was not to give me confidence that this vision appeared, for I had confidence in those who promised me the victory, but so that no one should believe that I invented this dream in my desire to fight. That is why He who protects my empire sent this vision to this man also, that he might bear witness to the authenticity of my story. Hence fear no more! Follow those who are protecting us and fighting at our head, and let no one think that victory depends on numbers, for in reality it is in the power of those who lead us!' He said the same thing to the soldiers, and having thus filled them with ardor ordered them to descend from the height of the mountain." Victorious, Theodosius of course became the second founder of the Christian Empire.

Brasseur notes that this story is strikingly reminiscent of two examples of military stratagems given by Frontinus in his treatise *Strategy*. On the eve of battle two generals, one Roman, the other Greek, allegedly told of having seen visions of Castor and Pollux mounted on horseback and proclaiming their readiness to aid in the fight.[64] But this is irrelevant to my purpose here. My point is simply that Christianity adapted the tradition of the royal dream for its own purposes, and that the triumph of Christianity on earth was associated with two dreams.

Chronicles and chansons de geste would also make use of royal dreams. One of the best-known examples occurs in the *Chanson de Roland*, where at four crucial moments in the plot Charlemagne has a prophetic dream.

In addition to the royal dreamer, however, Christianity introduced a new member of the dream elite: the saint. The hagiography of late antiquity and the early Middle Ages is filled with saints' dreams. Here I shall discuss only one case, that of Saint Martin, which is very important in view of the role played by this saint in medieval hagiography and religion.[65]

Martin's hagiographers from Sulpicius Severus to Gregory of Tours placed great stress on the saint's dreams. Consider those reported by Sulpicius Severus. In a first dream (3.3–5) Martin, while still a catechumen, sees Christ appear to him on the night after he has shared his cloak with a pauper. Christ is wearing the half of the cloak that Martin had given to the pauper and says to a host of angels: "This is Martin, a catechumen, who covered me with his cloak." The words of the Gospel, whatsoever thou doest to the most humble thou doest to me, are thus confirmed. Martin understands that he has given his cloak to Jesus disguised as a pauper and has himself baptized.

This is clearly a conversion dream, and it functions as a miracle. It confirms both the saintliness of Martin, "raised well above human glory" by Christ himself, and the truth of the Gospel.[66]

In a second dream Martin receives an order (whether from God or an angel it is impossible to say, but the dream is clearly of divine origin) to "visit" his native country and his parents, who remain caught in the toils of paganism. This dream of exhortation initiates Martin's work as a missionary.[67]

Martin sees numerous apparitions of angels as well as the devil, but he is awake when he sees them and I do not think that these visions can be classified as dreams (6.1–2, 21.1–4, 22.1–5, and 24.4–8).[68]

Finally, Sulpicius Severus himself learns of Martin's death from a vision. To place an irrefutable seal of authenticity on his work, the author of the *Vita* credits himself with a vision, which happens to be the last and highest confirmation of Martin's sainthood (Ep. 2.1–6). In his cell in the early morning hours, Sulpicius Severus has turned his mind to thoughts of the future and especially to fear of the Judgment and dread of the punishments of Hell. Lying down on his bed, he falls asleep, but it is a light morning sleep (hence more susceptible to dreams according to Tertullian's theory in chapter 48 of *De anima*). While sleeping he sees Saint Martin wearing a white toga, his face as hot as fire, his eyes shining like stars, and his hair as radiant as a sunset. Smiling, Martin indicates that he is carrying in his right hand a copy of his *Vita* by Sulpicius Severus. The latter kneels and asks the saint for a benediction, which Martin gives, laying his hand on Sulpicius's head in such a way that the hagiographer smells its fragrance. Suddenly, Heaven opens and Martin ascends and disappears, followed by his disciple, the priest Clair. Sulpicius also tries to follow, but in vain. He wakes up. His servant enters his cell and sadly announces that two monks have come from Tours with the news that Martin is dead.

This is not the place to analyze this dream, which became a topos of many other dreams: a saint ascends to heaven at the moment of his death. The dream simply caps a "popular" canonization.

It is worth noting the particular words that Sulpicius uses to refer to dreams involving Saint Martin. To be sure, he calls his own dream a vision: somnoque excitus congratulari coeperam *visioni* quam viderfam (suddenly awakened, I congratulated myself on the vision I had had, Ep. 2.5). For the three other dreams, however, he uses the word *sopor*. This denotes the type of sleep during which dreams occur, but it directs our attention to a series of inaccurate translations. The reference here is in fact to Genesis 2:21 and to the sleep to which God subjects Adam while removing the rib from which he will make Eve. The Vulgate reads: Immisit ergo Dominus Deus *soporem* in Adam. The Hebrew text reads תַּרְדֵּמָה, *tardema*, which has been understood to mean torpor or deep sleep ("And the Lord God caused a deep sleep to fall upon Adam"), translated in the Septuagint as *ecstasis* and by Jerome as *sopor*, even though this meant light sleep.[69] This passage of Genesis cannot be interpreted as an account of a dream. Nevertheless, Tertullian in *De anima* (45.3), interpreting *sopor* to mean *somnus cum ecstasi*, ultimately gives the *sopor* of Genesis the sense of ecstasy, which for him is the highest form of dream: "Hanc vim ecstasin dicimus, excessum sensus et mentis instar. Sic et in primordio somnus cum ecstasi dedicatus et misit Deus ecstasin in Adam et dormiit." (We call this force ecstasy, an escape from the senses and sort of dementia. Thus in the beginning sleep was revealed with ecstasy and God sent ecstasy to Adam, who slept). In Sulpicius Severus, by contrast, *sopor* refers to a kind of dream, that which occurs during the light sleep of the early morning hours.

In Gregory of Tours we find dreams incorporated into a Christianized version of incubation. In *De Virtutibus sancti Martini* (2.56), for example, a woman whose hands are bloody and gangrenous as a result of a contracture sinks her nails into them down to the bone. After sleeping next to the saint's tomb in Tours, apparently in vain, she falls asleep on the banks of the Cher and has a dream in which she sees the saint, wreathed in swan feathers and covered with purple and carrying a cross. He tells her that her hand is healed, and when she wakes up she finds that it is. The suddenness of the dream-apparition is underscored by the word *ecce:* "Iterum obdormivit. Et *ecce* vir crine cycneo. . . ." (She fell asleep once again. And there was a man with hair like swan feathers. . . .)

Such incubation dreams occur frequently in the work of Gregory of Tours (circa 538–594). In *De miraculis sancti Juliani* (9) is the story of a paralyzed woman, Fedamia, who comes one Sunday night to the saint's sanctuary and lies down in the portico of the basilica. After falling asleep she sees "a man" (*a viro quodam*), who asks why she is not keeping a vigil. She exhibits her infirmity, and the man carries her over to the tomb. Then she sees many chains fall from her body onto the ground. Upon waking she discovers that she is cured. Later she describes the man who appeared and spoke to her and helped her, and it turns out to be Saint Julian himself.

In both stories Gregory uses the ancient word *visum,* which previously referred to an illusory apparition: "dum haec in visu videret evigilans" (while seeing this in a pseudo-apparition, she awoke); "a viro quodam per visum correpta atque increpita est" (a man, in a pseudo-vision, attacked and reprimanded her). Gregory, too, uses the word *sopor* in describing the miracle of Saint Julian: "dum in sopore fundit orationem" (while in deep sleep she prayed to him from the bottom of her heart). Thus, the ancient vocabulary of dream interpretation lost its meaning, and the pair of words *visio* and *somnium* gradually came into use.

The increasingly close relation between dreams and saints is also evident in the hagiographical topos of the discovery of a saint's (often a martyr's) body as a result of a dream. Greek Christians were quick to adopt this topos, which also became influential in the West. The first instance of its use in Latin literature was apparently Saint Ambrose's "invention" of the bodies of the holy martyrs Gervasius and Protasius.[70] Saint Augustine said that Ambrose received the idea from God in a *visum* (*Confessions* 9.7.16.1) or a *somnium* (*Epistola ad catholicos de secta Donatistorum* 19.50). Yet Augustine was in general quite dubious of these "inventions *per somnia,*" which he judged to be more often than not fanciful. To the Council of Carthage in 401 he dictated a harsh condemnation of the practice (canon 14 in Mansi, *Sacrorum conciliorum . . . collectio,* vol. 3, p. 971): "nam quae per somnia et inanes quasi revelationes quorumlibet hominum ubique constituuntur altaria, omnimode reprobentur" (for the altars that are established everywhere by dreams and by the vain pseudorevelations of all sorts of men are something to be condemned absolutely).

*b. The poverty of dream theory compared with the luxuriance of dream accounts.* Between the fifth and seventh centuries the Christian typology of dreams, based on origins, became rigid and dogmatic and lost much of its content. The two leading theorists were Gregory the Great and Isidore of Seville, both instrumental in transmitting the encyclopedic culture of late antiquity to the Middle Ages.

Gregory, having set forth his views on dreams in *Moralia in Job* 8.42, returned to the subject in his *Dialogues* (4.50), written in 593–594. He has Peter ask him the following question: "Doceri velim si hoc quod per nocturnas visiones ostenditur debeat observari" (Would you please tell me whether what is revealed in nocturnal visions is to be taken into account). Gregory's answer is quite lengthy. He states his typology at once: "Oneiric images affect the soul in six ways. Dreams sometimes originate with a full or empty stomach, sometimes with an illusion, sometimes with a thought, reflection, or revelation. We know the first two categories from experience. We find the other four in the Holy Bible."[71]

Gregory then indicates that illusion is produced by the "hidden enemy" (*ab occulto hoste*), that is, the devil, and he cites two biblical texts (Ecclesiasticus 34:7 and Leviticus 19:26) that warn against *somnia*. He justifies the existence of mixed dreams, of dual origin, by citing Ecclesiastes 5:3 as proof that some dreams originate in both reflection and illusion and by invoking the story of Daniel explaining the dream of Nebuchadnezzar (Daniel 1:17, 2:16). Proof that some dreams come from God (revelation) is found in the dreams of Joseph in the Old Testament and of the other Joseph, Mary's husband, in the New Testament.

The old tripartite typology has been multiplied by two: dreams can be caused by man (stomach or reflection, body or thought), God (revelation), or the devil (illusion). The subtlety of Gregory the theologian in analyzing mixed dreams actually serves the purposes of Gregory the moralizing pastor: to dissuade Christians from the interpretation of dreams. In effect, the mixed categories make it more difficult to identify the origin of dreams. Man, a compound of good and evil, often produces ambiguous dreams, but these are without great danger. If some dreams are inspired by the devil, however, and therefore to be rejected, while others are in part of divine origin and therefore to be retained, one's qualms are aggravated. Gregory observes: "The more diverse the qualities at work in dreams, the more difficult it must be to believe in them. It is that much more difficult to explain the magnitude and nature of the forces that cause them." [72]

Only an elite of saints (*sancti viri*) is capable of determining which dreams come from "good spirits" (sent by God) and which are illusions (sent by the devil). Gregory borrows a phrase from Augustine: "an inward savor (*intimo sapore*) enables them to distinguish between illusions and revelation in the words and images of visions" (*ipsas visionum voces aut imagines*).

As is his wont in the *Dialogues*, Gregory ends with an edifying anecdote: "This in all truth is what recently happened to one of our friends. He paid undue attention to dreams. In one dream he was promised a long life. He set aside money for the expenses of a prolonged existence. Suddenly he died, leaving this fortune untouched, and he took with him not the least good work." [73]

Brief moralistic anecdotes of this sort ultimately developed into the medieval exempla, in which dreams played a part. Dreams also contaminated miracles. But the saints who performed miracles could always distinguish between true and false dreams (or, in Christian terms, between divinely and diabolically inspired dreams). In exempla, generally associated with a negative morality, the point was usually to warn others by holding up certain sinners as bad examples. Hence they are filled with people who attached too much importance to dreams and who allowed themselves to be deceived by the devil. [74]

In the first third of the seventh century Isidore of Seville turned his attention to dreams in chapter 6 of book 3 of the *Sententiae*, which according to Jacques Fontaine pointed the way to the summas of the Middle Ages. The chapter is entitled "On the Temptations of Dreams" and placed between a chapter "On the Temptations of the Devil" and another "On Prayer," prayer being the remedy for dreams.[75]

Isidore first shows demons assailing sleeping men with dreams: "per visiones conturbant, ut formidoloso et timidos faciant . . . per soporem conturbant" (they assailed them with visions to make them fearful and timid . . . they overwhelmed them with torpor). He places particular stress on the demons' use of illusory and tempting dreams (*variis illusionibus intentantes*). Like Gregory the Great, Isidore maintains that only saints can ward off these illusions (*illusionum vanitates despiciunt*). Isidore has borrowed Gregory's typology: certain dreams come from man's body through excess (*ex saturitate*) or want (*seu inanitione*); other visions are merely *illusions* caused by unclean spirits, that is, demons; still others are mixed (*permiste*) and originate in reflection and illusion or reflection and revelation. Some dreams are true (*Quamuis nonnulla vera sint somnia*), but others are forged by the mind (*mentes enim non nunquam ipsae sibi somnia fingant*).

Extreme caution and suspicion are therefore required when dealing with dreams. Even true dreams "must not be believed readily, for they stem from various qualities of the imagination and attention is rarely paid to their origin. We must not believe easily in dreams lest Satan . . . deceive us." Dreams are to be "despised" even if they appear to come true, for they may stem from illusion, from demons capable of mingling the true with the false the better to deceive. As stated in Matthew 24:23, "Si dixerint vobis, et ita evenerit, non credatis" (Then if any man shall say unto you, Lo, here is Christ, or there; believe it not).

Finally Isidore considers lustful dreams. If they occur during sleep against a person's will, they are no sin, but if, as is usually the case, they simply reproduce images that a person has entertained during the day, then the dreamer is committing a sin. Nocturnal emissions that may result from these dreams are sins, and upon awakening the dreamer must wash away the sin with tears.

The inability of the Church to establish criteria for determining the origin and hence the value of dreams compelled people to repress their dreams. Early medieval society was composed of frustrated dreamers. Antidream propaganda found its way even into the liturgy. At compline, the hymn *Te lucisante terminum* (attributed to Saint Ambrose) contains the words: "Procul recedant somnia et noctium phantasmata" (May dreams and phantasies of the night subside).

Even though dream theory was limited and essentially negative in its tenor, accounts of dreams were prevalent in ecclesiastic, hagiographic, and didactic literature. An excellent catalog of dreams in Gregory the Great's *Dialogues* has been compiled by Father Adalbert de Vogüé (*Sources chrétiennes* no. 265, vol. 3 [1980], pp. 357–359). In it we find first of all dreams that "herald coming events," of which 18 out of 33 concern an impending death and 10 of these pertain to the death of the "prophet" himself, that is, of a saint. It is not always clear whether the apparition occurs in the form of a vision or a dream during sleep. Usually, however, a nighttime setting or the use of the word *revelatio* indicates that the dream in question is "true." Saints commonly dreamed of their own deaths. Since the heroes of the *Dialogues* are saints, they are particularly favored with "true" dreams, "divine" revelations. They are also able to resist the oneiric temptations of the devil. When the saint is as great as Benedict, to whom the whole of book 2 of the *Dialogues* is devoted, he enjoys the privilege of being vouchsafed a "clear vision" of Satan rather than an obscure or dream vision: "Non occulte vel per somnium, sed aperta visione eiusdem patris se oculis ingerebat" (*Dialogues* 2.8.12).

Father de Vogüé draws a further distinction between "visions of the blessed" (of angels, supernatural figures, God, Jesus, the Virgin and her retinue, Saints Peter and Paul, Inticus, Juvenal and Eleutherus, Pope Felix, Jonah, Ezechiel, Daniel, Faustina), "visions of souls," "visions of objects" (some in the other world, others in this one, including signs in heaven, a cloud in church, a road ascending from earth to heaven, glowing radiances), and "dreams and nocturnal visions," primarily of the blessed.

Also to be numbered among the oneiric visions are accounts of voyages in the other world, which under the influence of Judeo-Christian apocalyptic literature were quite common in the first few centuries of the Christian era. These generally began with a statement that the visionary had left his body (*eductus e corpore*). This was the case with the soldier Stephen, who, while lying mortally wounded on the verge of death, made a journey to the other world. There he saw a bridge, which he described when contrary to all expectation he returned to the world of the living (*Dialogues* 4.37.8ff.). Sometimes a word such as *revelatio* indicates that the dream is a visionary one (as in 4.38.1). To the group that de Vogüé calls "dreams and nocturnal visions" we should therefore add certain "miracles" that he classifies as "visions," although visions that are said to be "direct" and "clear" (*aperte*) should not, I think, be counted as visionary dreams.

Evidently there was a need to edify the faithful by discussing the fate of the damned as well as the blessed, for certain infamous souls number among those authorized to return as ghosts to the world of the living (as in *Dialogues* 4.53).

Consider one dream that was used to support restrictions on the right of laymen to be buried in church. A modest ecclesiastical servant, the *custos ecclesiae,* probably a layman, was chosen to receive a revelation or divine vision justifying the new practice.

Perhaps the most striking thing about the visions recounted by Gregory the Great is the importance of the role ascribed to salvation, that is, to death and the afterlife. The dream and the vision become the vehicle of a journey in the other world. The thematic range of dreams may have diminished, but a vast field was thus opened up, and dreams became a place where Heaven and Hell almost touched, like the narrow bridge that every soul had to cross.[76]

*c. Monks' dreams.* While martyrs and saints were the quintessential dreamers in Christian dream theory, during the early Middle Ages a larger but still limited group gained prominence in the production of dreams for literary and pastoral purposes: namely, the regular clergy, which, while not as prestigious as saints and martyrs because not yet possessed of heavenly glory, was nevertheless a prestigious and exemplary group, a sprinkling of angels scattered among men and rooted in this world.

From John Cassian in fifth-century Marseilles to Bede the Venerable in the British Isles in the seventh and eighth centuries, monks produced ever more numerous and detailed accounts of their dreams. Monastic orders and the Church hierarchy kept a close eye on these tales, but in general they were welcomed. Dream accounts were worked and reworked, for the genre had no fixed form. Cassian brought dreams from the Orient and the desert to the West. Monks in their scriptoria read, copied, meditated and commented on dreams in scripture and hagiography. And Bede and others enriched the monastic imagination with tales from the Celts and other barbarian peoples. Young monks, lay brothers, and the lay *familia* of monastery servants added to the monastic corpus dreams from oral tradition and folklore. Some but not all of these dreams later filtered out from the monasteries into the wider world, for the monks were careful about what they preached outside the cloister to bishops and powerful laymen. Bede, for example, played a major role in popularizing visions of the other world. But monks amassed more dreams than they told, hoarding them behind their monastery walls. When the urban revolution,

Gregorian reform, and changes in the monastic orders themselves, coupled with the emergence of the new mendicant orders, made those walls more permeable, the treasure stored within increasingly entered into circulation. Changes in Christian theory and practice with respect to dreams encouraged this process, which helped to shape the imagination of the newly emerging society.

## Conclusion

In late antiquity and the Middle Ages the imaginations of men and women first in the Mediterranean region and later throughout western Christendom were shaped by two long-lived phenomena connected with dreams and their interpretation. Although the roots of these phenomena can be traced to the Jews, Greeks, and Romans of antiquity, they became truly important only after the rise of Christianity.

*a. The repression and manipulation of dreams.* The repression of dreams, like the repression of sexuality, was the work of the Church, and we are not yet entirely liberated from its consequences. (Among which is psychoanalysis. For lack of competence I have not ventured onto this terrain, but a more thorough approach to the history of dreams would need to make use of psychoanalytic discoveries.) Historically, dreams and fears have gone hand in hand, as Jean Delumeau has shown in his history of the "Christianity of fear," whose roots can be traced far into the past. Because the dream was seen as an instrument of the devil, it became part of the syndrome of *contemptus mundi* or rejection of the world so tirelessly elaborated by the monks of the early Middle Ages. It was no accident that the young cardinal Giovanni Lotario (who later became Pope Innocent III) devoted a chapter of his *De contemptu mundi* (ca. 1196) to the "fear of dreams," for this was the time of the first great liberation of the dream.

The more neurotic forms of Christianity created a nightmarish world in which not even darkness brought repose and man was reduced to the situation of Job at the time of his worst trials. Echoing his words the future pope proclaimed: "The time conceded to rest is not necessarily conceded to be restful: dreams terrify, visions attack." [77]

Yet dreams also seem to have become part of the counterculture and to have played a part in heretical protest. According to Raoul Glaber, the Champenois peasant Leutard became the first "popular" heretic some time after 1000 when he fell asleep in a field and had a vision.

And Emmanuel Le Roy Ladurie has shown the fascination that dreams exerted on the Cathari of Montaillou.[78]

*b. Dreams and individuals.* Dreaming is a collective phenomenon (which is of course why historians should be interested in dreams). As Hennigsen has pointed out, the seventeenth century was even plagued by "epidemics of dreams." Yet even though dreams are shaped by social and cultural forces, they are also an important means of individual self-assertion. Oneiric autobiography was born in late antiquity, as we have seen. From the pagan Aelius Aristides and the bishop Augustine it evolved slowly up to the time of the Benedictine abbot Guibert of Nogent (early twelfth century). The development of dreaming was closely associated with the fashion for journeys in the other world and the growing importance of *individual judgment* after death.

In conclusion let me cite from a text that considerably predates the period with which I have chiefly been concerned in this essay. It is from fragment 89 of Heraclitus: "The world of the waking is unique and common, but each sleeper returns unto himself."

## Appendix: Dreams in the Old Testament

Genesis

1. 15 Yahweh speaks to Abraham in vision.
2. 20 Yahweh appears to Abimelek in a nocturnal dream.
3. 26:24 Yahweh appears to Isaac in a dream.
4. 28:29 Dream of Jacob's ladder.
5. 31:10–13 Jacob's dream.
6. 31:24 Laban's nocturnal vision.
7. 37:5, 37:10 Joseph's dreams.
8. 40 Dreams of pharaoh's butler and baker.
9. 41 Pharaoh's dream.
10. 42:9 Joseph's dream.
11. 46:1–5 Yahweh reveals himself to Jacob in a vision.

Leviticus

12. 19:26 Laws given to Moses and the Jews: Yahweh prohibits divination by dreams.

Numbers

13. 12:6–8 To a prophet Yahweh speaks in a vision or dream (*invisione apparebo ei, vel per somnium loquar ad illum*) but to Moses he speaks face

to face and not in riddles and figures (*non per aenigmata et figuras*).

14. 22:8–21 Yahweh appears twice to Balaam.

## Deuteronomy

15. 13:1–6 Yahweh warns Israel against prophets and dreamers (*propheta aut fictor somniorum*).
16. 23:10–12 Purification ritual in the camps after a nocturnal pollution (*qui nocturno pollutus sit somnio*).

## Judges

17. 7:13–15 A Midianite tells Gideon a premonitory dream.

## I Samuel

18. 3 Yahweh calls the sleeping young Samuel three times.
19. 18:15 Yahweh ceases to speak to Saul through dreams (*per somnia*).

## I Kings

20. 3:5–15 Yahweh appears to Solomon in Gibeon.

## II Chronicles

21. 33:6 The impious Manasseh and other evildoers practice divination through dreams.

## Esther

22. 1:1 Dream of Mordecai.
23. 10:3b–3k Mordecai explains his dream.

## II Maccabees

24. 15:11–16 Dream of Judas Maccabeus

## Job

25. 4:12–21 Terrifying dreams told by Eliphaz: a ghost.
26. 7:13–14 Job cannot rest because Yahweh sends him frightening dreams and visions.
27. 20:8 The wicked "shall fly away as a dream" or "be chased away as a vision of the night."
28. 33:15–17 Yahweh torments man with dreams and nocturnal visions.

## Psalms

29. 73:20 "As a dream when one awaketh, so O Lord, when thou awakest thou shalt despise their image," i.e., the image of the wicked.

## Ecclesiastes

30. 5:3, 5:7 Dreams are a source of worry and vanity.

Wisdom

31. 18:17–19 Terrifying dreams and visions are among the plagues that Yahweh visits upon the Egyptians.

Ecclesiasticus

32. 34:1–8 Dreams are lies.
33. 40:5–7 Man in his misery cannot lie easy at night because of dreams and visions.

Isaiah

34. 29:7–8 The enemies of Jerusalem will be dispersed as a dream.

Jeremiah

35. 14:14 Against false prophets who tell of false visions.
36. 23:25–32 Against prophets who dream false dreams.
37. 27:9–10 Yahweh against dreamers of empty dreams.
38. 29:8–9 Yahweh asks Israel to ignore false prophets who interpret dreams.

Daniel

39. 2 Nebuchadnezzar's dream: the statue.
40. 4 Nebuchadnezzar's dream: the tree.

Joel

41. 2:28 Yahweh will send dreams to the old and visions to the young.

Zechariah

42. 1:7–6:15 Zechariah sees visions and hears voices by night.
43. 10:2 Vanity of false dream interpreters (*somniatores*).

# THE DREAMS OF
# HELMBRECHT THE ELDER

I hope that a medieval historian who is not a specialist in German history may be forgiven for offering this modest contribution in homage to Jörg Zink, a great scholar, professor, and teacher. My essay concerns certain dreams dreamt by the father of young Helmbrecht. More than twenty years have passed since I first noticed that these dreams contained remarkable evidence about the condition of the peasantry in southern Germany and about the image of the peasant in thirteenth-century literature and ideology.[1] When I returned to *Helmbrecht* a few months ago, I found that since 1964 it has been the subject of several major studies.[2]

In trying to repair my ignorance, I found that my reading, though instructive, only revealed my incompetence to engage in debate with specialists. I shall therefore limit myself, as an outsider, to a few perhaps naive remarks about the elder Helmbrecht's dreams, in the light of my long-standing interest in dreams and their interpretation in the Middle Ages.[3]

Four dreams of Helmbrecht the Elder are briefly recounted in lines 577 to 639 of the epic, each followed by the reaction of his son (which is always negative).[4] In the first dream (lines 580–586) the elderly peasant sees his son carrying two very bright torches, which remind him of a dream he dreamt a year earlier in which another person had carried torches. Since then that person had gone blind. "I would be quite a coward if I allowed myself to be impressed by such tales (*maere*)," says the son. The father then recounts two other dreams, one not only more frightening than the other but also easier to interpret. In one the father sees his son with a mutilated arm and leg (lines 592–600), but the young man says that this dream heralds "happiness and prosperity and abundant joys." The father then says that he watched as his son attempted to fly, but someone clipped his wings and he fell (lines 603–610). He conjures up an image of his son's battered body: "owê hende, füeze und ougen din." But young Helmbrecht stubbornly persists in interpreting the dream in a favorable light: "All the dreams foretell my fortune" (*saelde*). Then the old peasant recounts his

Originally published as "Quelques remarques sur les rêves de Helmbrecht père," *Mélanges Zink*, G.A.G. no. 364 (Göppingen, 1984), pp. 123–141.

final and most ghastly dream (lines 617–634), and this account is the longest, most detailed, and most realistic of all. He says that he saw his son hanged, with a crow and a raven pecking at his brains (an image that would be used two centuries later by François Villon in his *Ballade des pendus*). The son admits that this could be a sign of death. But until death comes he proposes to continue with his plan. He will leave home and escape the miserable fate of the peasant.

Later in the story, after young Helmbrecht's fall and in the course of his punishment, Wernher der Gartenaere alludes to these dreams, which can now be seen to be coming true. In lines 1786–1791 the father sees his brigand son, his eyes plucked out by the executioner and a hand and a foot cut off, and attempts to hide his grief behind laughter. The son having become a stranger, his father addresses him using the formal "you": "Now tell me whether my dreams have come true! But it will get worse, and you will suffer worse ills. Before the fourth dream comes true, leave this place at once!" And at the end of the story (lines 1910ff.), after young Helmbrecht has been hanged, the poet concludes: "I believe that the father's [last] dream had come true."

Notice, first of all, the status of old Helmbrecht, the dreamer in this tale. Since ancient times a distinction had been drawn between two sorts of dream interpretation: on the one hand there were learned oneiromancers, on the other "public soothsayers," often referred to as "impostors, charlatans, and clowns." The author of the best known ancient treatise on the interpretation of dreams, Artemidorus of Daldis (or Ephesus), who lived in Asia Minor in the second century A.D., states that he collected dreams not only from learned scholars and interpreters but also from popular soothsayers, whom he did not disdain to consult.[5]

In pagan antiquity a person who wished to know the meaning of a dream went to see a specialist, a learned scholar or popular soothsayer. But at the end of the fourth century, the pagan Synesius of Cyrene, who was baptized in 410 and later became a bishop, wrote a treatise *On Dreams* in which he argued that everyone, regardless of status or education, was capable of interpreting his or her own dreams. This attempt to democratize the dream was, however, doomed to failure.[6]

Christian doubts about dreams increased in the fourth century. The Church proscribed the professional dream interpreters and taught that only a small elite was blessed with meaningful dreams, dreams worthy of interpretation. In the Old Testament the interesting dreams were those of kings (Pharaoh, Nebuchadnezzar, Samuel, Solomon), patriarchs, prophets, and "overdetermined" figures such as Job. Most

Jewish dreams in the Old Testament have clear interpretations. And certain Jews, such as Joseph and Daniel, are endowed by God with a special ability to interpret the obscure dreams of pagan kings.[7]

The New Testament contains only a few dreams, which may be grouped into two sets. One of these is associated with the birth of Jesus and involves persons of the first rank (Joseph, the three Magi, and the wife of Pilate). The other (in Acts of the Apostles) is associated with Paul and reflects the influence of Hellenistic culture and the exaltation of the militant apostle.[8]

In the Middle Ages for a long time only the dreams of a small elite were believed worthy of interpretation. This elite included, among ecclesiastics, monks, bishops, and above all saints and, among laymen, chiefly kings. Royal dreams were described either in chronicles (as in the case of Henry I of England, whose early twelfth-century dream was recorded in the chronicle of John of Worcester) or in literary works (such as the dreams of Charlemagne reported in the *Chanson de Roland*).[9] Bede in the early eighth century was virtually the only medieval dream interpreter to consider the relatively obscure dreams of laymen.[10]

In the twelfth century the privilege of dreaming meaningful dreams began to be extended. Any Christian, male or female, could be blessed with a dream worthy of interpretation.[11] Old Helmbrecht, a peasant, enjoyed the benefits of this social broadening of the dream. But let me make three remarks. First, Helmbrecht Senior was no ordinary peasant but a model of the old virtues. Second, he calls attention to his own incompetence to interpret dreams and suggests calling upon men of learning, *wîsen* (line 579) or *wîse liute* (line 600). Third, he experienced not visions but dreams (*somnia, trôume*), which according to Christian doctrine constituted a lower order of experience, fit for relatively unimportant pagans or Christians, precisely those who were incapable of interpreting their own dreams. By contrast, visions were a higher form of message from the other world and generally revealed a hidden reality.[12]

The hierarchy of dreamers was still respected. The Old Testament implied that dreams were obscure, in contrast to visions, which were clear. In Numbers 12:6–8 God says that to Moses, who has always been faithful, he will "speak mouth to mouth, even apparently, and not in dark speeches." The distinction is fundamental in works such as Artemidorus's *Oneirocriticon,* which establishes two classes of dreams, the *theorematic* ("those which come to pass in such a way that they resemble in every way what was shown") and the *allegorical* ("which signify certain things by means of other dreams").[13]

Old Helmbrecht's first dream is allegorical. The son carries two torches, but in the real episodes of the story he does not carry torches. The dream reminds Helmbrecht Senior of an earlier dream, in which the man who was carrying the torches actually went blind.

This type of dream was of particular interest to Artemidorus, who in one of his typologies classifies dreams according to the relation they bear to what eventually comes to pass: "Certain dreams are good as to the inside and as to the outside; others bad as to both; others good as to the inside but bad as to the outside; and still others bad as to the inside but good as to the outside." [14]

Artemidorus was especially interested in the latter two types, that is, in deceptive dreams, because their interpretation required much learning, experience, and skill. He gives numerous examples in the catalog of dreams collected for his son in book 5. In one of these the "allegory" is similar to that in the dream of Helmbrecht Senior: "A man dreamed that he lit his lamp with the moon. He went blind. In fact he took his light to a spring, where he could not light it. It is also said that the moon has no light of its own." [15]

Both dreams contain the same contrast between a luminous object and blindness. [16] But no interpretation is given in the poem; Helmbrecht is no scholar and is incapable of explaining his dreams. Artemidorus, on the other hand, offers two objective explanations: the distance of the moon and the fact that it is a "dead star." Nevertheless, if the poet does not explain Helmbrecht's dream, he does suggest that blindness is punishment for the vanity of the young peasant who wished to "shine" (by his choice of cap and clothing, for example), that is, to strike the eyes of others. If moral intentions are not entirely absent from Artemidorus's text, they are perfectly clear in Wernher der Gartenaere's. Although there are few direct signs of Christianity in *Helmbrecht,* dreaming is Christianized in the poem. The subjective replaces the objective, and punishment of sins replaces fate. Man is the hero responsible for the dream.

The next two dreams are rather paradoxical. Old Helmbrecht continues to insist that they are allegorical, somewhat enigmatic, when in fact they are *theorematic,* revealing their message directly. The literary device is quite effective. On the one hand the shift from an enigmatic dream to a vision marks a dramatic progression in the representation of young Helmbrecht's future. On the other hand the psychological truth of this dramatization reinforces its effect.

Abandoning hope that he can convince his son with a dream whose meaning is obscure though actually quite easy to divine (for the listener or reader could not be expected to grasp anything but a simple riddle), old Helmbrecht resorts to more direct and disturbing means. He first describes a maimed person who is clearly identified with his son. But he pretends that, as an illiterate, he cannot decipher the meaning of his dreams and urges the young man to consult the scholars to find out what it means (lines 598ff.): "sol dir der troum wesen frum / oder waz er bediute / des frâge wîse liute."

The young man's answer demonstrates Wernher der Gartenaere's art at its finest. He makes use of his understanding of both the theory of dreams and human psychology. The son obviously does not believe or refuses to believe in dreams (a sign of his youth). He responds to his father's first dream by invoking his courage and determination. He shows that he is already imbued with the warrior ideals shared by the adventurous and devil-may-care class to which he wishes he belonged: the nobility.[17]

His response to the second dream is still provocative but above all ironic. With great skill he inverts the theory of Artemidorus upon which the previous dream was constructed. This time he invokes the category of "dreams bad as to the inside but good as to the outside." Accordingly he argues in substance that this horrible dream is surely a harbinger of good fortune and riches. Note, by the way, that the second book of Artemidorus's *Oneirocriticon* is largely devoted to the interpretation of dreams involving the body and its parts.[18]

Helmbrecht's third dream is again theorematic, albeit tinged to some degree with allegory. Combining two of Artemidorus's basic categories, this dream propels the narrative forward, as does the total failure of the son's enterprise. The model here is the dream of Icarus. For us, of course, it also conjures up Brueghel's famous painting, the foreground of which portrays a peasant at his plow.

In the chapter on dreams of flight (5.68) Artemidorus gives both favorable and unfavorable interpretations, as was his wont. Old Helmbrecht's dream clearly falls into one of Artemidorus's categories: "The saddest and most inauspicious thing in the world may be to wish to fly and to be unable to do so."[19] Under Christianity the dream of flight was interpreted primarily in terms of *superbia,* or pride. As the father says to the son (lines 605ff.): "dû soldest fliegen hôhe / über welde und über lôhe."

When the father pretends to wonder whether this is a good sign ("sol dir der troum guot sîn?"), the son stubbornly clings to his ironic interpretation: "All your dreams foretell my [good] fortune," but his sentiments are plain when he says "I am leaving *in spite of all your dreams!*" (swie vil dir sî getroumet, line 616). Like a young knight, an

Erec or Lancelot, Helmbrecht sets out on the path of knightly adventure despite the almost certain risk of death (indeed because of it, such is young Helmbrecht's death wish).

The escalation of horror and heightening of realism continues with the fourth dream. At this point, old Helmbrecht, unable to think of any other way to convince his son, makes an astonishing statement. All his previous dreams were unimportant, he says, but now he is going to relate a *true* dream. This, I think, is the correct interpretation of the third line in this passage, which begins with line 617: "Sun, al die tröume sint ein wint / dir mir noch getroumet sint: / nû hoer von einem troume."

Apart from the literary and psychological artifice, the poet is here using a dream typology that was well known from the Old Testament and ancient literature (compare Penelope's dream in the *Odyssey* 4.795–841 and Aeneas's statements in book 6 of the *Aeneid*) and that took on particular importance under Christianity. According to this typology, true dreams are sent by God, and false dreams are inspired by the devil. (Note, however, that this Christianized form of the ancient distinction is never mentioned in the poem.) And the dream, as was mentioned earlier, relates in grisly detail the story of a hanging.

Although the dream is quite clear, an important and to my mind unambiguous auxiliary symbolism is also used: the raven (*rabe*) and the crow (*krâ*). Literature and folklore traditionally made use of these highly charged symbols, whose meaning for a long time remained ambivalent. The birds could stand for either favor or misfortune.[20] In the early centuries of the Christian era, first in the East and later in the West, the raven was often a sign of divine protection. It fed the hermit in his solitude (witness Saint Benedict's raven in the *Dialogues* of Gregory the Great). In the thirteenth century, however, the raven was affected by a general "diabolization" of symbols[21] that was associated with an ecclesiastical pedagogy based on fear.[22] Thus echoes of Helmbrecht's hanged man can be heard not only in Villon but also in Poe's *The Raven*.

After the father has related his four dreams, young Helmbrecht reveals his desires, for which he is prepared to brave death (lines 638–639): "ich gelâze nimmer mînen muot / hinnen unz an mînen tôt." His character is summed up in this rhyme. Helmbrecht's dreams are clearly linked to a tradition, to an ancient and learned typology. They owe virtually nothing to Christian theories of dream interpretation, though of course in the late thirteenth century no one could explicitly contradict those theories.

Broadly speaking, the difference between pagan and Christian dream interpretation was this: the ancients based their interpretations on the dream's structure and content (ultimately developing the five-part typologies of Chalcidius[23] and Macrobius), whereas Christians, adapting a far less widely accepted Stoic tradition, gauged the *value* of a dream by its source (God, Satan, or the human body).

The elder Helmbrecht's dreams are dictated by knowledge of this pagan tradition. Of the third dream it is legitimate and even necessary to say that it is reminiscent not only of the flight of Icarus but also of the dream of Polycrates's daughter as reported by Herodotus.[24] This idea of Lunzer and Schmitz's is scornfully dismissed in the notes of the Speckenbach edition (p. 99) and in the eighth Panzer-Ruh edition (p. 84), but no valid grounds for such dismissal are cited. There is in fact every reason to believe that the father's dreams ought to be interpreted in the light of a tradition that can be traced back to Greek antiquity.

It is most unlikely that Wernher der Gartenaere knew Herodotus or Artemidorus directly, but I am certain that he was influenced by the ancient traditions they expressed and, in the case of Artemidorus, helped to shape. Further research is needed to uncover the literary tradition that enabled twelfth- and thirteenth-century Christians to continue or revive this ancient theory of dreams.

The theory of dream interpretation in Macrobius's *Commentary on the Dream of Scipio* was of course suppressed by Christianity up to the thirteenth century, when it was revived by scholars in the universities.[25] I suspect that it would be more fruitful to focus research on the tradition of "dream keys" that developed at about the same time. This drew on oriental (Arab and especially Byzantine) sources as well as on folklore and popular traditions. Several scholars have looked into this tradition and proposed a comparison between *Helmbrecht* and *Daniel's Book of Dreams*.[26] Research of this kind promises to shed light on the sources of old Helmbrecht's dreams.

I do not feel, however, that Wernher was greatly influenced by folklore or popular culture. Learned man that he was, Wernher der Gartenaere surely knew a great deal about the peasantry, and *Helmbrecht* has much detailed information to offer the historian. But these details are in some sense external to the work, not an essential part of its *meaning*.

It would be useful to catalog systematically the folkloric elements in *Helmbrecht* for comparison with Stith Thompson's *Motif Index of Folk Literature* and F. C. Tubach's *Index exemplorum*. It would also be interesting to apply Vladimir Propp's method of structural analysis. The story lends itself very well to this kind of reading, because it begins with the hero's departure and its characters represent most of the Proppian "functions."

But the essence of the tale lies elsewhere, I think. I realize that the interpretation of *Helmbrecht* is a subject of much controversy, and I hope that I may be forgiven for the mounting audacity of my claims.[27] It is quite clear that the work contains abundant information about the condition of peasants in southern Germany and elsewhere and that it is a valuable source for historians of material culture, social class, and *mentalités*. Horst Wenzel, for example, has compared the picture of rural society in *Helmbrecht* with that derived from the work of Karl Bosl, who worked with sources other than imaginative literature.

In attempting to understand the meaning of the work, it is of course legitimate to analyze it in sociological and political terms, and such an analysis may yield interesting hypotheses. But there are, I think, certain pitfalls to be avoided in this kind of approach. It is most unlikely that we will ever know more than we do now about the life of Wernher der Gartenaere, the exact date of composition of his work, his place of birth, or his social and political background. Although scholars have attempted with great subtlety and energy to answer these questions, their search is in vain. It is in the *nature* of many of the literary works of this period that we will never know much about how they were conceived, written, or received. There is no point in regretting these gaps in our knowledge. Instead we must accept them as essential characteristics of the relationship between early medieval literature and society, culture, and ideology. Analysis must focus primarily on the work itself.

As for *Helmbrecht,* I shall simply offer a few suggestions for other scholars to consider. My hypotheses are neither subtle nor new, but they do take account of basic facts about the production and function of literature in this period. The first question to ask is what is the *genre* of the work, and the answer is that it is a moralizing tale. It was written to amuse and to edify. In large part it therefore depends (as did most works written in this period) on the dominant ideology, namely, that of the Church. It borrows its methods from those commonly in use at the time: it amuses by means of *narrative* and teaches and edifies by inculcating an orthodox, not to say official, position. The meaning of *Helmbrecht* must be interpreted in light of the ideological and cultural aims of the Church. It is entirely a secondary matter that its setting should be Bavaria or the Tyrol or any other part of Christendom.

In unraveling its meaning it is of little importance whether its message served the interests of this or that dynasty or was used or manipulated for dynastic political ends. All that is merely *histoire événementielle,* political history in the most traditional and superficial sense; it is an epiphenomenon. As far as the *moral* message is concerned (and in the thirteenth century virtually every message was moral), it is uniformity that matters most. Regional and even social nuances are of secondary concern. Hence scholars have rightly examined the principal means by which the new Christian orthodoxy was spread in the thirteenth century, namely, the mendicant orders. In this respect the preaching of the Franciscan Berthold von Regensburg in the region is quite relevant.

The orthodox meaning of *Helmbrecht* is perfectly clear: that one must not seek to escape from one's estate, particularly if one is a member of the "peasant class" (and it is perfectly legitimate in this context to say peasant *class,* because the Church in both its doctrine and its pastoral mission tended to group all peasants together, always referring to them as *rustici* or by some other general and uniform term).

This truth is illustrated by the sad tale of one young peasant. More precisely, the work is able to fulfill its purpose because of its *structure,* namely, the opposition between the younger and the elder Helmbrecht. The father is an almost ideal model of the hardworking peasant, good husband, and good father, respectful of the Church's moral teachings and of his social superiors, particularly lords. By contrast, the son is a rebel who seeks to destroy the established order by abandoning his estate, his rural roots, his ecological niche (the farm), his family, and his home. Most serious of all, perhaps, is that he wishes, at least initially, to destroy the ruling class of lords, not by combatting it directly but from within, by entering into its bosom. As a result of these impious desires young Helmbrecht becomes a caricature of both the peasant and the lord: he is a brigand, an angry and rapacious criminal, a rapist and a murderer, who vents his wrath not only on the nobility that he wishes to join but also on the peasantry that he wishes to flee.

The result is a terrible punishment: exclusion from society and even from his own family, for the son, blind, maimed, and penniless, is cast out by his own father and thus condemned to certain death. His disgrace ends in an ignominious death by hanging, in which not even his corpse is spared from humiliation.

Clearly, this is a lesson in social conservatism that could only have served the two dominant orders, the nobility and the clergy. The interesting thing for the historian, however, is that the story is immersed in time, in history, if you will. The clash between father and son is a clash between two generations, two periods. Hence it is quite likely that the difference in age coincides with a change in society, a structural and cultural crisis, whose effects were particularly severe on the peasantry. The social dimension, which is internal to the work, is an *a priori*.

There would be nothing more to say if it were simply true that literature had no choice but to comply with the dominant ideology. But we must also ask whether the author, either on his own initiative or at the behest of his entourage, did not cast the work in such a way as to permit a second interpretation. (Here society and politics come back into the picture, albeit still in an indirect way.) Was not the contemporary listener or reader (hence also the modern historian) justified in interpreting the work on the basis of its witting or unwitting implications?

We know that because of the conditions under which medieval literary works were produced, many are *masked*. Thus we must venture upon the always subjective ground of interpretation. The best we can hope for is to arrive at a more or less credible hypothesis.

Central to the work is the father/son couple. Both have the same name, as Wernher himself emphasizes, and even if this was customary for the time and place, it is nevertheless significant. What we have here is a portrait of the two faces of the peasant, one idealized, the other rendered diabolical. And as in a Picasso portrait the two faces are skewed; between them are differences of age and history.

Thus, it is reasonable to ask whether old Helmbrecht could have become a brigand and whether young Helmbrecht could have remained a peasant. Was not the fact that the younger man left home more a sign of the times than a trait of nature or social character? Had it not become intolerable for most young peasants, good or bad, to remain peasants? A caricature of the nobleman as well as the peasant, young Helmbrecht reveals the darker side of the nobility whose brilliance entices him to his death. Is he a peasant thief or a knightly brigand? Is not the hideous corpse of the justly punished criminal also the cry of a social class?

Does not the appeal for stability and obedience mask a call to rebellion? And if such a rebellion had come to pass, it would not necessarily have been a crime, for the very impenetrability of the nobility had made it necessary.

Each reader must draw his own conclusions, based in part on scientific analysis of the text but in part on his personal commitments. Hypotheses must not be introduced from outside the text, however, but must come from within. In my view Helmbrecht's dreams lead us straight to the heart of the poem. The father dreams through his son and recounts what he has dreamt as if his dreams constituted a mirror in which both were reflected. His dreams belong to a literary genre born in antiquity and forgotten since the Middle Ages: oneiric autobiography.[28]

# NOTES

## INTRODUCTION

1. Pierre Bourdieu, *La Distinction: Critique sociale du jugement* (Paris, 1979), translated by Richard Nice as *Distinction* (Cambridge, Mass.: Harvard University Press, 1986); Roger Chartier, "La culture populaire en question," *Histoire* 8 (1981): 85–96; Peter Brown, *The Cult of the Saints* (Chicago: The University of Chicago Press, 1981), and *The Making of Late Antiquity* (1978), which cites Arnaldo D. Momigliano, "Popular Religious Beliefs and the Roman Historians," *Studies in Church History* 8 (1971): 18.

2. See the two works by Peter Brown cited in note 1 above.

3. Emile Mâle (1862–1954) was the author of *L'Art religieux de la fin du Moyen Age en France: Etude sur l'iconographie du Moyen Age et sur ses sources d'inspiration* (Paris, 1908); *L'Art religieux du XIIe siècle en France: Etude sur les origines de l'iconographie du Moyen Age* (Paris, 1922); *L'Art religieux du XIIIe siècle en France: Etude sur l'iconographie du Moyen Age et sur ses sources d'inspiration* (Paris, 1925). Numerous editions of all three volumes exist [as do English translations].

4. Erwin Panofsky, *Gothic Architecture and Scholasticism* (New York: New American Library, 1976); *Studies in Iconology* (New York: Harper & Row, 1972); *Meaning in the Visual Arts* (Woodstock: Overlook, 1955).

5. Meyer Schapiro, *Words and Pictures: On the Literal and the Symbolic in the Illustration of a Text* (Paris–The Hague, 1973). Also invaluable for the historian of the imagination is the posthumous work of Rudolph Wittkower, "Idea and Image: Studies in the Italian Renaissance," in Wittkower, *The Collected Essays,* vol. 4 (1978); and especially for my purposes Gerhard B. Ladner, *Images and Ideas in the Middle Ages,* vol. 1 (Rome, 1983).

6. In particular I am thinking of research carried on under the auspices of the Group for Historical Anthropology of the Medieval West at the Ecole des Hautes Etudes en Sciences Sociales under the leadership of Jean-Claude Bonne and Jean-Claude Schmitt.

7. I am thinking in particular of Gilbert Durand, *Les Structures anthropologiques de l'imaginaire* (Paris, 1960).

8. Barbara Obrist, in her excellent study *Les Débuts de l'imagerie alchimique (XIVe–XVe siècle)* (Paris, 1982), has shown the inanity of Jungian interpretations of astrological images. Carl Gustav Jung (1875–1961) was of course the psychoanalyst who invented the theory of archetypes.

9. Evelyne Patlagean, "L'Histoire de l'imaginaire," in J. Le Goff, et al., eds., *La Nouvelle histoire* (Paris, 1978), pp. 249–269.

10. Emmanuel Le Roy Ladurie, *Histoire du climat depuis l'an Mil* (Paris, 1967).

11. Robert Delort, *Les Animaux ont une histoire* (Paris, 1984).

12. Paul Alphandéry and Alphonse Dupront, *La Chrétienté et l'idée de Croisade,* 2 vols. (Paris, 1954–1959).

13. M.-D. Chenu, *L'Éveil de la conscience dans la civilisation médiévale* (Montréal-Paris, 1969).

14. Cited by P. Kaufmann in his excellent article "Imaginaire et Imagination," *Encyclopaedia Universalis* (Paris, 1968), vol. 8, pp. 733–739. For a philosophical point of view, see Jean-Paul Sartre, *L'Imaginaire* (Paris, 1940) and, above all, the works of Gaston Bachelard.

15. G. B. Ladner, *Ad imaginem Dei: The Image of Man in Mediaeval Art,* 1965.

16. From an abundant literature I recommend: R. Bradley, "Backgrounds of the Title 'Speculum' in Mediaeval Literature," *Speculum* 29 (1954): 100–115, and J. Margot Schmidt, "Miroir," *Dictionnaire de spiritualité,* vol. 10, cols. 1290–1303 (1980). On the mirror in medieval iconology see G. F. Hartlaub, *Zauber des Spiegels* (Munich, 1951).

17. The citation from Cattaneo is taken from Eugenio Garin, *Moyen Age et Renaissance,* French trans. (1969), p. 12. On the idea of progress, see Jacques Le Goff, "Progresso/reazione," in *Enciclopedia Einaudi* (Turin, 1980), vol. 11, pp. 198–230.

18. Two recent works offer similar views of the period: Henri I. Marrou, *Décadence romaine ou Antiquité tardive? IIIe–VIe siècle* (Paris, 1977), and Peter Brown, *The Making of Late Antiquity.* See also the admirable piece by Armando Sapori, "Moyen Age et Renaissance vus d'Italie: Pour un remaniement des périodes historiques," *Annales ESC* (1956): 433–457. To be deliberately provocative, one might say that Sapori's views are at least partly explained by the fact that Italy never experienced the Middle Ages but made the transition from antiquity to Renaissance between the tenth and twelfth centuries.

19. For a broad view of "renaissance" as an artistic and cultural phenomenon in history and especially in the history of art, see Erwin Panofsky, *Renaissance and Renascences in Western Art,* 2 vols. (Stockholm, 1960). For a delicate, subtle, and scholarly treatment of the Renaissance, see André Chastel, *Le Mythe de la Renaissance* (Geneva, 1969) and *Le Sac de Rome: 1527* (Paris, 1984).

20. Jacques Le Goff, *La Naissance du Purgatoire* (Paris: Gallimard, 1982), translated by Arthur Goldhammer as *The Birth of Purgatory* (Chicago: The University of Chicago Press, 1984).

21. Aaron Gourevitch, "Conscience individuelle et image de l'au-delà au Moyen Age," *Annales ESC* (1982): 255–275.

22. Lucien Febvre, *Le Problème de l'incroyance au XVIe siècle: La religion de Rabelais* (Paris, 1942).

23. On the miraculous in literature see Pierre Mabille, *Le Miroir du merveilleux* (Paris, 1962) and Tzvetan Todorov, *Introduction à la littérature fantastique* (Paris, 1970). On the miraculous in a broader sense see Michel Meslin, ed., *Le Merveilleux: l'imaginaire et les croyances en Occident* (Paris: Bordas, 1984). Concerning the Middle Ages in particular see Daniel Poirion, *Le Mer-*

veilleux dans la littérature française du Moyen Age (Paris: Presses Universitaires de France, 1982).

24. Jack Goody, The Domestication of the Savage Mind (Cambridge, England: Cambridge University Press, 1977).

25. See for example Marie-Christine Pouchelle, Corps et chirurgie à l'apogée du Moyen Age (Paris, 1983); Jacques Gélis and Odile Redon, eds., Les Miracles, miroirs des corps (Paris, 1983); two special issues of the review Razo: Cahiers du Centre d'Etudes médiévales à Nice, no. 2, 1981, entitled "The Image of the Human Body in Medieval Literature and History," and no. 4, 1984, entitled "The Suffering Body: Maladies and Medications"; a special issue entitled "Concern for the Body" of the review Médiévales, no. 8, 1985, published by the University of Paris VIII–Vincennes; and Marie-Thérèse Lorcin, "Le corps a ses raisons dans les fabliaux, corps féminin, corps masculin, corps de vilain," Le Moyen Age (1984): 433–453.

26. On the prehistory of Satan, see the two important books of Bernard Teyssèdre, Naissance du Diable: De Babylone aux grottes de la mer Morte (Paris, 1985) and L'Enfer au temps de Jésus (Paris, 1985).

27. On the urban imagination see the very interesting book of Chiara Frugoni, Una lontana città: Sentimenti e immagini nel Medioevo (Turin, 1983), which has an excellent iconographic index.

28. On medieval mathematics see Guy Beaujouan, "Le Moyen Age: L'héritage," and "Le Moyen Age: Originalité," in Émile Noël, ed., Le Matin des mathématiciens: Entretiens sur l'histoire des mathématiques (Paris: Belin/France Culture, 1985), pp. 171–189.

29. Jacques Le Goff, "Les rêves dans la culture et la psychologie collective de l'Occident médiéval," Scolies 1 (1971): 123–130, reprinted in Pour un autre Moyen Age (Paris: Gallimard, 1977), pp. 299–306 [in the English translation Time, Work and Culture in the Middle Ages, trans. Arthur Goldhammer (Chicago, 1978), pp. 201–24].

30. Jean-Claude Schmitt is currently working on the iconography of medieval dreams.

## FOR AN EXTENDED MIDDLE AGES

1. C. Brémond, Jacques Le Goff, and Jean-Claude Schmitt, L'Exemplum, Typologie des sources du Moyen Age occidental, pamphlet 40 (Turnhout, 1982).

2. Krzysztof Pomian, "Périodisation," in La Nouvelle Histoire, ed. Jacques Le Goff, R. Chartier, and Jacques Revel (Paris, 1978), pp. 455–457.

## THE MARVELOUS IN THE MEDIEVAL WEST

1. The problems discussed in this essay and the catalogue of marvelous occurrences suggested here were first proposed in a paper delivered to a conference held in March 1974 at the Collège de France on the theme "The Strange

and the Marvelous in Medieval Islam." My contribution was therefore comparative in intent, and it was unfortunate that no paper at the conference was devoted to the question of marvels in Byzantium. Hélène Ahrweiler and Gilbert Dagron attempted to fill this gap in the discussion. In revising this essay for publication, I have eliminated any direct comparison with Islam. For my remarks on this topic, see the proceedings of the colloquium *L'Étrange et le merveilleux dans l'Islam médiéval* (Paris: Editions J.A., 1978), pp. 61–79.

2. Frantisek Graus, *Volk, Herrscher und Heiliger im Reich der Merowinger: Studien zur Hagiographie der Merowingerzeit* (Prague, 1965).

3. Erich Köhler, *Ideal und Wirklichkeit in der höfischen Epik* (1956, second edition 1970), and "Observations historiques et sociologiques sur la poésie des troubadours," *Esprit und arkadische Freiheit—Aufsätze aus der Welt der Romania* (Frankfurt, 1966).

4. See the second part of this chapter, "A Preliminary Catalogue of the Marvelous in the Medieval West."

5. Ibid.

6. Although it is true that no clear distinction was made between *miraculum* and *mirabilia* until the twelfth century, I do not agree with D. Bouthillier and J.-P. Torrell, "'Miraculum,' une catégorie fondamentale chez Pierre le Vénérable," *Revue thomiste* 80 (1980): 357–386, who propose translating the word *miraculum* in Peter the Venerable's *De miraculis* as *marvel* or *marvelous fact*.

7. J. G. Frazer, *Folklore in the Old Testament*, 3 vols. (London, 1918); P. Saintyves, *Essais de folklore biblique: Magie, mythes et miracles dans l'Ancien et le Nouveau Testament* (1923); P. Gibert, *Une théorie de la légende: Hermann Gunkel et les légendes de la Bible* (Paris: Flammarion, 1979).

8. Also known as Giraud le Gallois or Giraud de Barri.

9. Bradford Broughton, *The Legends of King Richard I, Coeur de Lion: A Study of Sources and Variations to the Year 1600* (Paris–The Hague, 1966).

10. My friend Prof. Franco Alessio points out that there is a very interesting passage on "technological marvels" in Roger Bacon's *De secretis*.

11. On what is real and what is imaginary in Marco Polo's account, see J. Heers, *Marco Polo* (Paris, 1983).

## THE WILDERNESS IN THE MEDIEVAL WEST

1. See X. de Planhol, "Le désert, cadre géographique de l'expérience religieuse," in *Les Mystiques du désert dans l'Islam, le Judaïsme et le Christianisme* (L'Association des Amis de Sénanque, 1974).

2. See P. Gibert, *La Bible à la naissance de l'histoire* (Paris, 1979), p. 141, n. 3.

3. See A. Abecassis, "L'expérience du désert dans la mentalité hébraïque," in *Les Mystiques du désert*, pp. 107–129.

4. See especially J. Pedersen, *Israël, Its Life and Culture* (London–Copenhagen, 1926), p. 470, and N. J. Tromp, *Primitive Conceptions of Death and the Netherworld in the Old Testament* (Rome, 1969), p. 132.

5. See X.-L. Dufour, "Désert," in *Dictionnaire du Nouveau Testament* (Paris, 1975).

6. For Saint Paul temptations could occur anywhere: "in perils in the city, in perils in the wilderness, in perils in the sea" (2 Corinthians 11:26).

7. J. Décarreaux, *Les Moines et la civilisation* (Paris, 1962), pp. 64–109; J. Lacarrière, *Les Hommes ivres de Dieu* (Paris, 1975).

8. A. Guillaumont, "La conception du désert chez les moines d'Egypte," in *Les Mystiques du désert*, p. 38.

9. J. Pricoco, *L'Isola dei santi: Il cenobio di Lerino e le origini del monachismo gallico* (Rome, 1978).

10. D. J. Chitty, *The Desert a City* (Oxford, 1961), and G. J. M. Bartelink, "Les oxymorones *desertum civitas* and *desertum floribus vernans*," in *Studia Monastica* 15 (1973): 7–15.

11. P.-A. Février, "La ville et le 'désert'," in *Les Mystiques du désert*, pp. 39–61.

12. See J. M. MacKinlay, "In Oceano desertum: Celtic Anchorites and Their Island Retreats," in *Proceedings of the Society of Antiquaries of Scotland* 33 (1899), and L. Gougaud, *Les Chrétientés celtiques* (Paris, 1911).

13. O. Loyer, *Les Chrétientés celtiques* (Paris, 1965), p. 37.

14. C. Selmer, *Navigatio Sancti Brendani abbatis* (Notre Dame, 1959).

15. B. Mérignac, in *Un pays de Cornouaille, Locronan et sa région*, ed. M. Dilasser (Paris, 1979), p. 110. *La Vita de Saint Ronan* dates from the thirteenth century. Concerning the wolf, so important a figure in medieval reality as well as legend and the animal par excellence of the forest wilderness, see G. Ortalli, "Natura, storia e mitografia del lupo nel Medioevo," *La Cultura* (1973) pp. 257–311.

16. Gaston Roupnel, *Histoire de la campagne française* (Paris, 1932, 1974), chap. 3: "The Forest," pp. 91–116. Gaston Bachelard, in *La Poétique de l'espace*, pp. 171–172, echoes Roupnel in his evocation of the "ancestral forest," which is "prior to I and thou." The forest was a place in which people lost themselves. But others, intrepid explorers of the wilderness, went hopefully in search of themselves.

17. C. Higounet, "Les forêts de l'Europe occidentale du Ve au XIe siècle," in *Agricoltura e mundo rurale in Occidente nell'alto medioevo*, proceedings of the XIIIa Settimana di studio del centro italiano di studi sull'alto medioevo, 1965 (Spoleto, 1966), pp. 343–398.

18. "In foresta nostra nuncupata Arduenna, in locis vastae solitudinis in quibus caterua bestiarum geminat."

19. Marc Bloch, "Une mise au point: les invasions," *Annales d'histoire sociale*, 1945, reprinted in *Mélanges historiques* (Paris, 1964), p. 128.

20. Marc Bloch, *Les Caractères originaux de l'histoire rurale française* (Oslo, 1931), new edition (Paris, 1951), p. 6.

21. Charles de La Roncière, Philippe Contamine, Robert Delort, and Michel Rouche, eds., *L'Europe au Moyen Age*, vol. 2 (Paris, 1969), pp. 71–75.

22. "*Nulla erat habitacio hominum excepta latronorum in silvis.*"

23. Louis Gougaud, *Ermites et reclus* (Ligugé, 1928), p. 16.

24. Guibert of Nogent, *De vita sua*, 1. 9. Because of this story Evrard was claimed by the nineteenth-century *carbonari* as their founder.

25. One useful guide is *L'Eremitismo in Occidente nei secoli XI e XII*, Atti della Settimana internazionale di studio, Mendola, 1962 (Milan, 1965).

26. *Le Saga de Harald l'impitoyable*, trans. by R. Boyer (Paris, 1979), pp. 35–36.

27. See E. Köhler, *L'Aventure chevaleresque: Idéal et réalité dans le roman courtois*, French trans. (Paris, 1974).

28. See H. Braet, "Les amants dans la forêt, à propos d'un passage du 'Tristan' de Béroul," in *Mélanges Terno Sato* (Nagoya: Center of Medieval and Romanesque Studies, 1973), pp. 1–8.

29. Jacques Le Goff and Pierre Vidal-Naquet, "Lévi-Strauss en Brocéliande," abridged version published in *Critique* 325 (1974): 541–571. The complete version may be found in *Claude Lévi-Strauss*, ed. R. Bellour and C. Clément (Paris, 1979), pp. 265–319. On the medieval forest and its symbolism see M. Stauffer, *Der Wald: Zur Darstellung und Deutung der Natur im Mittelalter* (Zurich, 1958), and the still unpublished thesis of Roberto Ruiz Capellan, a summary of which can be read in *Bosque e Individuo: Necación y destierro de la sociedad en la epopeya y novela francesas de los siglos XII y XIII*, Universidad de Salamanca, Facultad de filosofía y letras, Departamento de filología francesa (1978).

30. On the important theme of man as savage in the Middle Ages, see Bernheimer, *Wild Men in the Middle Ages: A Study in Art, Sentiment, and Demonology*, 2d ed. (New York, 1970).

31. Le Goff and Vidal-Naquet, "Lévi-Strauss en Brocéliande," p. 284 of the complete version (see n. 29 above).

32. Gougaud, *Ermites et reclus*, p. 52: "The man who lived a holy life in a hermitage therefore became the true type of the ascetic for the common man. In folktales and legends the hermit was always described as a man of 'very saintly life.' That is why he was chosen in preference to all other men of religion to fill the role of champion in the struggle with the devil."

33. *Ibid.*, p. 19. An English translation of the poem was published by Kuno Meyer, *King and Hermit* (London, 1901).

34. Le Goff and Vidal-Naquet, "Lévi-Strauss en Brocéliande," pp. 272–273 of the complete version (see n. 29 above).

35. As Paule Le Rider points out in her admirable book, *Le Chevalier dans le Conte du Graal de Chrétien de Troyes* (Paris, 1978), pp. 160–164.

36. All the more crucial because it is the final scene in which the hero appears in Chrétien's unfinished work. Whatever the conclusion might have been, this would no doubt have remained a key episode.

37.                 En boscermita m.vol faire,
                     Per zo qe ma domma ab me.s n'an

Lai de fueill' aurem cobertor.
Aqi vol viurë e murir
Tot autre afar guerpis e lais.

From a poem by Bernard Marti, cited by J.-C. Payen, *L'Espace et le temps de la chanson courtoise occitane*, p. 155.

38. Jacques Le Goff, "Guerriers et bourgeois conquérants: l'image de la ville dans la littérature française du XIIe siècle," in *Culture, science et développement, Mélanges Charles Morazé* (Toulouse, 1969), p. 127. This essay is translated in part 4 of this book.

39. See Jacques Le Goff, "Ville et théologie au XIIe siècle: Une métaphore urbaine de Guillaume d'Auvergne," in *Razo,* Cahiers du centre d'études médiévales de Nice (June 1979), p. 33, translated in part 4 of this book. On the contrast between men of the city and men of the woods in Italy, a country where urbanization was advanced but where there was also a great vogue of eremitism in the Middle Ages, see W. M. Bowsky, "*Cives silvestres:* Sylvan Citizenship and the Sienese Commune (1287–1355)," *Bulletino senese di storia Patria,* 1965.

40. Frederick Antal, *Florentine Painting and Its Social Background* (London, 1948), attributes to this work an antibourgeois ideological and political significance.

41. Hervé Martin, "L'implantation des franciscains bretons en milieu marin," in *Annales de Bretagne et des Pays de l'Ouest* (1980), pp. 641–677. On the reasons why Francis of Assisi and the first Franciscans abandoned the hermit's life and took to the cities, see J. Paul, "L'érémitisme et la survivance de la spiritualité du désert chez les franciscains," in *Les Mystiques du désert*, pp. 133–146.

## THE PERCEPTION OF CHRISTENDOM
## BY THE ROMAN CURIA

1. *Ut interim haberi possit competens discussio et plena deliberatio ad opportuna exquirenda, ut decet, antidota circa illa per approbationem eiusdem adhibenda* (letter of 11 March 1273, Guiraud, Registers, 1, p. 91, n. 220).

2. A. Callebaut, "Le voyage du Bienheureux Grégoire X et de saint Bonaventure au concile de Lyon et la date du sacre de saint Bonaventure," in *Archivum Franciscanum Historicum* 18 (1925): 169–180.

## THE TIME OF PURGATORY

1. Father P.-M. Gy has kindly shared with me his compilation of sources concerning the "receptacles of souls."

2. Interested readers may refer to my *Naissance du Purgatoire* (Paris: Gallimard, 1981), translated by Arthur Goldhammer as *The Birth of Purgatory* (Chicago: The University of Chicago Press, 1984), for further details and a bibliography.

3. Robert Bultot, *Christianisme et valeurs humaines: La doctrine du mépris du monde en Occident de saint Ambroise à Innocent III,* vol. 4 (Paris, 1963–1964).

4. A. Murray, *Reason and Society in the Middle Ages* (Oxford, 1978).

5. Father P.-M. Gy drew my attention to this delicate but important connection.

6. H. Dondaine, "L'objet et le medium de la vision béatifique chez les théologiens du XIIIe siècle," in *Revue de théologie antique et médiévale* 19 (1952): 60–130.

7. M. Dykmans, *Les Sermons de Jean XXII sur la vision béatifique* (Rome, 1973).

8. Jean-Claude Schmitt, "Temps, folklore et politique au XIIe siècle: A propos de deux récits de Walter Map, *De nugis curialium,* I. 9 et IV. 3," *Le temps chrétien de la fin de l'Antiquité au Moyen Age* (Paris: Centre National de Recherche Scientifique, 1984), pp. 489–515.

9. See J. Chiffoleau, *Le Comptabilité de l'au-delà: Les hommes, la mort et la religion dans la région d'Avignon à la fin du Moyen Age* (Rome, 1980).

10. See Le Goff, *La Naissance du Purgatoire,* chap. 8.

11. See Le Goff, "Au Moyen Age: Temps de l'Eglise et temps du marchand," *Annales ESC* 1960: 417–433, reprinted in *Pour un autre Moyen Age* (Paris, 1977), pp. 46–55.

12. See J.-L. Lemaître, *Répertoire des documents nécrologiques français* (Paris, 1980), vol. 1, especially pp. 23–24.

13. See the works discussed by J. Wollasch in "Les obituaires, témoins de la vie clunisienne," *Cahiers de Civilisation médiévale* 86 (April–June 1979): 139–171.

14. On this point my interpretation differs from that of A. Gourevitch, who focuses exclusively on Purgatory as it relates to the individual. (Because of the author's involuntary absence I read a summary of his paper to the colloquium. It has now been published as "Conscience individuelle et image de l'au-delà au Moyen Age," *Annales ESC* [1982]: 255–275.)

## THE TIME OF THE *EXEMPLUM*

1. See the roundtable organized in 1979 by the Ecole française de Rome on the subject "Rhétorique et histoire: L'exemplum et le modèle de comportment dans le discours antique et médiéval," *MEFRM* 112 (1980–81): 7–179.

2. See C. Brémond, Jacques Le Goff, and Jean-Claude Schmitt, *L'Exemplum,* pamphlet 40 in the series *Typologie des sources du Moyen Age occidental,* edited by Léopold Génicot and R. Bultot (Turnhout, 1982).

3. Definitions given by intellectuals, formed by book learning and the influence of antiquity, illustrate continuity rather than change. The Middle Ages followed Cicero: "*Exemplum est quod rem auctoritate aut casu alicuius hominis aut negotii confirmat aut infirmat*" (*De inventione,* 1, 49). Even more they followed a work then attributed to Cicero, the *Rhetorica ad Herennium:* "*Exemplum est*

*dictum vel factum alicuius autentice persone dignum imitatione"* (4, 49, 62). See G. Mari, ed. "Poetria . . . de arte prosaica, metrica et rithmica," *Romanische Forschungen* 13 (1902): 888.

4. The study on which this essay is based was carried out by the Group for Historical Anthropology of the Medieval West at the Ecole des Hautes Etudes en Sciences Sociales. It focused primarily on the following works: Caesarius of Heisterbach, *Dialogus miraculorum;* the unpublished (except for the exempla cited by Crane) *sermones vulgares* and *ad status* of James of Vitry; Stephen of Bourbon's *Tractatus de diversis materiis praedicabilibus* (unpublished except for the exempla collected by Lecoy de la Marche); and Arnold of Liège's *Alphabetum narrationum* (also unpublished).

5. Bernard Guenée, *Histoire et culture historique au Moyen Age* (Paris: Aubier, 1981).

6. F. Hartog, *Le Miroir d'Hérodote* (Paris: Gallimard, 1980).

7. See Francis Yates, *The Art of Memory* (Chicago: The University of Chicago Press, 1966).

## BODY AND IDEOLOGY IN THE MEDIEVAL WEST

1. These brief remarks should be read as annotations to the important work of Marie-Christine Pouchelle, "Savoir médical et symbolique du corps dans la seconde moitié du Moyen Age: La Chirurgie d'Henri de Mondeville (1306–1320)," thesis, University of Paris X, 1980, and of Jean-Claude Schmitt on medieval gestures.

## GESTURES IN PURGATORY

1. See my *La Naissance du Purgatoire* (Paris: Gallimard, 1982), translated by Arthur Goldhammer as *The Birth of Purgatory* (Chicago: University of Chicago Press, 1984).

2. Jean-Claude Schmitt, "Le geste, la cathédrale, et le roi," in *L'Arc,* special issue devoted to Georges Duby, 72 (1978).

3. Jean-Claude Schmitt, "*Gestus, gesticulatio:* Contribution à l'étude du vocabulaire latin médiéval des gestes," in La Lexicographie du latin médiéval et ses rapports avec les recherches actuelles sur la civilisation du Moyen Age (Paris: CNRS, 1981).

4. See Le Goff, *The Birth of Purgatory,* chap. 6, for a bibliography concerning the *Purgatorium Sancti Patricii.* I used the edition of K. Volmöller, *Zur Geschichte der Legende vom Purgatorium des heil: Patricius in Romanische Forschungen* (Mall, 1891), pp. 139–197.

5. See V. Turner and E. Turner, *Image and Pilgrimage in Christian Culture* (Oxford, 1978), chap. 3, "Saint Patrick's Purgatory: Religion and Nationalism in an Archaic Pilgrimage," pp. 104–139.

6. See Gérard Le Don, "L'imagerie des enfers," thesis, Centre d'Etudes sur l'Imaginaire, Chambéry.

7. See Carlo Ginzburg, "High and Low: The Theme of Forbidden Knowledge in the Sixteenth and Seventeenth Centuries," in *Past and Present* 73 (Nov. 1976): 28–41.

8. Dante of course chose another way of representing progress in Purgatory: a mountain, which souls ascend as they are purified. See my *Birth of Purgatory,* chap. 10.

9. For an example of medieval theology constructed around the *redditus* theme, see M. Corbin, *Le Chemin de la théologie chez Thomas d'Aquin* (Paris, 1974).

## THE REPUDIATION OF PLEASURE

1. For references see the select bibliography at the end of this article.

2. Cited in J.-L. Flandrin, *Un Temps pour embrasser,* pp. 8–9.

## LEVI-STRAUSS IN BROCELIANDE

1. The title of this essay is obviously inspired by Edmund Leach's well-known paper "Lévi-Strauss in the Garden of Eden: An Examination of Some Recent Developments in the Analysis of Myth," *Transactions of the New York Academy of Science* 2(23)1967. We wish to thank Claude Gaignebet, a true savage, and the very civilized Paule Le Rider for the valuable information they provided.

2. For this date and general information about the sources and composition of the romance, see J. Frappier, *Etude sur "Yvain ou le Chevalier au lion" de Chrétien de Troyes* (Paris, 1969), which contains a nearly complete bibliography. We use and cite from, with minor correction, the modern French adaptation by André Mary (Paris, 1944). [The English translations here are from the French cited in the original text.—Trans.] Not until it was too late to make use of it did we learn of the translation by C. Buridant and J. Trotin (Paris, 1972). The numbering of the verses is that of the "edition" (based on Guiot de Provins's copy) of Mario Roques, *Les Romans de Chrétien de Troyes,* vol. 4: *Le Chevalier au lion* (Paris, 1967). The best edition is still that of W. Foerster, 2d ed. (Halle, 1891); cf. P. Jonin, *Prolégomènes à une édition d'Yvain* (Aix-Gap, 1958).

3. See C. Brémond, *Logique du récit* (Paris, 1973), which builds on the work of Vladimir Propp.

4. This was noticed by R. Bezzola, *Le Sens de l'aventure et de l'amour (Chrétien de Troyes),* 2d ed. (Paris, 1968), pp. 81–134. See also W. S. Woods, "The Plot Structure in Four Romances of Chrestien de Troyes," in *Studies in Philology* (1953), pp. 1–15; J. C. Payen, *Le Motif du repentir dans la littérature française médiévale* (Geneva, 1968), p. 385; and W. Brand, *Chrétien de Troyes* (Munich, 1972), pp. 72–73, which clearly summarizes the different views concerning the two parts of *Yvain.* Comparative structural analysis of Chrétien's five ro-

mances can be found in the fundamental work of Eric Köhler, *Ideal und Wirklichkeit in der Höfischen Epik* (Tübingen, 1956), pp. 257–264 (a second edition with an important appendix was published in 1970).

5. Published in English translation by J. J. Parry in the *University of Illinois Studies in Language and Literature,* vol. 10, no. 3 (Urbana, 1925). For a recent comment on Merlin's madness see D. Laurent, "La gwerz de Skolan et la légende de Merlin," in *Ethnologie française* 1 (1971): 19–54. On Merlin as a man of the woods and on a similar figure in Scottish mythology who was taken up by Christianity in the legend of Saint Kentigern see M. L. D. Ward, "Lailoken or Merlin Sylvester," in *Romania* (1893) pp. 504–526.

6. See the examples collected in the excellent work of R. Bernheimer, *Wild Men in the Middle Ages: A Study in Art, Sentiment, and Demonology,* 2d ed. (New York, 1970), pp. 12–17. As Bernheimer rightly notes, "to the Middle Ages wildness and insanity were almost interchangeable terms" (p. 12). Merlin is of course mentioned numerous times in this work.

7. Frappier, *Etude,* p. 19.

8. Ibid., p. 178. The psychologization of the episode dates as far back as the Middle Ages. The German poet Hartmann von Aue in his *Iwein* gives a sort of interpretation of Chrétien's romance that frequently emphasizes its structural aspects. Nevertheless, he insists that courtly love, or "Minne," is so powerful that a member of the weaker sex can reduce a valiant warrior to madness. See J. Fourquet, *Hartmann d'Aue: Erec-Iwein* (Paris, 1944), and for a comparison of the two poems and a commentary on Hartmann's work, see H. Sacker, "An Interpretation of Hartmann's Iwein," in *Germanic Review* (1961), pp. 5–26, and M. Huby, *L'Adaptation des romans courtois en Allemagne aux XIIe et XIIIe siècles* (Paris, 1968), especially pp. 369–370. We are indebted to Raymond Perrenec for several useful comments on Hartmann's poem.

9. J.-C. Payen, *Le Motif du repentir,* goes so far as to compare Yvain's remorse with "that . . . of Cain hiding in a grave to escape from his bad conscience."

10. Few structural analyses of medieval literature have been attempted in France. See, however, F. Barteau, *Les Romans de Tristan et Iseut* (Paris, 1972). A recent bibliography and a brief general introduction may be found in P. Zumthor, *Essai de poétique médiévale* (Paris, 1972), pp. 352–359.

11. Hartmann von Aue underscores the opposition between cultivated fields and wild forest by systematically rhyming *gevilde* (cultivated rural lands) with *wilde* (the wilderness), as in lines 3237–3238 in the Benecke, Lachmann, and Wolff edition: "Thus he crossed the fields (*über gevilde*) and headed for the wild (*nach der Wilde*)." The German poet is also playing on the relation between *Wilde* and *Wald* (forest).

12. See Jacques Le Goff, *La Civilisation de l'Occident médiéval* (Paris, 1964), pp. 169–171.

13. Charles Petit-Dutaillis, *La Monarchie féodale,* 2d ed. (Paris, 1971), pp. 140–142, citing *De necessariis observantiis scaccarii dialogus,* ed. A. Hughes,

C. G. Crump, and C. Johnson (Oxford, 1902), p. 105. Compare H. A. Cronne, "The Royal Forest in the Reign of Henri I," in *Essays in Honor of J. E. Todd* (London, 1949), pp. 1–23.

14. Petit-Dutaillis, *La Monarchie féodale.*

15. This park remains rather mysterious. In the Welsh version of Yvain's adventures the park is the place where the mad knight meets the lady who will save him. It thus becomes a kind of seigneurial "paradise."

16. It is tempting to speculate that this episodic lad has a female counterpart in the person of the "Wild Damsel" (line 1624), who warns Laudine of the impending arrival of King Arthur and his court in her mysterious domain in the heart of Broceliande, which will establish contact between the City and the Forest.

17. *Heracles,* lines 157–164. On these questions see Pierre Vidal-Naquet, "Le Philoctète de Sophocle et l'Ephébie," *Annales ESC* (1971), pp. 623–638, reprinted in Jean-Pierre Vernant and Pierre Vidal-Naquet, *Mythe et tragédie en Grèce ancienne* (Paris, 1972), pp. 167–184, especially pp. 170–172.

18. Georges Dumézil, *Mythe et épopée* (Paris, 1968), vol. 1, p. 64.

19. Béroul, *Le Roman de Tristan,* ed. E. Muret and L. M. Defourques (Paris, 1972); translated into modern French by D. Grojnowski (Lausanne, 1971).

20. This point bears emphasis because certain modern and widely known versions of *Tristan* (such as those of Joseph Bédier and René Louis) portray King Mark threatening Tristan with an arrow in the famous scene of the observed rendez-vous. But nothing like this can be found in the versions of Béroul or Eilhart of Obert or Gottfried of Strasburg. The scene is also absent from what has survived of Thomas's version. See J. Bédier, *Le Tristan de Thomas* (Paris, 1902), pp. 198–203, an instructive text for anyone interested in knowing how a medieval romance is reconstituted or fabricated.

21. *Merlin's Prophecies,* ed. L. A. Paton (New York, 1926).

22. The names suggest bears.

23. *Merlin's Prophecies,* pp. 424–425.

24. An erotic song by Jean Bretel d'Arras (G. Raynaud, ed., *Bibliothèque de l'Ecole des chartes* 41 (1880): 203–202) has as its refrain "Je sui li ars qui ne faut" (I am the unerring bow). On the theme and image of the unerring bow, see M. D. Legge, "The Unerring Bow," *Medium Aevum* (1956): 79–83.

25. Geffrei Gaimer, *Estoire des Engleis,* ed. A. Bell (Oxford, 1960), line 4392.

26. Galbert of Bruges, *Histoire du meurtre de Charles le Bon, comte de Flandre,* ed. Henri Pirenne (Paris, 1891), p. 59; see also pp. 121–122.

27. See Georges Duby, *Le Dimanche de Bouvines* (Paris, 1973), pp. 103ff.

28. Bertrand of Bar, *Girard de Vienne,* ed. P. Tarbé (Paris, 1850), p. 7.

29. R. Foreville, *Latran I, II, III et Latran IV* (Paris, 1965), p. 89.

30. Benedict of Sainte-Maure, *Le Roman de Troie,* ed. L. Constans (Paris, 1905), vol. 2, lines 12354–12374, pp. 231–232. See also A. M. Crosby, *The Portrait in Twelfth-Century French Literature* (Geneva, 1965), pp. 21–22 and 87.

31. R. L. Thomson, ed., *Owein or Chwedl Iarlles y Ffynnawn* (Dublin,

1968). Very likely the two versions shared a common source. The works of Frappier, *Etude*, pp. 65–69, and A. C. Brown, "Iwain, A Study in the Origins of Arthurian Romance," in *Studies and Notes in Philology and Literature* (Cambridge: Harvard University Press, 1903), pp. 1–147, may also be consulted, though both works suffer from nationalist and pro- or anti-Celtic prejudice.

32. Morgan Watkin, *La Civilisation française dans les Mabinogion* (Paris, 1963). Jean Marx, not one to minimize the importance of Celtic sources, also recognizes "the influences of Franco-Norman romances and mores" on the Welsh *Owein*. See his *Nouvelles Recherches sur la littérature arthurienne* (Paris, 1969), p. 27, note 5. Neither of these authors has considered the role of the bow in *Yvain* or *Owein*, however.

33. Cf. Thomson, *Owein or Chwedgl Iarlles y Ffynnawn*, pp. xxx–xxxi. These are sumptuous bows, strung with the muscles of stags and equipped with whalebone handles.

34. Claude Lévi-Strauss, *Annuaire de l'Ecole pratique des Hautes Etudes*, Sections des sciences religieuses (1958–1959), pp. 3–43; reprinted in *Anthropologie structurale II* (Paris, 1973), pp. 175–233.

35. The nature/culture, savage/courtly dialectic was a feature of the period's mental and literary schemata. In a text roughly contemporary with *Yvain*, an *exemplum* taken from the Cistercian Geoffroy of Auxerre's commentary on Revelation, we find a process of acculturation of a savage woman that is more or less the exact opposite of the process of deculturation that Yvain undergoes. Yvain first abandons the company of the civilized, then sheds his clothing, then changes his diet. In Geoffroy's text a young man returning from a swim in the ocean brings with him a Melusina, to whom he gives clothing, food, and drink in the company of his relatives and friends: "*Suo nihilominus opertam pallio duxit domum et congruis fecit a matre sua vestibus operiri. . . . Fuit autem cum eis manducans et bibens, et in cunctis pene tam sociabiliter agens, ac si venisset inter convicaneos, inter cognatos et notos*" (see F. Gastaldelli, ed., *Super Apocalipsim* [Rome, 1970], p. 184). Compare G. Lobrichon, "Encore Mélusine: un texte de Geoffroy d'Auxerre," *Bulletin de la société de mythologie française* 83 (1971): 178–180.

36. This nudity is mentioned five times, in lines 2834, 2888, 2908, 3016, and 3024. See M. Stauffer, *Der Wald: Zur Darstellung und Deutung der Natur im Mittelalter* (Zurich, 1958), p. 79.

37. Béroul, *Le Roman de Tristan*, lines 1285–1296.

38. Claude Lévi-Strauss, "Le triangle culinaire," *L'Arc* 26 (1966): 19–29.

39. That it is important not to reify these concepts is a point made by Serge Moscovici, *La Société contre nature* (Paris, 1972), as well as by Claude Lévi-Strauss, *Structures élémentaires de la parenté*, 2d ed. (Paris–The Hague, 1967), p. xvii.

40. On the relation between *silva* and *silvaticus* (or *Wald* and *Wild* in German), see W. von Wartburg, *Französiches Etymologistes Wörterbuch* 11 (Basel, 1964), pp. 616–621, and especially J. Trier, *Venus, Etymologien und das Futterlauf*, in *Münsterische Forschungen* 15 (Cologne, 1963), pp. 48–51.

41. See M. D. Chenu, "La nature et l'homme: La Renaissance du XIIe siècle," in *La Théologie au XIIe siècle* (Paris, 1957), pp. 19–51.

42. The semantic commonality is among the most disturbing. *Silva* meant both forest and matter (from the Greek *hyle*), and medieval thought played on this fact. J. Györy has attempted to use this as the basis for an interpretation of Chrétien's romance in "Le cosmos, un songe," in *Annales Universitatis Budapestinensis, Sectio philologica* (1963), pp. 87–110.

43. See P. Gallais, *Perceval et l'initiation* (Paris, 1972), especially pp. 28–29 and 40–43, whose conclusions need to be verified by close examination of the text.

44. See M. Zink, *La Pastourelle: Poésie et folklore du Moyen Age* (Paris-Montreal, 1972), especially pp. 100–101, whose conclusions are similar to ours in a number of respects.

45. Chretién de Troyes, *Perceval le Gallois ou le Conte du Graal,* translated by L. Foulet (Paris, 1972), p. 147.

46. This episode is commented on several times in Gallais, *Perceval et l'initiation* (see the index under *ermite*).

47. See J. B. Williamson, "Elyas as a Wild Man in Li Estoire del Chevalier au Cisne," *Essays in Honor of L. F. Solano* (Chapel Hill, N.C.: University of North Carolina Press, 1970), pp. 193–202.

48. See A. Dickson, *Valentine and Orson: A Study in Late Medieval Romance* (New York, 1929).

49. Ibid., p. 326; Bernheimer, *Wild Men,* p. 18.

50. Think of the centaurs of antiquity and their role as educators. Bernheimer's *Wild Men* is an initial attempt to pursue this theme, which bears further investigation.

51. *Quête du Graal,* edited by A. Pauphilet (Paris, 1923), translated by A. Béguin as *Quest for the Grail* (Paris, 1965).

52. Tzvetan Todorov, "La Quête du récit," in *Critique* (1969), pp. 195–214 (the passage cited here is on p. 197). There is in thirteenth-century literature an allegorical reading of an episode involving Yvain: Huon de Méry, *Le Tornoiemenz Antecrit,* ed. G. Wimmer (Marburg, 1888). On the transition from symbolism to allegory, see for example H. R. Jauss, "La transformation de la forme allégorique entre 1180 et 1240: d'Alain de Lille à Guillaume de Lorris," in A. Fourrier, ed., *L'Humanisme médiéval dans les littératures romanes du XIIe au XIVe siècle* (Paris, 1964), pp. 107–144.

53. P. Haidu, *Lion-Queue-Coupée: L'Ecart symbolique chez Chrétien de Troyes* (Geneva, 1972); see especially the classic pages of M. D. Chenu, "La mentalité symbolique," in *La Théologie au XIIe siècle,* pp. 159–190.

54. Overviews for a single era are relatively rare. On the Middle Ages, see Bernheimer, *Wild Men,* whose interests are extremely broad. Also worth consulting is L. L. Möller, "Die Wilden Leute des Mittelalter," the catalogue compiled for an exposition at the Museum für Kunst und Gewerbe of Hamburg (1963); W. Mulertt, "Der Wilde Mann in Frankreich," *Zeitschrift für französische Sprach und Literatur* (1932), pp. 69–88; O. Schultz-Gora, "Der Wilde

Mann in der provenzalischen Literatur," in *Zeitschrift für Romanische Philologie* 44 (1924): 129–137.

55. In Europe, for example, there was both a wild man of the winter, naked, hairy, wielding a club, and often likened to a bear, and a wild man of the spring, or "May man," girt with a symbolic belt of leaves. Concerning the rites associated with the capture of the wild man, that is, the subsumption of the forces that he represents, see A. Van Gennep, *Manuel de Folklore français*, vol. 3 (Paris, 1947), pp. 922–925, and vol. 4 (Paris, 1949), pp. 1488–1502.

56. See A. Aarne and S. Thompson, *The Types of the Folktale*, 2d ed. (Helsinki, 1964), FFC 184, T. 502, pp. 169–170, and, for France, P. Delarue and M. L. Ténèze, *Le Conte populaire français*, vol. 2 (Paris, 1964), countertype 502, "l'homme sauvage," pp. 221–227. On the wild man as a motif in folktales, see S. Thompson, *Motif-Index of Folk Literature*, vol. 6 (index) (Copenhagen, 1958), under the head "Wild Animal," especially III, F. 567.

57. Not everyone made such interpretations, but this was the majority attitude.

58. See the fine study of R. Marienstras, "La littérature élisabéthaine des voyages et *La Tempête* de Shakespeare," in Société des Anglicistes de l'enseignement supérieur, *Actes du Congrès de Nice* (1971), pp. 21–49. For a colonial interpretation of *The Tempest*, see R. Fernandez Retamar, *Caliban cannibale*, translated by J. F. Bonaldi (Paris, 1973), pp. 16–63.

59. Bernheimer's *Wild Men* lacks a chapter on the wild man and the devil.

60. We are not, of course, proposing a comprehensive interpretation of *Yvain* but merely attempting to bring out one level of meaning.

61. See the special May–August 1971 issue of *Annales ESC*, devoted to "History and Structure."

62. On the forest as the natural setting of knightly adventure, see Stauffer, *Der Wald*, especially pp. 14–115 (on Broceliande, cf. pp. 45–53). "Were the handsomest forms of prowess those of the city or those of the forest?" seems to have been a standard question in the Middle Ages, the answer to which was obviously that "the prowess of the city is worthless." See C. V. Langlois, *La Vie en France au Moyen Age*, vol. 3 (Paris, 1927), pp. 239–240.

63. Haidu, *Lion-Queue-Coupée*, emphasizes the symbolic value of this "Christian moral topos" (p. 37). See also the lucid comments of Eric Auerbach, *Mimesis*, trans. W. Trask (Princeton, 1953).

64. These lines are omitted from the Mary translation.

65. Haidu, *Lion*, p. 38, which draws upon a chapter in the celebrated work of E. R. Curtius, *European Literature and the Latin Middle Ages*, trans. W. Trask (Princeton, 1953).

66. In speaking of the knight or the hero we are referring to both Calogrenant and Yvain.

67. The translation is based on the text as established, we think in convincing fashion, by F. Bar, "Sur un passage de Chrétien de Troyes (*Yvain*, v. 276–285)," *Mélanges I. Siciliano* (Florence, 1966), pp. 47–50. In any case, it has been known since Foerster's edition that line 278 of the Guiot manuscript

(*tors salvages, ors et lieparz*) should not be read as "wild bulls, *bears and leopards*," for the latter animals are never mentioned again. The word *orz*, plural of *ord* (frightful, terrifying) was originally misread as *ors* (bear), and this mistake led to others. Buridant and Trotin, *Yvain*'s most recent translators, were also persuaded by this emendation (see p. ix of their version).

68. Hartmann borrows this comparison: "*Er was einem Möre gelich*" (line 427), but in a striking detail, which underscores the kinship between the mad Yvain and the wild man, he also applies it to the "mad noble" (*der edele Töre*, line 3347). The master of the bulls, though not "mad" in the psychological sense, is described in line 440 as a "*walttör*," a "madman of the woods."

69. Many of these features were a topos of medieval romance, and some can be traced back to late Latin literature. See Crosby, *The Portrait*, index under "giant herdsman."

70. Despite what is said by Gallais, *Perceval*, pp. 132–139, the "hideous damsel" of the *Grail* (lines 587–612, Lecoy edition, pp. 109–111 of the Foulet translation) does indeed offer Perceval a salutary warning, which is later completed and corrected by the hermit. Her portrait parallels that of the "peasant."

71. See especially Bernheimer, *Wild Men*, pp. 1–48. Note, however, that sexual aggressiveness is missing. On the other hand, the character's declaration that he is human is part of the medieval topos of the wild man. Among the many comparisons that one might make, one seems inevitable because it is with another herdsman who is also a helper of the hero: see *Aucassin et Nicolette*, Dufournet edition, chap. 24, pp. 15–16.

72. The corresponding figure in the Welsh tale reigns over true wild animals: serpents and mountain lions. As is common in Celtic tales, fantastic features are accentuated. The herdsman has only one foot and one eye, for example. See Loth, p. 9. In Hartmann there are no mountain lions, bears, serpents but there are bison and wild oxen, in other words, wild counterparts of the bull.

73. Cultivated lands are mentioned in lines 1619, 1808, 2086, and 2472.

74. The tree is a pine, and apart from the great oak mentioned in line 3012, near which Yvain regains his mental health, it is the only tree in the forest that is described. Because the pine is an evergreen, there is something magical about it (lines 384–385).

75. Such passages (and there are many others) provide some justification for Huon de Méry's allegorical interpretation, according to which Heaven precedes Hell on the approach to the fountain, as well as for A. Adler's modern interpretation, "Sovereignty in Chrétien's *Yvain*," in *Publications of the Modern Language Association of America* (1947), pp. 281–307, which attempts to identify instances of the philosophical concept of *coincidentia oppositorum* throughout the romance.

76. On this subject see the pertinent remarks of Tzvetan Todorov, *Introduction à la littérature fantastique* (Paris, 1970), pp. 21–24, criticizing Northrop Frye, *The Anatomy of Criticism* (Princeton, 1957).

77. As noted by E. Köhler, "Le rôle de la coutume dans les romans de

Chrétien de Troyes," in *Romania* (1960), pp. 386–397: "The misuse of the fountain is stopped by incorporating it into Arthur's kingdom" (p. 312). Of course this incorporation is not actually effected until the end of the romance.

78. This change of sign is characteristic of initiation rituals and of the stories told in connection with or in place of such rituals. The initiatory wilderness is brought into the world of culture. See on this matter the enlightening remarks of A. Margarido, "Proposiçòes teoricas para a leitura de textos iniciáticos," *Correio do Povo* (Porto Alegre), 21 August 1971.

79. Except that when he nearly goes mad again, he is compared to a "frenzied boar" (line 3518).

80. Chrétien's German "translator" actually makes the serpent a dragon. On the significance of dragons in medieval art and literature, see Jacques Le Goff, "Culture ecclésiastique et culture folklorique au Moyen Age: Saint Marcel de Paris et le dragon," in *Mélanges C. Barbagallo* (Bari, 1970), pp. 53–90, which contains a lengthy bibliography; reprinted in *Pour un autre Moyen Age* (Paris: Gallimard, 1978), pp. 236–279; English translation, pp. 159–188.

81. The comparison between the soul's concupiscent parts and the serpent was a twelfth-century topos. Yet a positive image of the serpent persists in medieval symbolism: even that creature was ambiguous. See Le Goff, "Culture ecclésiastique et culture folklorique."

82. On the symbolism of the lion and its origins in the legend of Saint Jerome and the story of Androcles, see J. Frappier, *Etude sur Yvain*, pp. 108–111, and Haidu, pp. 71–73. We do not believe, however, that Yvain's lion is a symbol of Christ, although the lion commonly figured as such in medieval symbolism. In the *Queste del Saint Graal*, ed. A. Pauphilet, pp. 94–98 and 101–104, Perceval repeats Yvain's adventure with the lion and the serpent and then, in a dream, sees two ladies, one riding a serpent, which is identified with the synagogue, the other riding a lion, which is identified with Christ. The two systems of images were thus combined.

83. This has been analyzed by G. Sansone, "Il sodalizio del leone e di Ivano," in *Mélanges I. Siciliano* (Florence, 1966), pp. 1053–1063. Concerning the eastern and monastic background of this friendship, see G. Penco, "L'amicizia con gli animali," in *Vita monastica* 17 (1963): 3–10, and M. J. Falsett, *Irische Heilige und Tiere im mittelalterlichen lateinischen Legenden* (Diss. Bonn, 1960).

84. This was noted by Brand, p. 78.

85. Here we omit the detail of the narrative, which is quite complex: in particular, Yvain intervenes in a quarrel between two heiresses. We are emphasizing only what is pertinent to the main line of our analysis and certainly one of the main lines of the story, namely, Yvain's relations with the wild.

86. The giant intends to turn the girl over to *garçons* (servants of the lowest sort) for their pleasure (lines 3866, 4110, and 4114). On the erotic connotations of the savage, see Bernheimer, *Wild Men*, pp. 121–175.

87. On possible meanings of the word *plain*, see p. xx below.

88. The parallel is carried to great lengths in the Welsh *Owein* (cf. Thom-

son, pp. xx and lii–liv). Both castles are inhabited by twenty-four maidens. In Chrétien's version both Pême-Aventure and the vavasor's castle have orchards (lines 5345, 5355). In both the heroes eat sumptuous meals. Sexual temptation is also present, but rejected. Yvain, faithful to Laudine, refuses to marry the girl he delivers, though she, too, is "beautiful and gentle" (line 5369). One point of difference is that there is no wife in the vavasor's castle, but there is one at Pême-Aventure.

89. Netun is derived by phonetic evolution from the Latin name of the god Neptunus.

90. Netun's son wields a sort of club "covered with metal and brass wire." Concerning this "horned club," normally proscribed in knightly combat, see F. Lyons, "Le bâton des champions dans *Yvain,*" in *Romania* (1970), pp. 97–101.

91. Here we are referring to characters that live *in* the wild, not to those who are merely passing through, such as the lady of Noroison whose magic ointment cures Yvain.

92. In Delarue and Ténèze's brief analysis of the "Conte de l'homme sauvage," the polarity between savage helper and savage enemy is clearly noted. In this story a child delivers a captive savage. Threatened with death and banished to the wild, the child encounters giants against whom the savage helps to protect him. The story ends with the child's return and the reintegration of the savage into society. It is clear, however, that this final sequence is redundant with respect to what goes before.

93. Obviously it would be possible to give a general anthropological reading of the text based on the theory of rites of passage and initiatory schemes, but such a reading is not within our area of expertise and in any case beyond the scope of this essay.

94. For a comprehensive and up-to-date introduction to the subject, see P. Le Gentil, *La Littérature française du Moyen Age,* 4th ed. (Paris, 1972), pp. 24–29.

95. The controversial issues are well stated in the anthology entitled *Chanson de geste und Höfischer Roman* (Heidelberg, 1963) (*Studia Romanica* 4), especially in the contributions of E. Köhler, "Quelques observations d'ordre historico-sociologique sur les rapports entre la chanson de geste et le roman courtois," pp. 21–30, and H. R. Jauss, "Chanson de geste et roman courtois au XIIe siècle (Analyse comparative du *Fierabras* et du *Bel Inconnu*)." See also R. Marichal, "Naissance du roman," in *Entretiens sur la renaissance du XIIe siècle,* ed. M. de Gandillac and E. Jeauneau (Paris and The Hague, 1968), pp. 449–482; J. Le Goff, "Naissance du roman historique au XIIe siècle," in *Nouvelle Revue française* 238 (1972): 163–173.

96. Léon Gautier, *La Chevalerie,* new edition (Paris, undated), p. 90.

97. Lévi-Strauss, *La Geste d'Asdiwal,* pp. 30–31.

98. "Explain structurally what can be explained structurally, which is never everything. As for the rest, try insofar as possible to grasp a determinism of another kind, which must be gleaned from statistics and sociology and

which has to do with individual history, the society, and the environment."
Claude Lévi-Strauss, *L'homme nu* (Paris, 1971), p. 560.

99. Claude Lévi-Strauss, *L'Origine des manières de table* (Paris, 1968), pp. 105–106.

100. Especially in his magisterial work, *Ideal und Wirklichkeit in der Höfischen Epik.*

101. Ibid., pp. 37–65.

102. *Roman de Thèbes,* ed. G. Raynaud de Lage (Paris, 1966).

103. Chrétien de Troyes, *Cligès,* ed. A. Micha (Paris, 1970), lines 3105–3124.

104. Erich Köhler, "Quelques observations," p. 27.

105. See Jauss, "Chanson de geste et roman courtois," pp. 65–70.

106. The comparison was first made, as far as we know, by J. Lafitau, *Moeurs des sauvages amériquains comparées aux moeurs des premiers temps* (Paris, 1724), vol. 1, pp. 201–256, and vol. 2, pp. 1–70, 283–288.

107. The point can be made without relying on the rather dubious comparisons with oriental material suggested by P. Gallais in *Perceval et l'initiation.*

108. On dubbing see Marc Bloch, *La Société féodale,* vol. 2 (Paris, 1940), pp. 46–53, and J. Flori, "Sémantique et société médiévale: Le verbe *adouber* et son évolution au XIIe siècle," *Annales ESC* (1976), pp. 915–940.

109. "Au XIIe siècle: les 'jeunes' dans la société aristocratique," *Annales ESC* (1964), pp. 835–896, reprinted in *Hommes et structures du Moyen Age* (Paris, 1973), pp. 213–226; references here are to the paper in the *Annales.* See also E. Köhler, "Sens et fonctions du terme 'jeunesse' dans la poésie des troubadours," in *Mélanges René Crozet* (Poitiers, 1966), pp. 569ff.

110. Duby, "Au XIIe siècle," pp. 835–836.

111. Ibid., p. 839.

112. Ibid., p. 843. On the complexity of courtly attitudes toward marriage, see E. Köhler, "Les troubadours et la jalousie," in *Mélanges Jean Frappier* (Geneva, 1970), pp. 543–559.

113. Duby, "Au XIIe siècle," p. 844.

114. Gawain has a brother, but he plays the role of antihero in the story of the Grail.

115. We make these brief remarks in the hope that someone will undertake a systematic study of kinship structures in courtly romance.

116. Duby, "Au XIIe siècle," p. 839.

117. On this subject see the illuminating remarks of J. Frappier, *chrétien de Troyes: L'homme et l'oeuvre* (Paris, 1957), p. 15.

118. There is a conflict over an inheritance in *Yvain,* but it is between sisters, both daughters of the Seigneur de la Noire Espine (lines 4699ff.). Yvain restores the rights of the dispossessed younger sister.

119. We are here borrowing and to some extent elaborating upon a suggestion made by J. Györy in his previously cited article, pp. 107–108. On the matter of land-clearing itself, see Georges Duby, *L'Économie rurale et la vie des campagnes dans l'Occident médiéval* (Paris, 1962), pp. 142–169 and, more briefly,

*Guerriers et paysans* (Paris, 1973), pp. 225–236. Duby places the "moment of maximum intensity of the phenomenon" between 1075 and 1180 (*Guerriers et paysans*, p. 228). The latter date is roughly when *Yvain* was written.

120. Wace, *Le Roman de Rou*, ed. A. J. Holden (Paris, 1971), lines 6372ff. The text has often been cited and commented on, notably by Frappier, *Etude sur Yvain*, pp. 85–86, and Stauffer, p. 46.

121. Note that our reading is based on the hero's encounters with three characters of the male sex (including the lion). Another reading, which would stress encounters with female characters, is surely possible.

122. This detail is found only in Chrétien's version. Whatever relations there may be between the Welsh tale and the French romance, the text of *Owein*, in which the hermit does not appear, places the savage in a clearing but situates the fight between the lion and the serpent on a low hill. See Loth, pp. 9 and 38. Harmann von Aue's interpretation is again interesting: Calogrenant comes to a vast clearing (*geriute*) whose paradoxical character is underscored by the absence of any humans (*âne die liute*, lines 401–402). The savage herdsman is in a field (*gevilde*, line 981). The hermit is not grubbing for roots but is standing on newly cleared land (*niuweriute*, line 3285). The encounter with the lion and the serpent takes place in a clearing (*bloeze*), to which the hero comes after "crossing a huge pile of felled trees," (lines 3836–3838). The trees do not appear to have been felled by the man but by natural and magical means, as after the storm unleashed by Yvain.

123. The word *essart* (clearing) occurs again in line 4788 when the elder daughter of the Seigneur de la Noire Espine announces that she will not share with her sister "either castle or city or clearing or wood or plain or any other thing."

124. Adler, p. 295, notes the parallel between the hermit and the savage guardian: "The Gestalt of the Hermit assumes the feature of a spiritualized replica of the Herdsman."

125. Duby, *L'Économie rurale*, pp. 146–47.

126. The argument could be pursued further by comparing *Yvain* with tales and myths in which land-clearing plays an essential role, such as the story of Melusina. See J. Le Goff, "Mélusine maternelle et défricheuse," *Annales ESC* (1971), pp. 587–622, and E. Le Roy Ladurie, *Le Territoire de l'historien* (Paris, 1973), pp. 281–300. In the authentic peasant folklore of Kabylie, the land clearer, the one who "clears away brush to create a garden or orchard," is none other than Sultan Haroun al-Rashid, "here promoted to almost supernatural rank," according to Camille Lacoste-Dujardin, *Le Conte kabyle* (Paris, 1970), p. 130.

127. See P. Le Rider's remarkable *Le Chevalier dans le conte du Graal de Chrétien de Troyes* (Paris: S.E.D.E.S., 1978).

## VESTIMENTARY AND ALIMENTARY CODES

1. I have tried to show this in my "Rituel symbolique de la vassalité," in *Simboli e Simbologia nell'Alto Medioevo* (Settimane di studio del Centro italiano

di studi sull'alto Medioevo, vol. 23 (Spoleto, 1976), pp. 679–788, reprinted in *Pour un autre Moyen Age,* pp. 349–420, especially pp. 365–384 [English translation, pp. 237–287].

2. In this case I make an exception and preserve the *oisiax* of the text, meaning birds, rather than interpret by substituting "fowl." The word may refer to game birds, worthier of a noble dinner table, or it may mean mere fowl, on account of the vavasor's poverty. Compare line 5538.

3. See Jacques Le Goff and Pierre Vidal-Naquet, "Lévi-Strauss en Brocéliande," earlier in this volume.

4. Insufficient attention has been paid, in my view, to the fact that the celebrated *Vers de la mort* by the Cistercian Hélinand of Froimont has alimentation as its primary reference.

## WARRIORS AND CONQUERING BOURGEOIS

1. I have used the following editions and translations. *Le Charroi de Nîmes,* ed. J. L. Perrier (Paris: Honoré Champion, 1963). A later edition by D. McMillan (Paris: Klincksieck, 1972) is also available, as is a translation by F. Gégou (Paris: Honoré Champion, 1977), based on the Perrier edition. For *La Prise d'Orange,* I used the edition of C. Régnier (4th ed., Paris: Klincksieck, 1972) and the translation of C. Lachet and J.-P. Tusseau (Paris: Klincksieck, 1974). For the *Lais de Marie de France,* I used the edition of J. Rychner (Paris: Honoré Champion, 1966) and the translation by P. Jonin (Paris: Honoré Champion, 1972). For *Perceval,* the edition of F. Lecoy (Paris: Honoré Champion, 1975), 2 vols., and the translation of L. Foulet (Paris: Stock, 1947), reprinted by A. G. Nizet (Paris, 1972), which is largely based on the edition of A. Hilka (Halle, 1932). I am greatly indebted to the work of historians of literature, including many whom I do not cite. In particular I have been helped by M. Mancini's study of *Le Charroi de Nîmes* and by the work of E. Köhler and P. Le Rider on Chrétien de Troyes and *Perceval.*

2. Line 11. The original text is: *Et desoz Rome ocist Corsolt es prez.* I shall refer to the original only on rare occasions, when the literary expression is particularly interesting or the existing modern French translation seems to me inaccurate. The walls of Rome are mentioned not in this line but in line 243, where F. Gégou I think rightly accepts the word *mur* (wall) from the BCD manuscripts rather than *marbre* (marble) from the manuscript used in the preparation of the Perrier edition.

3. In paraphrasing texts I shall try not to introduce anything that may alter what the originals have to say about cities. Of necessity I must omit episodes in which cities are not discussed. In order to properly appreciate the "urban presence" in these works, the reader must bear in mind that my summaries and paraphrases inevitably concentrate the urban image.

4. Lines 450–453:

> Demandez li Espaigne le regné,
> Et Tortolouse et Porpaillart sor mer,

Et apres Nymes, cele bone cité,
Et puis Orenge, qui tant fet a loer.

Tortolouse is generally identified as Tortosa, but Portpaillart remains mysterious. J. L. Perrier's index mentions the *pagus Pallariensis* in the vicinity of Urgel. Valsure, mentioned in the next paragraph, is also a mystery. The attempt to identify these places seems to me of secondary importance and possibly futile. The chansons de geste are famous for mingling real and imaginary places, proper names and distorted ones. This was the way memory worked, and the chansons both exploited and distorted it. Spain in this chanson includes Nîmes and Orange because it was thought of as the land of the Saracens. Here again we encounter a geography that is both historical and imaginary.

5. The enumerative formulas in which cities are mentioned are repeated several times: Orange in lines 452–453, 502–503; Nîmes in lines 452, 495, and 502; Chartres and Orléans in lines 529 and 541. These repetitions are clearly related to the techniques of epic and served as aids to memorization. They are especially important for the historian of the imagination and of *mentalités* and sensibilities and as such deserve close study. They are a key element in the formation of collective memory. Linguists, semiologists, and structuralists have taught us the importance of reiteration and redundancy. Now it is up to historians to add historical content and meaning to their lessons.

6. *Cors,* meaning bodies, but here with the sense of *person,* although the physical dimension is implicit in the ambiguity of the term.

7. Here we touch once again on the difficult interpretation of the word *cors.* It is to be hoped that a good semantic study of this fundamental word will soon be forthcoming.

8. Here beauty (*beauté*) is in the original (line 258).

9. Se ge nen ai la dame et la cité (line 266).

10. Lachet and Tusseau plausibly translate *riche* as *magnificent.* The ideas of beautiful, good, and rich, carefully distinguished in modern usage, were of course partly confounded in the Middle Ages.

11. "Nymes, la fort cité vaillant" (line 482).

12. See below, n. 31.

13. In the 234 final lines of the chanson, Nîmes is mentioned five times, and Paris, Algiers, and the Saracen Royaumont-sur-mer (?) are all named in addition, of course, to Orange.

14. Line 361 says that William was disturbed and upset by Orange, beset by thoughts of the city: "Or fu Guillelmes por Orenge *esmaiez.*"

15. I shall have more to say later on about the chronology of the works in question.

16. For some time I have been considering how leading twelfth- and thirteenth-century families, the most illustrious being the Plantagenets and the most successful in this regard the Lusignans, could in a Christian society have proudly laid claim to a Melusina or diabolical female as an ancestor. In the face of the city's bourgeoisification, might they not have been trying to affirm their roots in savage nature, in a sense the natural element of the warrior as well as

the chosen refuge of the monk? True, Melusina in turn also became urbanized and in the fourteenth century joyfully constructed cities and castles.

17. The original text says *chastel,* but Jonin's translation as fortified city is justified by what follows, since there is discussion of the spread of news of the death of the lady and of Yonec's decapitation of his stepfather in the city: "Puis ke si fu dunc avenu et par la cité fu sceü" (lines 547–548).

18. Perceval's adventures are set either in the forest or in simple castles. As Foulet points out in the notes to his translation (p. 220), however, while castle generally means fortress it could also mean "a small fortified city containing, in addition to the castle proper, houses, streets, and squares." Lecoy, on page 128 of volume 2 of his edition, mentions that lines 6421–6422 allude to Pavia, "the Italian city cited as a model of opulence." There is discussion of a *chastiax* (castle) that is hardly less splendid than Pavia.

19. The following episode, which comprises 140 lines, is summarized in four lines (5821–5824) in manuscript A (French ms. 794, Bibliothèque Nationale, Paris), written by the copyist Guiot in the second quarter of the thirteenth century, which most editors have followed even though fourteen other manuscripts of *Perceval* give it *in extenso.* In my view this is a problem that warrants further study. Lecoy follows manuscript A in his edition but gives the entire episode in an appendix (vol. 2, pp. 114–117), following the version given by A. Hilka in lines 5887–6026 of his edition.

20. In the original "scum" is *vilenaille* and "whoreson rabble" is *pute servaille.* Guibert of Nogent's phrase "communio autem novum ac pessimum nomen" occurs in book 3, chapter 8 of *De vita sua.*

21. This is not the place to explain the relation of the concepts of culture and *mentalité.* Culture refers primarily to works, while *mentalité* refers to discourse. Learned traditions therefore play a more coherent part in the former than in the latter, yet the two are drawn together by their collective, transsocial, spontaneous character. Historians must elucidate and specify but also respect this relationship.

22. There is one striking exception to this statement, namely, Rome. But the Roman image is polysemous and ambiguous. Was it a city or an empire? Pagan or Christian? Glorious or ruined? Rome must therefore be regarded as a special case. Concerning the medieval myth of Rome, see A. Graf's old but still great *Roma nella memoriae imaginazioni del Medio Evo* (Turin, 1915), and the numerous works cited in my *Storio d'Italia,* volume 2 (Turin: Einaudi, 1975).

23. Of course conflict was not out of the question when the traditions and interests of the warrior class and the Church diverged, as in regard to sexual and matrimonial practices, attitudes toward violence, the importance of physical virtues, and so on. In the twelfth century, moreover, although the knightly class accepted a Christianization of some of its military ideals, it also encouraged the development of a more secular culture, not to say a counterculture. Courtly culture was one in which Christian influence was limited and which was open to pre- and para-Christian popular culture.

24. This text served as the theme for a series of seven sermons delivered

over the course of a week at Augsburg in 1257 or 1263 by the Dominican Albertus Magnus, who set forth a theology, ideology, and imagery of the city in which contemporary realities, biblical and Augustinian themes, and the political philosophies of Plato, Aristotle, and Cicero (as understood by urban scholastics) all converged. This important document for the study of medieval urban ideology has been published by J. B. Schneyer, "Alberts des Grossen Augsburger Predigtzyklus über den hl. Augustinus," *Recherches de théologie ancienne et médiévale* 35 (1969).

25. The importance of so-called apocryphal literature in medieval culture and religion is well known. One such text, the "Vision of Saint Paul" or "Apocalypse of Paul," had a particularly important influence on medieval imagery of the other world. In it Paul visits Paradise, guided by an angel: "Post hec [angelus] duxit eum [Paulum] in civitatem pulchram nimis, ubi terra erat aurea et lux clarior luce priori; habitatores quoque eius splendidiores auro. Et in circuitu eius duodecim muri et duodecim turres in ea, et quattuor flumina intus currencia. Et sciscitatus est Paulus nomina ipsorum fluminum. Et angelus ait: unum dicitur Phison de melle, alterum Eufrates, quod et lacteum est, tercium Geon de oleo, quartum Tigris de vino. Qui in mundo recti sunt, ad hos rivos perveniunt post mortem. Hic remunerantur a domino." (*Visio Pauli*, Silverstein edition, The Vienna Fragment, Vienna Codex 302, p. 150.) In this significant text the urbanization of Paradise is pushed to the limit, for the City incorporates within its walls the Garden and its four rivers.

26. These of course also stand for the first two functions of the Indoeuropean trifunctional ideology elucidated by Georges Dumézil. The third function, the economic or reproductive function, does not occur in the Bible in connection with the urban theme. The episode in the New Testament in which Jesus drives the merchants out of the Temple has another meaning entirely. This should come as no surprise, since Dumézil has shown that trifunctional ideology remained alien to the Bible and to ancient Jewish culture. But the medieval West did revive the trifunctional theme, as is clearly shown by our texts' insistence on the marketplace, trades, and urban prosperity. This was a medieval innovation, an example of the creativity of medieval thought.

27. Success is enhanced when literary or mental images are joined by figurative representations. The importance of urban imagery in medieval painting (especially miniatures) and sculpture corroborates this conclusion. See P. Lavedan, *La Représentation des villes dans l'art du Moyen Age* (Paris, 1954); C. Heitz, *Recherches sur les rapports entre architecture et liturgie à l'époque carolingienne* (Paris, 1963); W. Müller, *Die heilige Stadt, Roma quadrata, himmliches Jerusalem und Mythe von Weltnabel* (Stuttgart, 1961).

28. As has been shown by Georges Dumézil with respect to the origins of Rome and by Pierre Vidal-Naquet with respect to Atlantis.

29. Recall, as Georges Duby showed in *Le Dimanche de Bouvines*, that in twelfth-century Latin the same word, *nundinae*, was used for fairs and tournaments; the two were closely associated, and a tournament was as much an economic event as an occasion for knightly combat.

30. A great specialist in the history of the medieval city, E. Ennen, writes: "A typically Italian and south-European phenomenon was the immigration of the nobility into the cities. North of the Alps the nobility built castles outside the cities, but Italian nobles willingly or unwillingly lived in the cities" (*Die europäische Stadt des Mittelalters* [Göttingen, 1972], p. 129). In the case of Marie de France it is particularly surprising to find "Breton" cities inhabited by knights.

31. The *mirabilia* literature of the twelfth century was strictly imaginary. At the beginning of the thirteenth century Latin Christians experienced an extraordinary shock in the realm of urban imagery. Unable to recognize the ideal city in either their modest new cities or in ancient Rome or in the ruins of Jewish Jerusalem, suddenly they found it as they stared in amazement at Constantinople, conquered in 1204 in the course of the Fourth Crusade. Reality at last rivaled fiction. In describing the real Constantinople, Geofroy de Villehardouin and Robert de Clari saw the imaginary city, the marvelous city imagined a half-century earlier by Western writers in the grip of urban fever.

## AN URBAN METAPHOR

1. "William of Auvergne gives a locally based definition: 'Those who inhabit a city and the citizens of a city are said to be a single people because of the unity of the place in which they reside,' despite differences of sex, condition, and profession (*De universo* 1.12, p. 606 a H). Here we see the empirical outlook and practical character of the bishop of Paris: a city is defined by its location, but the insistence with which he then repeats the formula *una civitas, unus populus* shows that he has not lost sight of the conditions of moral and legal unity that the members of this group must satisfy." Pierre Michaud-Quantin, *Universitas: Expressions du mouvement communautaire dans le Moyen Age latin* (Paris, 1970), p. 115, n. 26.

2. William of Auvergne, *Opera omnia* (Orléans-Paris, 1674), pp. 407–416: "De sacramento in generali." I am grateful to Father P.-M. Gy for calling my attention to this text.

3. William of Auvergne is not cited by J. Comblin in his interesting *Théologie de la ville* (Paris, 1968).

4. See the essays "Lévi-Strauss in Broceliande" and "Warriors and Conquering Bourgeois" earlier in this volume. Roberto Ruiz Capellian's still unpublished thesis is summarized in "Bosque e Individuo: Negación y destierro de la sociedad en la epopeya y novela francesas de los siglos XII y XIII," Universidad de Salamanca, Facultad de filosofia y letras, Departamento de filología francesa, 1978.

5. "*Cives civitatis procul dubio sunt veri nominis homines,*" while other men are not true men "*sed potius animalia sint habendi.*" *Opera omnia*, p. 409.

6. See R. Bernheimer, *Wild Men in the Middle Ages: A Study in Art, Sentiment, and Demonology,* 2d ed. (New York, 1970).

7. "Hic coetus, vel civitas et templum dicitur propter Dei cultum, seu

honorificentiam cui principaliter se impendit, atque finaliter, et civitas propter saluberrimam pacem; et jucundissimam societatem, quibus sub Deo rege secundum sacratissimam legem ejusdem vivant. . . ." *Opera omnia,* p. 409.

8. For a recent treatment see the enlightening remarks of Georges Duby in *Les Trois Ordres ou l'imaginaire du féodalisme* (Paris, 1979).

9. See A. Vauchez, "Une campagne de pacification en Lombardie autour de 1233: L'action politique des ordres mendiants d'après la réforme des statuts communaux et les accords de paix," in *Mélanges d'archéologie et d'histoire* (Paris, 1966), pp. 503–549.

10. J. C. Payen was working on a study of happiness in the Middle Ages when he died in 1984.

11. ". . . qui civitatem istam ingrediuntur ita, ut cives ejus efficantur, necesse habent civilitatem ejus suscipere, hoc est leges et statuta, moresque subire." *Opera omnia,* p. 409.

12. "Et omnis inaequalitas lapidum deponitur, alioquin in illam non admittuntur. Quemadmodum frondositas lignorum ac fortitudo ac tortuositas, aliaque omnia, quae ligna aedificiis inepta faciunt, nisi omnino essent amota, in ipso ingressu in aedificium necessario deponentur." *Opera omnia,* p. 410.

13. ". . . et civitatem istam, velut membra gratuita, societate sibi invicem colligata esse, sive compacta, voluntariaque subservitione sibi invicem submistrantia, manifestum est intueri volentibus." Ibid.

14. "De rure et vita rusticana ad civitatem transeuntibus, et cives effici volentibus, necesse est, mores agrestes, et habitationem deserere, civitatemque inhabitare, civilesque mores, et urbanitem civilem, atque socialissimam assumere." Ibid.

15. Michaud-Quantin, *Universitas,* p. 111.

16. Albert's sermons have been published by J. B. Schneyer, "Alberts des Grossen Augsburger Predigtzyklus über den hl. Augustinus," *Recherches de théologie ancienne et médiévale* 35 (1969): 100–147. I am indebted to Father J.-L. Bataillon for my knowledge of this other important source of medieval urban imagery. Did Albert draw his inspiration from William? At first sight it would appear not. A precise comparison of the two texts would be interesting.

## SOCIAL REALITIES AND IDEOLOGICAL CODES

1. See for example Charles V. Langlois, *La Vie en France au Moyen Age, de la fin du XIIe au milieu du XIVe siècle,* vol. 1 (Paris, 1924); vol. 2 (Paris, 1925).

2. This is what T. F. Crane does, for example, in "The Exempla or Illustrative Stories from the Sermones Vulgáres of Jacques de Vitry," *Publications of the Folklore Society* 26 (London, 1890), reproduced by Kraus Reprint (Nehdeln, 1967), no. 161, and what A. Lecoy de La Marche does in *Anecdotes historiques, légendes et apologues tirés du recueil inédit d'Etienne de Bourbon, dominicain du XIIIe siècle* (Paris, 1877), extracting from James's sermons whatever is useful for the study of folklore or from Stephen of Bourbon's "Treatise on the Seven Gifts of the Holy Spirit" a variety of anecdotes. Salvatore Battaglia,

"L'esempio nella retorica antica," *Filologia Romanza* 6 (1959): 45–82 and "Dall'esempio alla novella," *Filologia Romanza* 7 (1960): 21–82, reprinted in *La coscienza litteraria medievale,* characterizes exempla as bibles of everyday life.

3. See for example Erich Köhler, *Ideal und Wirklichkeit in der höfischen Epik,* 1st ed., 1956, 2d revised ed., 1970; Georges Duby, "Histoire sociale et idéolgie des sociétés," *Faire de l'histoire,* vol. 1, ed. J. Le Goff and P. Nora (Paris, 1974), pp. 147–168, for the theoretical perspective, and for practical illustrations, see *Le Dimanche de Bouvines* (Paris, 1973), and *Les Trois Ordres ou l'imaginaire du féodalisme* (Paris, 1978).

4. See Jacques Le Goff and Jean-Claude Schmitt, "Au XIIIe siècle: Une parole nouvelle," in *Histoire vécue du peuple chrétien,* vol. 1, ed. Jean Delumeau (Toulouse, 1979), pp. 257–279.

5. On exempla see J. T. Welter, *L'Exemplum dans la littérature religieuse et didactique du Moyen Age* (Toulouse, 1927); R. Schenda, "Stand und Aufgaben der Exemplaforschung," *Fabula* 10 (1969): 69–85; H. Pétri, R. Cantel, and R. Ricard, "Exemplum," in *Dictionnaire de spiritualité,* vol. 4/2 (Paris, 1961), columns 1885–1902; C. Brémond, Jacques Le Goff, and Jean-Claude Schmitt, *L'Exemplum, typologie des sources du Moyen Age occidental,* pamphlet 40 (Turnhout: Brepols, 1982).

6. The three principal theologians of the twelfth century, whose views concerning the sacraments were most influential in the first half of the thirteenth century, were Hugh of Saint-Victor (*De sacramentis [PL, 176, 173–618]*); Peter Lombard (*Libri IV sententiarum,* 2 vols. [Collegium S. Bonaventurae ad Claras Aquas, 1916]); and Peter the Chanter (*Summa de sacramentis et animae consiliis,* 5 vols., ed. J. A. Dugauquier [1954–1967]).

7. On confessors' manuals see C. Vogel, *Les Pénitentiels, typologie des sources du Moyen Age occidental,* pamphlet 27 (Turnhout: Brepols, 1978); A. Teetaert, *La Confession aux laïques dans l'Eglise latine depuis le VIIe jusqu'au XIVe siècle* (Bruges-Paris: Webern, 1926); Pierre Michaud-Quantin, "A propos des premières Summae confessorum," *Recherches de théologie ancienne et médiévale* 26 (1959): 264–306; Jacques Le Goff, "Métier et profession d'après les manuels de confesseurs du Moyen Age," *Miscellanea Mediaevalia,* vol. 3 (Berlin, 1964), pp. 44–60; reprinted in *Pour un autre Moyen Age,* pp. 162–180 [English translation, pp. 107–121].

8. On the importance and significance of classifications, see Jack Goody, *The Domestication of the Savage Mind* (Cambridge, 1977), and Pierre Bourdieu, *La Distinction, critique sociale du jugement* (Paris, 1979).

9. See M. W. Bloomfield, *The Seven Deadly Sins: An Introduction to the History of a Religious Concept, With Special Reference to Medieval English Literature* (East Lansing, Mich.: 1952); S. Wenzel, "The Seven Deadly Sins: Some Problems of Research," *Speculum* 43 (1968): 1–22; M. Corti, *Il viaggio gestuale: Le ideologie e le strutture semiotiche* (Turin, 1978), pp. 248–249.

10. Lester K. Little, "Pride Goes Before Avarice: Social Change and the Vices in Latin Christendom," *American Historical Review* 75 (1971).

11. Concerning the abundant literature on *états du monde,* see Jean Batany's thesis, University of Paris IV–Sorbonne, 1979.

12. Jacques Le Goff, *La Civilisation de l'Occident médiéval* (Paris, 1965), p. 347.

13. J. F. Hinnebusch, ed., *Historia Occidentalis* (Freiburg, 1972), chapter 7: "De statu parisiensis civitatis." Cf. Corti, "Il viaggio", pp. 248–249.

14. T. F. Crane, *The Exempla,* no. 161, pp. 62–64.

15. I am indebted to Marie-Claire Gasnault for making available the complete transcript of sermon number 52, *Ad potentes et milites,* based on Paris BN Ms Lat 17509, which was used by Crane, and of another manuscript, Cambrai BM 534, which is valuable for its rubrics.

16. See the classic study of Karl Bosl, "'Potens' und 'Pauper': Begriffsgeschichtliche Studien zur gesellschaftlichen Differenzierung im frühen Mittelalter und zum 'Pauperismus' des Hochmittelalters," *Festschrift für O. Brunner* (Göttingen, 1963), pp. 60–87.

17. An instance of the image of the "secular arm."

18. On tournaments, the indispensable source is Georges Duby, *Le Dimanche de Bouvines* (Paris, 1973), pp. 110–137; the reader may also wish to consult O. Müller, *Turnier und Kampf in den altfranzösischen Artusromanen* (Erfurt, 1907); J. J. Jusserand, *Les Sports et les jeux d'exercice dans l'ancienne France* (Paris, 1901), pp. 41–98; F. H. Cripps-Day, *History of the Tournament in England and in France* (London, 1918). An important document is the *Histoire de Guillaume le Maréchal,* ed. P. Meyer (Paris, 1891–1901), especially vol. 1, lines 1471–5094 and vol. 3, pp. xxxv–xliv. This is the primary basis for the interesting article of Marie-Luce Chênerie, "Ces curieux chevaliers tournoyeurs," *Romania* 97 (1976): 326–368. See also M. Pastoureau, *Traité d'Héraldique* (Paris, 1979), pp. 39–41, and especially Georges Duby, *Guillaume le Maréchal ou le meilleur chevalier du monde* (Paris, 1984) [available in an English translation by Richard Howard, (New York: Pantheon, 1987)].

19. See Sidney Painter, *French Chivalry: Chivalric Ideas and Practices in Medieval France* (Baltimore, 1940), p. 36. Painter draws a parallel between William the Marshall's desire for glory and what Philippe de Novare wrote in his treatise *The Four Ages of Man:* "He works to acquire honor as well as to be renowned for his valor and to gain temporal goods, riches and inheritances."

20. Jean Renart, *Le Roman de la rose ou de Guillaume de Dole,* ed. F. Lecoy (Paris, 1962); translated into modern French by J. Dufournet, J. Kooijman, R. Ménage, and C. Fronc (Paris, 1979).

21. M. Zink, *Roman rose et rose rouge: Le Roman de la rose ou de Guillaume de Dole* (Paris, 1979).

22. *Aucassin et Nicolette,* edited and translated by J. Dufournet (Paris, 1973).

23. Rutebeuf, *Poésies,* translated by J. Dufournet (Paris, 1978), p. 54.

24. Lambert of Ardres, *Historia comitum Ghisnensium et Ardensium dominorum, Monumenta Germaniae Historica Scriptores,* vol. 24 (1879).

25. See Chênerie, "Ces curieux chevaliers tournoyeurs," p. 349.

26. *Redimere: peccunniam nomine redemptionis extorquere, injuste exigere.* Du Cange. Only MS Latin 17509 reads *non redimit.*

27. Horace, *Epistles,* 1.2.14.

P.S. I wish to thank Daniel Rocher for his help with research and documentation. These pages were already written when Claude Lecouteux called my attention to Klaus Speckenbach, "Von den troimen: Uber den Traum in Theorie und Dichtung," in *Sagen mit Sinne,* ed. H. Rücker and K. O. Seidel, Festschrift für Marie-Luise Dittrich (GAG 180) (Göppingen, 1976), pp. 169–204.

## CHRISTIANITY AND DREAMS

1. Roger Caillois and G. E. von Grunebaum, *The Dream and Human Societies* (Berkeley: The University of California Press, 1966).

2. Saint Jerome, *Epistola ad Eustochium* 22.30. See R. Antin, "Autour du songe de saint Jérôme," *Revue des études latines* 41 (1963): 350–377.

3. E. L. Ehrlich, *Der Traum im Alten Testament,* 1953.

4. Martine Dulaey, *Le Rêve dans la vie et la pensée de saint Augustin* (Paris, 1973), pp. 231–232.

5. I have removed references that seemed to me erroneous or inadequate: from Ehrlich's list, Psalms 126:1 and Isaiah 65:4, and from Dulaey's, Genesis 2:21 (Adam's sleep during Eve's creation is not accompanied by dreaming) and Psalms 44:15.

6. A. Wikenhauser, "Die Traumgeschichte des Neuen Testaments in religionschichtlicher Sicht," in *Pisciculi,* Festschrift für Fr. Dölger, Antike und Christentum, 1939.

7. See André Coquot, *Les Songes et leur interprétation,* "Sources orientales II," (Paris: Editions du Seuil, 1949), passim.

8. André Caquot suggests that in Genesis visions correspond to the Yahwist verses whereas dreams in which God speaks derive from ancient Israel. See A. Caquot and M. Leibovici, eds., *La Divination,* vol. 1 (Paris, 1968), pp. 94–96. Cf. Caquot, *Les Songes et leur interprétation,* pp. 101–124; W. Richter, "Traum und Traumdeutung im Alten Testament," in *Biblische Zeitschrift,* undated. This distinction is roughly comparable to that of Artemidorus in his *Dream Key:* "Some dreams are theorematic, others allegorical. Theorematic dreams are those whose fulfillment fully resembles the prevision. By contrast, allegorical dreams are those that signify certain things by means of other things. In these dreams it is the soul which, in accordance with certain natural laws, yields an obscure comprehension of an event." Artemidorus, *Dream Key,* retranslated here from page 20 of the French translation, *Clef des songes.*

9. "Now a thing was secretly brought to me, and mine ear received a little thereof. In thoughts from the visions of the night, when deep sleep falleth on men, fear came upon me, and trembling, which made all my bones to shake. Then a spirit passed before my face; the hair of my flesh stood up: It stood still, but I could not discern the form thereof: an image was before mine eyes, there was silence, and I heard a voice. . . ." (Job 4:12–16). "Then thou scarest me with dreams, and terrifiest me through visions." (Job 7:14).

10. "And he dreamed, and behold a ladder set up on the earth, and the top of it reached to heaven: and behold the angels of God ascending and descend-

ing on it. And, behold, the Lord stood above it, and said, I am the Lord God of Abraham thy father. . . ." (Genesis 28 : 12–13).

11. On Greek attitudes toward dreams, particularly in the archaic and classical periods, see H. Kenner, "Oneiros," in Pauly-Wissowa, *Real-Encyklopädie der classischen Altertumswissenschaft,* vol. 18/1, 1939, cols. 448–459, and T. Hopfner, "Traumdeutung," in the same volume. A succinct account can be found in C. A. Behr, *Aelius Aristides and the Sacred Tale* (Amsterdam, 1968), pp. 171–195.

12. In Homer the dream is sometimes the image (ἔυψδωλον) of a living person (as in *Odyssey* 4.795ff.), sometimes the phantom soul of a dead person (as in *Iliad* 23.65ff.).

13. Hesiod, *Theogony,* lines 211–213.

14. Aristotle, in three short pamphlets entitled "On Sleep and Waking" (περὶ ὕπνου καὶ ἐγρηγόρσεως), "On Dreams" (περὶ ἐνυπνίων), and "On Divination in Sleep" (περὶ τῆς καθ' ὕπνου μαντικῆς). A French translation has been published, along with the original Greek, by René Mugnin (Paris: Les Belles Lettres, 1953).

15. See Hippocrates, *Du régime,* edited and translated by R. Joly (Paris, 1967).

16. See Galen, *Le diagnosi per mezzo dei sogni,* ed. G. Guidonizzi, in *Bollettino del Comitato per l'edizione dei classici greci e latini,* N.S. 21, 1973. Aline Rousselle (*Porneia: De la maîtrise du corps à la privation sensorielle, IIe–IVe siècle de l'ère chrétienne* [Paris, 1983]) shows what a good historian can do with ancient medical treatises.

17. On the Stoic fragments, see J. H. Waszink's note "The Classification of Dreams" in his edition of Tertullian's *De anima,* pp. 500–501.

18. ". . . sed tribus modis censet deorum adpulsu homines somniare: uno quod provideat animus ipse per sese, quippe qui deorum cognatione teneatur, altero quod plenus aer sit immortalium animorum, in quibus tanquam insignitae notae veritatis appareant, tertio quod ipsi di cum dormientibus conloquantur." Cicero, *De divinatione* 1.64.

19. Peter Brown (*The Making of Late Antiquity* [1978]) has cast doubt on the use of the term "popular." To be sure, its meaning is vague, and it ought to be used with caution. But given the facts that there is a constant circulation between "high" and "popular" culture and that the meaning of "popular" changes from society to society and period to period (illiterate, pagan, folkloric, mass, etc.), I see no reason to eliminate a concept that was often used by clerics in the past, that has provided sound historical results, and that remains serviceable today.

20. See Behr, *Aelius Aristides,* pp. 171ff. For an interesting study of the *phantasma* in the Middle Ages, see Massimo Oldoni, "A fantasia dicitur fantasma (Gerberto e la sua storia)," *Studi Medievali* 21 (1980): 493–622 and 24 (1983): 167–245.

21. Cf. D. Del Curno, *Graecorum de re onirocritica scriptorum reliquiae* (Milan: Varese, 1969).

22. On ancient oneiromancy several old works are still useful: B. Büchsen-schütz, *Traum und Traumdeutung in Alterthum* (Berlin, 1868) and A. Bouche-Leclercq, *Histoire de la divination dans l'Antiquité*, 4 vols. (Paris, 1882). See the recent summary by Raymond Bloch, *La Divination dans l'Antiquité* (Paris, 1984).

23. A. Brelich, "Le rôle des rêves dans la conception religieuse du monde en Grèce," in *Le Rêve et les sociétés humaines,* ed. R. Caillois and G. E. von Grünebaum (Paris, 1968), pp. 282–289.

24. E. R. Dodds, author of the classic *The Greeks and the Irrational* (Berkeley, 1963) which has much to say about dreams, made this argument in his *Pagan and Christian in an Age of Anxiety* (Cambridge, 1965); for a critique see Brown, *The Making of Late Antiquity*, p. 273, n. 1. Dodds's argument is only partly persuasive: although it is clearly simplistic to explain the triumph of Christianity in terms of a rise of irrationalism and "popular culture," it is undeniable that the general climate became one of anxiety in the second century, as Brown himself notes several times.

25. See especially Iamblichus, *De mysteriis* 3.2f.f (Paris: Edouard des Places, 1966).

26. On Artemidorus see W. Kurth, "Das Traumbuch des Artemidoros im Lichte der Freudschen Traumlehre," *Psyche* 4 (1950): 488–512 for a Freudian interpretation; Claes Blum, *Studies in the Dream-Book of Artemidoros* (Uppsala, 1936); and E. R. Dodds, *The Greeks and the Irrational.* The recent edition by Roger A. Pack, *Artemidori Daldiani Oneirocriticon* (Leipzig: Teubner, 1963), does not replace the earlier edition of J. G. Reiff, *Artemidori Oneirocritica* (Leipzig, 1805), which contains the valuable critical notes of N. Rigault and J. J. Reisk. Four translations of the *Oneirocriticon* have appeared in recent years: in German, a revision by M. Kaiser, with notes, of F. S. Krauss's translation *Symbolik der Träume* (Basel, 1965); in English, R. J. White has translated the work as *The Interpretation of Dreams* (Park Ridge, N.J., 1975); in French there is A. J. Festugière's *La Clef des songes* (Paris: Vrin, 1975); and in Italian, Dario del Corno's *Il libro dei sogni* (Milan: Adelphi, 1975).

27. Artemidorus, *Dream Key.* See also Mikhail Bakhtin's account of the cultural importance of the marketplace in the fourteenth, fifteenth, and sixteenth centuries in his *Rabelais* (Bloomington: Indiana University Press, 1984).

28. On Aelius Aristides and his *Sacred Tales:*
a) Text: E. B. Keil, *Aelii Aristides quae supersunt omnia* (Berlin, 1898), reprinted 1958, vol. 2, pp. 376–467, discourses 47–52; Latin translation by G. Canter (Basel, 1566), reprinted in Geneva in 1604 and again in *Aelii Aristidis Opera omnia graece et latine,* 2 vols., ed. S. Jebb (Oxford, 1722 and 1730); C. A. Behr, *Aelius Aristides and the Sacred Tales* (Amsterdam, 1968); and in Italian, Elio Aristide, *Discorsi Sacri,* ed. Salvatgore Nicosia (Milan, 1984).

b) Studies: A. Boulanger, *Aelius Aristides et la sophistique dans la province d'Asie au IIe siècle de notre ère* (Bibliothèque des Ecoles françaises d'Athènes et de Rome, pamphlet 126) (Paris, 1923), part 2, chap. 3, pp. 163–209; Dodds,

*Pagan and Christian,* chapter 2; A. J. Festugière, "Sur les 'Discours sacrés' d'A. Aristides," *Revue des études grecques,* 82 (1969): 117–153; G. Michenaud and J. Dierkens, Les Rêves dans les "Discours sacrés" d'A. Aristide: IIe siècle après J.-C., Essai d'analyse psychologique (University of Mons, 1972); G. Misch, *Geschichte der Autobiographie,* vol. 1, *Das Altertum* (1949); O. Weinreich, "Typisches und Individuelles in der Religiosität des Aristides," *Neue Jahrbücher für des Klassische Altertum* 17 (1914): 597–606; F. G. Welcker, "Inkubation: Aristides der Rhetor," in *Kleine Schriften,* vol. 3 (Bonn, 1850), pp. 89–157; M. Loison, "Les Discours sacrés d'Aelius Aristide: Un exemple de relations personnelles entre un paien et son dieu," master's thesis, University of Paris IV, 1975–1976.

29. See A. J. Festugière, *Personal Religion among the Greeks* (Berkeley, 1954), pp. 85–104.

30. Misch, *Geschichte der Autobiographie,* vol. 1, pp. 503–519.

31. Julio Caro Baroja, *Vidas mágicas y Inquisición,* 2 vols. (Madrid, 1967).

32. W. Lang, *Das Traumbuch des Synesius von Kyrene: Übersetzung und Analyse der philosophischen Grundlagen* (Tübingen, 1926); G. Lacombrade, *Synésius de Cyrène, hellène et chrétien* (Paris, 1951); *Synesii Cyrenensis Opuscula,* ed. N. Terzaghi (Rome, 1944); French translation in H. Druon, *Etudes sur la vie et les oeuvres de Synésius* (Paris, 1859).

33. Macrobius, *Commentarii in Somnium Scipionis: Saturnalia,* 2 vols. ed. James Willis (Leipzig, 1963). There is an English translation by William Harris Stahl, *Commentary on the Dream of Scipio* (New York, 1952, 2d ed., 1966). See also P. Courcelle, *Les Lettres grecques en Occident de Macrobe à Cassiodore* (Paris, 1943), and, by the same author, "La postérité chrétienne du *Songe de Scipion,*" *Revue des études latines* 36 (1958): 205–234; also, H. Silvestre, "Survie de Macrobe au Moyen Age," *Classica et Medievalia* 24 (1963): 170–180. The outline of Scipio's dream was known from book 6 of Cicero's *De republica,* the only book known in the Middle Ages. Scipio Aemilianus (Africanus Numantinus) had a dream in which he saw his father, Scipio Africanus, showing him Carthage and predicting victory. To spur him on, he also revealed that the souls of those who served the fatherland were rewarded by the supreme god (*princeps deus*) with a blessed life after death in the Milky Way. The supreme god inhabited the highest of the nine celestial spheres, which revolved in harmony. He further exhorted his son to turn his attention to those things of the heavens whose revolutions were very long, the so-called Great Years. Man's body is mortal, but his soul is to the body as god is to the world. (This summary is borrowed from Etienne Gilson.)

34. J. H. Waszink, *Studien zum Timaeus Kommentar des Chalcidius* (Leyden, 1964), and "Die sogennante Fünfteilung der Traüme bei Chalcidius und ihre Quellen," *Mnemosyne,* N.S. III, 1942, pp. 65–85.

35. Ernest Jones, *On the Nightmare,* 2nd edition (1949).

36. D. Grodzynski, "Par la bouche de l'empereur," in *Divination et rationalité,* ed. Jean-Pierre Vernant (Paris, 1974).

37. Origen, *Contra Celsum.*

38. "Et major paene vis hominum ex visionibus Deum discunt."

39. Cyprian, Epistle 9, *PL* 4, 253: "Castigare nos itaque divina censura nec noctibus desinit nec diebus. Praeter nocturnas enim visiones, per dies quoque impletur apud nos Spiritu Sancto puerorum innocens aetas, quae in ecstasi videt oculis et audit et loquitur de quibus nos Dominus monere et instruere dignatur."

40. See Jacques Le Goff, *La Naissance du Purgatoire,* (Paris: Gallimard, 1982), translated by Arthur Goldhammer as *The Birth of Purgatory* (Chicago: The University of Chicago Press, 1984).

41. See Louis Robert, "Une vision de Perpétue martyre à Carthage en 203," in *Comptes rendus de l'Académie des inscriptions et belles-lettres,* meeting of 7 May 1982 (Paris, 1983), pp. 227–276.

42. "Haec visiones insigniores ipsorum martyrum beatissimorum Saturi et Perpetuae, quas ipsi conscripserunt" (Van Beek edition, p. 34).

43. On Montanism see the still useful work of P. de Labriolle, *La Crise montaniste* (Paris, 1913).

44. Tertullian, *De anima,* ed. J. H. Waszing (Amsterdam, 1946), with an excellent commentary. On Tertullian see J. C. Fredouille, *Tertullian et la conversion de la culture antique* (Paris, 1972).

45. "Tenemur hic de somniis quoque Christianam sententiam expromere, ut de accidentibus somni et non modicis iactationibus animae, quam ediximus negotiosam et exercitam semper ex perpetuitate motationis, quod divinitatis et immortalitatis est ratio. Igitur cum quies corporibus evenit, quorum solacium proprium est, vacans illa a solacio alieno non quiescit et, si caret opera membrorum corporalium, suis utitur." (We must also state here the Christian doctrine on dreams, as they are born from the accidents of sleep and the significant movements of the soul, which as we have said is always busy and agitated because of its perpetual movement, due to its divine and immortal character. Hence when rest comes to the body as its peculiar comfort, the soul, for which this comfort is not intended, does not rest and, since it must do without the activity of the body's members, uses its own.) *De anima,* 45.

46. Tertullian holds that during the *interim* in Hell some souls are afflicted by *supplicia* while others benefit from *refrigeria,* a belief that he bases on the Gospel story of Lazarus and the wicked rich man. See Le Goff, *La Naissance du Purgatoire,* pp. 65–66 and 70–74.

47. Et utique non clausa vis est nec sacrariorum circumscribitur terminis: vaga et pervolatica et interim libera est. Quo nemo dubitaverit domus quoque daemoniis patere nec tantum in adytis, sed in cubiculis homines imaginibus circumveniri.

48. Superstitio, ut cum apud oracula incubaturis ieiunium inducitor, ut castimoniam inducat. *De anima,* 48.3.

49. P. Saintyves, *En marge de la Légende dorée* (Paris, 1930), pp. 3–163.

50. Nevertheless, in Christian doctrine the dead were not allowed to appear to the living in dreams, with the exception of saints in Heaven, who made few appearances in the early centuries of Christianity. The only autho-

rized apparitions from the other world were of God himself (rare) and, more commonly, of angels and archangels. When Purgatory was finally defined as a geographical place in the late twelfth century, it became possible for souls in Purgatory to appear to the living as well.

51. "Qui augeria vel auspicia, sive somnia vel divinationes quaslibet, secundum morem Gentilium observant, aut in domos suas huius modi homines introducunt in exquirendis aliquibus ante malifica . . . confessi, quinquennio poenitentiam agant." Text based on the "interpretation" of Isidor Mercator in Mansi, *Amplissima Collectio* (1960), vol. 2, p. 534.

52. Martine Dulaey, *Le Rêve dans la vie et la pensée de saint Augustin* (Paris, 1973); Pierre Courcelle, *Recherches sur les Confessions de saint Augustin* (Paris, 1950), 2d ed. (1968) and *Les Confessions de saint Augustin dans la tradition littéraire: Antécédents et postérités* (Paris, 1963).

53. A.-J. Festugière, "L'expérience religieuse du médecin Thessalos," *Revue biblique* 48 (1939): 46.

54. Courcelle, *Recherches,* pp. 127ff.

55. Dulaey, *Le Rêve,* pp. 76ff.

56. Ibid., pp. 80ff.

57. Ibid., pp. 90ff.

58. Ibid., pp. 93ff.

59. Ibid., p. 98, n. 54 and pp. 113ff.

60. Ibid., p. 127.

61. Compare Courcelle, *Recherches,* pp. 103–104, and Dulaey, *Le Rêve,* p. 210, n. 58. Augustine maintains that one does not really see the dead in dreams but only their *similitudines,* or likenesses. See *De cura pro mortuis gerenda* 12.15.

62. Dulaey, *Le Rêve,* pp. 135–139.

63. Constantine's vision has stirred enormous controversies among historians. The problem is not whether the vision was "real" (who can say?), but its tradition. Eusebius and Lactantius, the two chroniclers closest in time to the vision, give different versions. The state of the question is discussed in J. K. Aufhauser, "Konstantins Kreuzesvision," in *Kleine Texte,* ed. H. Lietzmann (Bonn, 1912). Cf. H. Grégoire, "La 'conversion' de Constantin," *Revue de l'Université de Bruxelles* 36 (1930–31).

64. See A. Brasseur, "Le songe de Théodose le Grand," *Latomus* 2 (1938): 190–195. Theodoretus's two texts recounting Theodosius's dream are translated on pp. 192–193 of this paper.

65. The indispensable reference is Jacques Fontaine's edition, with abundant commentary, of Sulpicius Severus's *Life of Saint Martin* in the series *Sources chrétiennes,* nos. 133, 134, and 135, 3 vols. (1967–1969). See in particular "Le problème historique des songes et les visions," vol. 1, pp. 195–198.

66. "Quo viso, vir beatissimus non in gloriam est elatus humanam, sed bonitatum Dei in suo opere cognoscens, cum esset annorum duodeviginti, ad baptismum convolavit." (By this dream the very holy man was not raised to the peak of human glory, but he recognized the goodness of God in his work

and, when he was twenty-two years old, he hastened to baptism.) Sulpicius Severus, *Vita Martini* 6.3–5.

67. "Nec multo post admonitus per soporem ut patriam parentesque, quos adhuc gentilitas detinebat, religiose sollicitudine visitaret." Ibid., 5.3.

68. On Saint Martin and the devil, see Fontaine's edition, vol. 1, pp. 191ff.: "Le problème historique du Diable dans la *Vita*."

69. I am grateful to Ilan Hirsch for this information.

70. Courcelle, *Recherches,* pp. 145ff.

71. "Sciendum, Petre, est quia sex modis tangunt animam imagines somniorum. Aliquando namque somnia ventris plenitudine vel inanitate, aliquando vera illusione, aliqando autem cogitatione simul et revelatione generantur. Sed duo quae prima diximus, omnes experimento cognoscimus. Subiuncta autem quatuor in sacrae scripturae paginis invenimus." Gregory the Great, *Dialogues,* vol. 3.

72. "Sed nimirum cum somnia tot rerum qualitatibus alternent, tanto eis credi difficilius debet, quanto et ex quo inpulsu veniant facilius non educet." Ibid., 4.50.6.

73. Ibid., 4.51.

74. See C. Brémond, J. Le Goff, and J.-C. Schmitt, *L'Exemplum,* in *Typologie des sources du Moyen Age occidental,* pamphlet 40 (Turnhout, 1982), and Jacques Le Goff, "Vita et pré-exemplum dans le deuxième livre des *Dialogues* de Grégoire le Grand," in *Hagiographie, Cultures et Sociétés, IVe–XIIe siècle* (Paris, 1981), pp. 105–120.

75. Isidore of Seville, *Sententiae* 3.6 in *PL,* vol. 83, cols. 668–671.

76. P. Dinzelbacher, *Vision und Visionsliteratur im Mittelalter* (Stuttgart, 1981).

77. Innocent III, *De contemptu mundi* 1.25. *PL.*

78. E. Le Roy Ladurie, *Montaillou, village occitan de 1294 à 1324* (Paris, 1975), pp. 608–609.

## THE DREAMS OF HELMBRECHT THE ELDER

1. Jacques Le Goff, *La Civilisation de l'Occident médiéval* (Paris, 1964), pp. 394–396.

2. See V. Seelbach, *Bibliographie zu Wernher der Gartenaere* (Berlin, 1981).

3. See Jacques Le Goff, *Pour un autre Moyen Age,* (Paris: Gallimard, 1977) pp. 299–306 [English edition, pp. 201–204].

4. For the text of *Helmbrecht* I used the eighth edition of F. Panzer, revised by K. Ruh (Tübingen, 1968). A ninth edition was published in 1974. Also valuable were the notes in the editions of K. Speckenbach (Darmstadt, 1974) and H. Brackert, W. Frey, and D. Seitz (Frankfurt, 1972). The Speckenbach edition has a brief but substantial note on *troum* on pp. 98–101, from which I took the following references: J. Lunzer, *Zum Meier Helmbrecht,* PBB 53 (1929): 195–207 and W. Schmitz, *Traum und Vision in der erzählenden Dichtung des deutschen Mittelalters* (Münster, 1934). See also S. R. Fischer, *The Dream in*

the *Middle High German Epic: Introduction to the Study of the Dream as a Literary Device to the Younger Contemporaries of Gottfried and Wolfram* (Berne, Frankfurt, Las Vegas, 1978).

5. See above, p. 273, n. 26.

6. N. Terzaghi, ed., *Synesii Cyrenensis Opuscula* (Rome, 1944).

7. E. L. Ehrlich, *Der Traum im Alten Testament* (1953).

8. A. Wikenhausen, "Die Traumgeschichte des Neuen Testaments in religionsgeschichtlicher Sicht," *Pisciculi*, Festschrift für Fr. Dölger (1939).

9. K. J. Steinmeyer, *Untersuchungen zur allegorischen Bedeutung der Träume im altfranzösische Rolandslied* (Munich, 1963).

10. Compare the vision of Drythelm in *Historia ecclesiastica* 5.12 and P. Dinzelbacher, *Vision und Visionsliteratur im Mittelalter* (Stuttgart, 1981).

11. See Le Goff, *Pour un autre Moyen Age*, p. 300, n. 3.

12. F. Schalk, *Exempla romanischer Wortgeschichte* (Frankfurt, 1966), pp. 295–337, and Schmitz, *Traum und Vision*, n. 4.

13. Artemidorus, *Dream Key*.

14. Ibid.

15. Ibid., dream no. 11.

16. Under the category of dreams that predict "many things by many things," Artemidorus imagines a dream very much like the third one of old Helmbrecht: "A man dreamed that he was flying and that, having raised himself by his own power, he reached the goal for which he was striving. Afterward he dreamed that he had wings and that he could climb into the air with the birds. . . . The result was that he left his country because of his flying." Artemidorus, *Dream Key*.

17. Compare the well-known and convergent views of Duby, "Les jeunes dans la société aristocratique," and Erich Köhler, "Sens et fonction du terme 'Jeunesse' dans la poésie des troubadours," *Mélanges offerts à René Crozet* (Poitiers, 1966), pp. 569ff.

18. Artemidorus, *Dream Key*.

19. Ibid.

20. See Stith Thompson, *Motif Index of Folk Literature* under *raven* as well as the *Handwörterbuch des deutschen Aberglaubens*.

21. Arturo Graf, "Artù nell'Etna," in *Leggende, miti e superstizioni del Medio Evo* (Turin, 1925).

22. See Jean Delumeau, *La Peur en Occident (XIVe–XVIIIe siècle)* (Paris, 1978).

23. J. H. Waszink, "Die sogenannte Fünfteilung der Träume bei Calcidius und ihre Quellen," *Mnemosyne* 9 (1941): 65–85.

24. Herodotus, *Histories* 3.124.

25. W. H. Stahl, ed., Macrobius, *Commentary on the Dream of Scipio* (1952).

26. Lynn Thorndike, *A History of Magic and Experimental Science* (London, 1923), vol. 2, pp. 290–302; W. Suchier, "Altfranzösischer Traumbücher," *Zeitschrift für französischer Sprache und Literatur* 67 (1957): 129–167; Graf-

funder, ed., "Daniels Traumdeutungen," *Zeitschrift für deutsches Altertum und Literatur* 48 (1906): 507–531.

27. Among the articles I have found most useful are those of H. Bausinger, "Helmbrecht, eine Interpretationsskizze"; G. Schindele, "*Helmbrecht:* Bäuerlicher Aufstieg und landesherrliche Gewalt," in *Literatur im Feudalismus,* a special issue of *Literaturwissenschaft und Sozialwissenschaft* 5 (1975); and H. Wenzel, "Helmbrecht wider Habsburg," *Euphorion* 71 (1977): 230–249.

28. See G. Misch, *Geschichte der Autobiographie* (Frankfurt, 1955–1969), vols. 2–4.

# INDEX